The Second Spring of Your Life

Other Books by Mel London

Getting into Film
Making It in Film
Getting into Video
Easy Going
Bread Winners
Bread Winners Too

With Sheryl London

The Fish Lovers' Cookbook
Creative Cooking with Grains and Pasta
The Herb and Spice Cookbook
Fresh Fruit Desserts: Classic and Contemporary

The
Second Spring
of Your Life

**How You Can Make Your Middle Years
Joyous and Productive**

Mel London

CONTINUUM · NEW YORK

1990

The Continuum Publishing Company
370 Lexington Avenue
New York, NY 10017

Printed in the United States of America

Library of Congress Cataloging-in-Publication Data

London, Mel.
The second spring of your life : how you can make your middle
years joyous and productive / Mel London.
p.   cm.
Rev. ed. of: Second spring. c1982.
ISBN 0-8264-0457-X
1. Middle age—United States.   2. Aging—United States.
I. London, Mel.   Second spring.   II. Title.
HQ1059.5.U5L59   1990
305.24′4—dc20   89-23967
                                                          CIP

To My Friend, Ernie Rieger

*No matter what his age, he always
remains younger than springtime*

Contents

PART III: The Changing Face of Aging

PART IV: New Beginnings, New Horizons

Acknowledgments

Even after the publication of so many books, the author still feels traumatic about this small section acknowledging the people who have helped so much. Some years ago, during the euphoria that accompanies seeing a first book in print, I made the disconcerting discovery that I had left out the name of a man who had been very valuable to me during the pregnancy period of trying to fill the empty pages. Luckily that particular book was updated just last year and I managed to correct the omission. But it has created a minor paranoia that stays with me until this very day as I attack the chore once again, this time complicated by the fact that the support list includes the original edition of *Second Spring* as well as the research that went into this update. My deepest thanks go to everyone who has provided that special degree of encouragement and knowledge, without which I could not have completed not only the original journey, but this time of revision and update as well. I hope I have omitted no one this time.

In analyzing the publications and the books that have been issued during these past eight years, I realize more than ever that those of us who attack the problems of aging, as well as the potential solutions, are much indebted to many of the same "original thinkers"—those who have managed to break the bonds of the stultifying past, of the prejudices related to aging, and of their awareness of the changing demography as we begin to reach a point in our history where those over sixty-five will soon outnumber the young. Indeed, in reviewing some of the material that went into the book in the first place, as well as the current crop of publications, I smile when I find the same statistics, anecdotes, and catch phrases (such as "boomerang") used in the works of others.

Thus, I am greatly indebted to the thinking of Dr. Bernice Neugarten, and especially of the special "chemistry" of Maggie Kuhn of the Gray Panthers. I am an ardent admirer of both. My thanks also go to the late Dr. Robert

Mendelsohn, to Dr. Stephen Z. Cohen and Marty Knowlton; to Dr. Richard Gruelich and Daniel Rogers of the Gerontology Research Center; to Dr. Richard H. Davis of the Andrus Gerontology Center; and to Dr. Manny Riklan and Janet Beard at St. Barnabas Hospital in the Bronx for their support and their invaluable and provocative information, much of which appears in the chapters that follow.

Before Geraldine Ferraro made the run for vice president of the United States, I had known her as a Fire Island neighbor and as a US Representative. It was she who first made me aware of the distortions taking place in the projections for the Social Security system. It was through her that I then found Robert M. Ball. I am grateful to both of them for helping to balance the discussion and to make me more aware of the attack on both the aged and their support system.

My thanks, too, for the help of the Older Women's League—especially to Dr. Ruby Benjamin and Jean Phillips—and to the Displaced Homemaker's Network, to Elderhostel and Michael Zoob. Much of my original research was aided by the staff of the unfortunately now defunct *Prime Time Magazine* through Barbara Hertz and Roberta Gerry. However, in this new edition, the slack has more than been made up by the gracious assistance and encouragement of Amy Krakow and Gerry Hotchkiss of *New Choices for the Best Years*, formerly *Fifty Plus*.

Dr. George Gerbner and his staff at the Annenberg School, University of Pennsylvania, made a superb contribution with their reporting and analyses of the media. Thanks to Tom Walker and Nina Kenny at Colonial Penn Group, to Dr. James C. Hall of Pace University, and to Dr. Jim Gallagher and my dear friend Joe Maloney for their help in the areas of education, outplacement, and career changing. Much of the research for the original book was done by Anne Luck, Ralph Bowers, and Irene Levitt of NRTA/AARP.

For this latest edition, I want to thank the people at Palm Coast for their encouragement and their support. Jerry Full, an occasionally master punster, along with John Gazzoli, and Tom Bailey from the same ITT unit, were invaluable in offering their information and advice about the issues involved with relocation and the change of careers in middle age. As a result of their graciousness, there is a new section in this edition of the book, totally devoted to advice and information for those of us who are ready to make the move to another home or to a change of job location. My appreciation, too, for the support and the encouragement of Yvonne Middleton, who happens to be my most favorite public relations person.

And finally, a nod to my family doctor, Robert Levin, who has since retired, leaving me drifting in the netherworld of impersonal medicine, and to Charles Inlander of the People's Medical Society, a group that has happily filled a troublesome gap in the area of consumerism in the medical field. My original editor was Charles Gerras. My new editor and publisher, Mike Leach, has been as delightful and as helpful in moving the new edition along. To him, and to all the others—listed and inadvertently forgotten—my deepest thanks for making this new journey so memorable.

Mel London
Fire Island, NY

The Author at a "Certain Age"

My mother used to say, "You can't chew your cabbage twice." As a child, I didn't really know what she meant, for she was filled with homilies, sayings, parables, and folklore that accompanied my growing years in the Bronx. Along with other half-remembered phrases, the one about cabbage eluded me until just recently, when it was decided that this book would be reissued, along with corrections, updates, new views of aging, and the reflections of a changing society over these past very critical eight years.

Having "chewed" my cabbage once, I finally had the opportunity to look back since I first saw a former incarnation of this book in print, and to muse over some things that were important to me as well as to the others in my generation. I could actually "chew my cabbage" twice!

- What had changed over these past eight years?
- What had not changed?

Well, in the first place, I celebrated my sixty-fifth birthday just this past year. In the past, I had never really thought much about the so-called milestones that were supposed to create havoc, or were supposed to be the catalyst for a fiesta. Each ten-year marker was certainly noted, toasted with champagne, and then quickly forgotten as I entered the next decade. But at sixty-five, there is a noticeable and very different punctuation that cannot be ignored. Where the other birthdays could be forgotten the next day, the arbitrary line that denotes the fact that we have become what the society delightfully terms "seniors" must be accompanied by a physical act that transcends the opening of birthday presents. Each of us must go down to the Social Security office and register for Medicare!

In itself, it becomes an almost unreal experience, since I first found that the office, in typical government efficiency, was no longer at the address listed in the telephone book. And then, having found my way into the labyrinth of bureaucracy, I could not believe that I was actually being told what my Social Security income would be should I decide to retire at that instant.

Other than that, I find that very little has changed in terms of the societal attitudes toward the aging population of this country. Eight years of a conservative and rather unsympathetic government have, indeed, magnified some of the problems of support systems, but the rigidity and the mean-spirited legislation of the period have also hurt the children and the disadvantaged of America, so we are not alone. At the same time, there has been a concerted attack on the rights and the benefits of the elderly, mostly from a cranky generation that has been spoiled almost since birth, and I shall have more to say about that later.

And yet, I am still optimistic and enthusiastic about the years of middle age. Looking back over the past eight years, I realize that I have not lost that optimism in spite of the anger that I sometimes feel over society's treatment of the elderly (usually starting around age forty!).

There have been changes. On a lighter level, I no longer need a token for the New York City transit system. I now travel half fare on buses and trains. I get into movie theaters at half price and I take full advantage of it, with no excuses.

On a more serious level, the small company that my wife Sheryl and I started ten years ago is thriving and we have been doing our documentary films around the world, with very special clients. About two years back, I became a consultant to ITT Community Development Corporation at Palm Coast, Florida, and finally it was my *age* that made me eligible to give advice on relocation and recareering for both retirees and for middle-aged men and women who wanted change at that part of their lives. The section in this book about those subjects is a direct result of that work for Palm Coast. It may well help some of my readers to look more carefully and intelligently at a change in life-style after the kids are gone and the job seems a dead end.

One of the most delightful results after the publication of *Second Spring* was that I was invited to appear at and conduct seminars for middle-aged participants across the country. Television and radio are always hungry for a new author, and it gave me a chance to articulate some of the feelings that were reflected in the book. The most marvelous discovery was that there are so many out there who had (and *have*) exactly the same feelings and responses about every subject covered here: about children, change of careers, gerontophobia and ageism, about aging parents, health, and sex. At the AT&T Pioneer's Convention in Montreal, our seminar participants told stories that had all of us holding our sides in laughter. On the Seattle television program, *Northwest Today,* both studio audience and call-in viewers discussed gray hair, children who were returning home to live, and the prejudices of the workplace. The letters that have come to me since the first publication of this book have been, for the most part, encouraging, feisty, and enthusiastic. There were, of course, a few reviews and letters that damned me and said that life was miserable.

But, the biggest problem in rewriting this book has been that my files have continued to grow at a tremendous rate during the process of collecting up-to-date materials, revising information, and culling the articles, news items, and statistics about the subject of middle age. For it has become a most popular topic over these past few years, both on the social level and in the area of marketing products and services to those of us who are reputed to have so much of the wealth of the economy. We have been "discovered" as a market, and the percentage of older Americans will increase by a hundred percent over the next thirty years, so you "ain't seen nothin' yet!" On the other hand—there is always an "on the other hand"—millions of us want to be productive but are not allowed to be. Most of the elderly who enter nursing homes are not sick, but have no other place to go. Nineteen out of twenty Americans over sixty-five are healthy, vigorous, and active, and yet old age—which should be the crowning achievement of a lifetime of hard work—is all too often a most intolerable burden.

And so, in "chewing my cabbage twice," I will try to cover both aspects of both middle age and aging. There are "new cabbages" that I have found in the garden of society, and some things have not changed very much. In trying to find an overview of today, this time in our lives, I suppose that the cynical curmudgeon takes over my better nature and I can only quote from a new and typical game that is now on the market: TRUMP: THE GAME. The cover reads: "It's not whether you win or lose, but whether you win!" This is the age in which all of us now live.

PART I

The Invisible
Generation

1 ✸ Welcome to Middle Age

Then we shall rise
And view ourselves with clearer eyes.

—Henry King, bishop of Chichester
"The Exequy"

It was bound to happen to me. It had never happened before, though I am certain that, in the deep, dark recesses of my mind, it was a possibility that had been pushed even deeper each time it threatened to surface. It was a first time, and I'm sure the look of anguish and distress mingled with the awful need to laugh aloud. It was obviously important to me, terribly, terribly important, or I would not have chosen to use it in the very first chapter of this book.

We were on the Third Avenue bus in New York, and it was a brilliant Saturday afternoon, filled with the promise of the vitality "uptown" and pre-Christmas shopping, the hum of kinetic energy that so characterizes every shopping area before the holidays. The bus, empty when we began our trip, soon became filled with bundled-up wintertime passengers, all of them bound for the department stores.

An elderly lady got on, making her way falteringly past the driver as she paid her fare, and I rose to give her my seat. She smiled at me, sat down, and I turned to move away. A young man, about twenty-five, then rose, nodded slightly, and *offered me his seat!*

Of course, I was startled. For an instant, I refused to realize that it was I to whom he was nodding. I was then, and still am, an active filmmaker and you must understand that there is no doubt in my mind that I could outlast that young man on an extended film trip through the world and, at age fifty-seven, I could carry more equipment and be less tired than he would be while working at an altitude of fourteen thousand feet in Bolivia. I could survive more easily in the funk of a jungle or the aridly oppressive heat of a desert, work longer hours, function more efficiently with less sleep, and then offer *him my seat* on a bus were he to get aboard last!

But that is not the point, is it? Arriving home, I looked carefully in the mirror. Undoubtedly, to that young man I looked middle-aged, at the very least; possibly he saw in me the early stages of a gerontological disintegration. Belatedly, I appreciated his kind and thoughtful gesture.

A short time later, while reading the late Malcolm Cowley's delightful minibook *The View from Eighty* (Viking Press: New York), I laughed when I came across his own description of just such an occurrence. It was on the Madison Avenue bus in his case, and it obviously made as strong an impression upon him as it had on me.

And so it comes to us in a variety of ways, for each of us at a different time in what we have begun to call our "middle lives." Possibly it happens when the children leave home or when a reassessment of a career becomes a vital emotional enigma. It is, whatever the personal catalyst, a realization that for some time we have been looking at middle age from the *opposite* side of the calendar. Whether on a bus, or by some chance remark, or by a stroke of inner genius, we suddenly realize, as the cartoon character Pogo might have said, "Them is us!" But, as this book took shape—I found to my surprise, that the norm was not a *negative* feeling about reaching middle age, but a very positive view of what we *are* rather than what we *were*, and a reassessment that occurs for the express purpose of determining *what it is we want to be* during these coming generations of our lives.

In setting the parameters, I decided to look carefully at the generations between the ages of forty-five and sixty-five, and especially now with "twenty-twenty hindsight" at the age of sixty-five, I would like to stick to those parameters. I hope that the people under the age of forty-five might read the book because they will soon join us, and I hope that people over the age of sixty-five would also read it, for some of the most dynamic personalities in my research were between that age and up to the age of eighty-five!

The generations between the ages of forty-five and sixty-five are, in fact, the most active, the most affluent, and in many respects the strongest group in American society, but you'd never know it from reading what's around, from watching television or from the jokes and stories that filter through the social gatherings. We've reached a stage where we have more freedom than we've ever had, and though the group represents about one-quarter of the population, and is growing rapidly, it earns more than 50 percent of the income in the country.

With people living longer than ever, career changing has become a dynamic part of the life-style of those who have passed the age of forty-five and it is much more prevalent than people think. More and more in the age group are going back to college either full-time for degree courses or part-time for myriad personal reasons. Indeed, parents and grandparents are now entering college to acquire degrees and their master's degrees now that they're free of the expenses of orthodontia and college fees.

The health problems of the generations have been terribly overemphasized. The myths of the "empty-nest syndrome" and "midlife crisis" are bandied about relentlessly, but, essentially, both are fallacies of our current societal thinking.

Of course, we are changing. When have we not? At what point in our lives did we not face change and the need for response to that change? For some reason, however, as we reach midlife, the word *change* seems to give way to the word *crisis* and society demands that we think differently about ourselves as we reach whatever magic age is decreed to be a "crisis" point. And we, gentle sheep that we are, begin to accept what society wants us to believe— that it is time to move aside and leave the harvest to the young. During the live interview on *Northwest Today* in Seattle, a man stood up and rather angrily asked if I didn't think it was time for those of us in middle age to move aside and let the young people climb the ladder. My answer to him was that no one did it for us, especially those of us who grew up during the Depression. Somehow they, too, will make it. I feel just as strongly about it today, almost seven years later.

And so, this is a book that not only speaks of change as it affects us. It, hopefully, is a book about *one person's* observations, one person's euphoria at having reached an age where we can no longer be put into neat categories, rigid "stages" of life; where we are discovering that our age groups are more confident, more adventurous, more interesting, more eager to enjoy the fruits of our labor, and more filled with a sense of growth than ever before in our lives. It is, in its own way a book that reflects my anger and distress at the inequity of a lack of social recognition for an entire and very large segment of our population. And I am not alone, for I have continued to hear this same anger during the past ten years, and that wrath has grown in volume. New groups and new voices are rising irately against the unfairness that relegates more than half of America to a pasture of distortion and myth—unobserved, unnoticed, unheard.

I am not, by any means, a Pollyanna. My first interest in the subject of aging dates back more than twenty years, when I was involved in a series of films that took me to chronic disease hospitals, nursing homes, and facilities for the aged, blind, and deaf. It has continued up to the present in my film work and, just this past year, we produced a documentary for the Little Sisters of the Poor, who care for the aged poor in their thirty residences around the country as well as overseas. I have seen enough pain and suffering to last a lifetime, and that is perhaps another reason that I wanted to write a book about the aging process, one that looks more optimistically at where we are in life and opens new avenues of discovery at this most exciting time.

I watched for five slow, agonizing years as my wife ministered to her own mother through senility, Alzheimer's disease, and the wasting away of the body and senses. During the original writing of the book, my sister-in-law died at the age of sixty after a debilitating and horrifying battle with cancer. During these interim years, too, my father died as the result of an automobile accident, in which he was an innocent victim in the passenger seat, and after six weeks in the hospital, the tough eighty-six-year-old spirit and vitality finally succumbed. I have written of him in another section of this book.

My Academy Award nomination for best documentary short film was for *To Live Again* (1963) on the subject of Parkinson's disease and aging. I am only too aware of just how vulnerable we are and I, like you, have watched close friends succumb to a variety of diseases, all the while hearing that we live longer now (and we do). But I suppose that if we live long enough, we are bound to see the passing of dear friends and family, and the feeling of indestructibility that is with us in our youth soon passes.

Problems? Of course there are problems with aging. But that is exactly my point. At what time in our lives did they *not* occur? If problems are the private domain of the aged, why is the suicide rate so high among teenagers and young adults? Too much of what has been written or said about us has been spelled out by "experts," many of them self-proclaimed and most of them younger than we are. At a conference on aging held in Iowa some time back, a discussion leader of about thirty was summing up some suggestions when a feisty, gray-haired older woman stood up and shouted, "I came to Des Moines to hear older women speak. I'm getting tired of having all you younger women telling me what my problems are, and patronizing me. How can you know what it's like to be old?"

And so, I, who am not a sociologist, psychologist, psychiatrist, geron-tologist, social worker, or medical doctor, ask you to share this personal journey with me, for it has taken me all of sixty-five years to "research" what is included in the chapters that follow. Indeed, it it just the fact that I am *not* one of the "ologists" listed above that brought some of the few complaints in the reviews of *Second Spring,* most of which were quite good. One reviewer, commenting upon the fact that this was only the account "of how one man . . . changed his life" and taking issue with the fact that being fifty-eight was not a qualification for writing the work, probably missed the whole point.

This *is* only one person's account. It can be nothing but that. It has been a personal journey and I share it with you, for whatever it's worth. I changed my career at the age of fifty-seven, the year in which the original book was first written. I found, to my surprise, that many of my friends were contemplating just such a change, and some were much, much older than I. My friends, Carmen and Helena bought an old, burned-out stone house in upstate New York, and they are reconstructing it stone by stone, while living there. The fact that Carmen is now close to seventy and is still an active filmmaker, sculptor, painter, animator, and ham radio operator, plus the fact that it may take him at least forty more years to complete the construction job, does not seem to faze him in the least. Not content with the monumental task ahead, he has just opened an art gallery on the highway, converted from an old schoolhouse and in it he displays and sells his own work. Most of all, for Carmen, there is time. Best of all, there is his attitude.

Through the reading of the book, you will possibly discover several things along with the author. We will not meet anyone who is getting younger! But there are distinct advantages to getting older. Most important of all, you will find—as I have—that the archaic theory of "life stages" is fast losing support or that the so-called categories and stages are fast being redefined to allow for the change in the demography of the country. I think you will find that your own journey, though very personal in its experiences, will have much in common with what I have found.

It was winter on Fire Island when I began writing this book. The village was once again empty and the wind was blowing from the south, hopefully placing even more sand on our fast-depleting beach. Now—as then—I can hear the hushed roar of the ocean just a few yards away. The deer, once so rare as they crested the dunes, have proliferated until it is no longer a rare sight to see the beautiful creatures, even as they nibble the foliage right outside the door. However, where the first words were written as snow was forecast for the evening, it is now spring and very close to the heat of summer as I finish. Possibly it is an omen that it is now spring rather than the ice of winter. And once again I am reminded with delight of a story that was told to me by my friend, Lewis Freedman.

George Santayana was invited to speak to the student body of Harvard University. It was early April a long, long time ago. The students, about three hundred of them, had assembled in the large, ramped lecture hall when Santayana entered and walked to the podium. He paused, looked around the hall, and then glanced out the window near the lectern. There, brilliant in their yellow glory, the forsythia had begun to bloom. Santayana looked again at the students, all of them waiting to hear what the great man would say. "Excuse me, gentlemen," he said with a smile. "I have a date with Spring." And he walked out of the lecture hall and into the garden.

And so, I—and you—have a date with spring. For the second time.

2 The Great American Disappearing Act

We've spent the last ten thousand years trying to grow old people, and now that we've done a pretty good job, we're embarrassed about it.

—Dr. Ken Dychtwald
"Age Wave"

As a child I was a great movie fan. Saturday morning was the beginning of an all-day odyssey that took me through three features, fourteen short subjects, a Flash Gordon (or Buck Rogers or Tarzan) serial, four games of Kid-Bingo or Keeno or Banko, plus door prizes of bicycles, Monopoly sets, or roller skates (none of which I ever won). All for ten cents! My only sustenance was a large bag of jelly beans, purchased for another five cents at the local Woolworth's, and by seven o'clock that evening, my mother might have the police out looking for the wayward son who had not yet returned from an "afternoon" at the Park Plaza Theater, only two blocks away.

So many years later, as a filmmaker, I think back to the motion pictures that still stay with me, and there are many that come to mind. Frederic March and his miraculous and spine-chilling transformation from Dr. Jekyll to Mr. Hyde. Lon Chaney as the original and unsurpassed Phantom of the Opera. My first loves and childhood passions: Fay Wray and Helen Twelvetrees. Above all, the "movie magic" of Claude Rains in *The Invisible Man*.

In glorious black-and-white and with scratchy sound, this film portrayed a figure bandaged to the top of his head, only the sculptured shape of the gauze indicating that there was a human face underneath. I remember sitting breathlessly as he unwound the strands of the bandage slowly, deliberately, revealing that under it all there was—nothing! He had disappeared, for beneath the bandage no flesh could be seen. He strode undetected through the real world, the only clue to his existence being the footprints he left in the snow.

During the intense and exciting year in which I researched this book, it all came back to me vividly and with a sense of impotent anguish. When we are children, adolescents, or young adults, the behavorial scientists study, analyze, and dissect us. They interpret everything we do or say or think, and even some of the things we never thought. Our rebellions are evaluated as normal and then reevaluated as abnormal if we dare to go too far.

As we grow, go out into the world of business, marry, or develop a relationship with someone else, or possibly have children and then send them on their way, the writers find it quite easy to categorize us and put us into little compartments. Some time after the age of forty, we seem to stabilize for the researchers, the sociologists, and the analysts, and they skip an entire generation, suddenly to *rediscover* us again at age sixty-five.

Unfortunately, sixty-five is a mystical, burdensome number that was forced upon us by legislative history and the arbitrary choosing of an age by Chancellor Otto von Bismarck of Germany. He pulled the magic figure of "sixty-five" out of his pointed steel helmet back in 1881. In those days, few people lived past the age of sixty-five, so it stood to reason that Bismarck—no fool he—would choose that age at which to reward his workers with the world's first funded retirement program. Our own Congress, never noted for its innovation, followed suit during the thirties, totally unprepared for the blossoming of the age group.

Even today, the scientists, sociologists, physicians, and philosophers pick us up again at sixty-five for a microscopic study of our emotional needs, our physical disintegration, our financial status, our sexual nonrequirements, our nutritional poverty, and our rapid slide into nursing home senility and Alzheimer's disease. Though only five percent of all people over sixty-five are in rest homes or nursing homes, while the remainder live comfortably and vitally within their communities or in their own homes, the myths of fragility and invalidism that have sprung up about the aging persist.

What, then, about the years in between? What happens to the age group between forty or forty-five and the magic number of sixty-five? What happens to those of us who feel that between those two ages we barely seem to exist? Through all the papers, the books, the monographs, the "scientific" studies, the surveys, the magazine articles and the projections of the self-proclaimed pundits, we begin to feel as Claude Rains must have felt. We are there under all the bandages of experience, but no one seems to see us *for twenty whole years!* Sometimes we get the feeling that we haven't even left our tracks in the snow. To put it yet another way, we are groundhogs who come up to see if our shadows are visible at the age of forty-five and, seeing nothing, we descend again under the forest floor, to reappear at sixty-five.

The more perceptive researchers, such as Dr. Bernice Neugarten of the University of Chicago, have also discovered this strange disappearance of millions of people. She has written that the years of maturity are, indeed, much less understood than those of early life experiences or the years that follow the onset of old age. Somehow, the scientists assume that all the decisions of any importance, all the significant events, all the emotional traumas (with the exception of the so-called midlife crisis, which I shall cover later) have already been lived. Obviously, nothing ever happens between the ages of forty-five and sixty-five!

I was a guest on a cable television show hosted by an old friend, Jean Phillips. Devoted to the problems, the life-style and the interesting people among older Americans, and called *Prime Time* (Manhattan Cable), the show is one of the few outlets on the subject. Commenting upon our invisibility, Jean said to me:

> So far as research, forget it. I've been to the Gerontological Library, the Public Library, and all the research you can get is about people who are institutionalized. I talked to the head of the Post Graduate Center on Mental Health and I said, "I've been trying to get some research on the psychology of the midlife person—people between forty-five and fifty." And she said, "There isn't any."

In our daily lives, the phenomenon continues and, especially for women, the entire generation is almost totally invisible. All our vitality, all our financial strength as consumers, all our achievements are barely touched on in the media (especially television and advertising) or in popular literature. And to make matters even worse for the women in our age group, the fact that the entire society is constantly aging, means the female population will grow even larger, since women live longer than men.

Several years ago, Gail Sheehy wrote her best-selling study on "Predictable Crises of Adult Life" in *Passages* (Bantam: New York. Still available in paperback). In it she covered 115 case histories of people in midlife. In 514 pages (a very thick book by any standards), she devoted *only 19* of them to people over forty-five years of age! In those final pages, one slight mention is made of someone over fifty-five, but other than that, we do not exist in her book. We simply are not there and all our "predictable crises" have already occurred. A friend of mine, interviewed by me for this book, angrily told me, "I was furious. I've just turned fifty and I couldn't find myself in her book." Possibly it's because Sheehy defines "midlife" as the middle thirties!

In still another best-seller, and a book that is quoted over and over again in articles and other books on the age group, *The Seasons of a Man's Life* (Ballantine), Daniel Levinson presupposes early in his preface that every middle-aged person is negative toward that stage in life. I thought the book would be a turnoff for me, but I must admit that I enjoyed it a great deal more than Sheehy's popular reportage.

Nevertheless, Levinson's study is based upon forty *men* (with women remaining invisible again, this time since the author had limited funding and felt that it was better to study forty men in depth than to divide the sexes at twenty apiece. Some women might disagree). All his male subjects were from the Northeast and all were in one of four categories: biologists, novelists, executives, or blue-collar workers. The rest of us are to assume that our "midlife" times are reflective of his subjects, no matter what our backgrounds, our jobs, our economic status, or our geographic location.

More important, perhaps, and more germane to my feelings of invisibility, is the fact that Levinson also stops at the other side of the dividing line, and in his period of "middle adulthood" age forty-five to sixty is not touched upon at all! We are passed off—the millions of us—with the statement that our bodily powers and our mental faculties will somewhat diminish after the age of forty. But then he goes on to state that many of humanity's most ingenious and brilliant achievements take place during those invisible years—in science, the arts, teaching, business, politics, international diplomacy, and philosophy. Indeed, as I read it, I could not for the life of me remember a brilliant philosopher who was even *eighteen* years of age. I will admit that there *were* some brilliant twenty-five- and thirty-year-olds on Wall Street before the big crash of October 1987, though some are now without jobs and some few others have ended up in prison. But, if you will, think of the names that come to your mind in the professions that I've listed. You'll find that almost all the names are in the age group of forty-five or older.

In a sense it is inconceivable that society almost totally disregards the projections that promise the "graying of America."

Though I normally resist reading statistics, I was fascinated by a book that was published by the US Senate Special Committee on Aging (in conjunction with the AARP, the Federal Council on Aging and the US Administration on Aging). Titled *Aging America: Trends and Projections*, the invisibility of the middle and older age groups in our country becomes even more startling:

- In 1986, the median age in this country was 31.8 years.

- By the year 2000, it will rise to 36 years.

- By the year 2040 it will jump to 42 years.

- By 2050, though the population will increase by a third, the 55-plus age group will *more than double!*

- By 2030, one in three people will be 55 years or older and one in five will be 65-plus.

- Even today, we have more people over the age of 65 in the United States than the *entire* population of Canada.

In most other surveys, even the more scientific ones, we are either "lumped" or "bumped." One of the best studies was conducted by Louis Harris Associates for the National Council on Aging back in 1975. It analyzes public attitudes on aging and it is titled *The Myth and Reality of Aging in America*. From what I can determine, much has not changed since then and I shall refer to many of its findings in later chapters. However, I was struck again by an interesting phenomenon as I reviewed the book just recently. Over four thousand in-person household interviews were conducted and there were two basic groups of interviewees: the "general public" and those over sixty-five, the former including everyone between the ages of eighteen and sixty-four! Somehow it became uncomfortable to think that I had exactly the same feelings about something as important as aging as did my young friends of eighteen or twenty or thirty. Nevertheless, the survey did much to uncover the myths and the prejudices that exist right across the demographics of our culture.

The final point that I'd like to make has nothing to do with our invisibility, but rather with the tendency of Americans to put everything and everyone into neat, gift-wrapped packages. I get the feeling that if we don't fit into a category, we somehow are discarded just to keep the statistics tidy and uncluttered. In the literature that exists, with a few outstanding exceptions (such as the works by Dr. Neugarten), the tendency to put everyone into stages, transitions, passages and life straitjackets began to upset me, for the more I read and the more people to whom I spoke, the more I realized that there is no average American, young, old—or middle-aged. The society has blended so rapidly across age groups in these past twenty years that it is well-nigh impossible to put any of us into a specific category once we reach a certain age. In fact, I genuinely doubt that there ever was such a time.

And, as I've already commented, if the male of our generation thinks he's invisible, the female of our group must be even angrier and more frustrated. One well-known study (by Dr. George Vaillant), for example, covers the lives of only ninety-five men—all Harvard graduates! It is no wonder that some of us feel that we have been assembly-lined as people, expected to perform the necessary changes as each age comes upon us.

It may be just a coincidence, but ever since that young man got up and offered me his seat on the bus, I have been doing a lot more walking! The other day, I was strolling uptown on my way to an appointment and I noticed the signs in the windows of the savings banks. Right along with the weekly rates for six-month certificates of deposit and the latest mortgage percentages, the bold, red signs in the windows proclaimed: NEW LOW RATES FOR SAVINGS BANK LIFE INSURANCE, INQUIRE WITHIN! I read on to find that there were new, lower rates for five-year renewable term policies and that the annual premium had been slashed (also in capital letters). Of course, since women live longer than men, their rates were even lower. I quickly skimmed the ages, past twenty, twenty-five, thirty, thirty-five, forty—and then it stopped, right at forty-five! No more. Ended. Finished. The bargain sealed, but only up to forty-five.

I looked in vain to see if, perhaps, they had slashed my rates, too. Nothing. Nothing older than forty-five. Of course, they had figures for me inside the bank. But no more bargains. Certainly not at fifty-five. And definitely not at sixty-five. Once again, I felt invisible.

3 "Excuse Me, Sir (or Madam), Could You Direct Me to Middle Age?"

> "Most of our customers are middle-aged."
> "How old is that?"
> "Over twenty."
>
> —Disco Manager

Long the butt of jokes, long reflective of the stereotypes and myths, middle age is actually impossible to define. At least it is absurd to try to categorize it at all in this generation. But that doesn't seem to stop anyone from trying. Most of the definitions tend to make me uncomfortable, especially when the speaker is trying to be humorous. President Reagan once gave his own illustration when he said, "Middle age is when you are faced with two temptations and you choose the one that will get you home by nine o'clock."

Think for a moment and then give your own definition of "middle age." Is it a chronological description? Some pun you heard? A joke? A personal, emotional one? A textbook or dictionary definition? If you succeed on the first one, try giving a definition of "old age." Easier? Not for most. It just depends upon which side of the fulcrum you swing from.

If you listen, if you read, if you watch television, if you are thirty or if you are thirteen, your perception and thus your answers will be quite different than if you are forty-five, or even sixty-five. Bear with me for some examples that will show exactly what I mean.

31

- I remember, with a smile, a cartoon that I saw a long time ago in a medical journal. An ancient man, sitting on a bench and being questioned about his age, retorts with, "Which age do you mean? Anatomic, psychologic, physiologic, moral, or chronologic?"

- My late mother-in-law, at the age of eighty-one, met an old friend who was just turning ninety-two. In describing the meeting, my mother-in-law took umbrage at the fact that I considered the two women contemporaries. "How can you compare *me* with *her?*" she asked haughtily. "*She's* middle-aged!"

- The Bureau of Labor Statistics considers the category of "older worker" anyone over forty-five!

- Bernard Baruch once observed, and it is a definition that I use quite frequently, "Old age is always fifteen years older than I am."

Back in the mid thirties my mother was a radio soap opera addict. The daily fare included a continuing saga about a woman named Helen Trent. Each day, to the accompaniment of sobbing organ music, the announcer intoned, "Helen Trent . . . can a woman over thirty-five find romance?" It was some years later that I laughed out loud when I heard someone refer to "Helen Trent" as the program that gave virtue a bad name!

Has it changed? Not on your life. I use my semimonthly visits to my barber shop to catch up on what I call the "Three P's": *People, Playboy,* and *Penthouse.* In an interview with Joan Collins, the *Playboy* questioner reminded me of good old "Helen Trent" when Ms. Collins was asked the following question:

Another thing you did . . . in your next film, *The Bitch,* was appear in erotic nude scenes. Why, in your forties, are you still taking off your clothes?

She responded wonderfully, saying that she had taken a good, hard look in the mirror and "it looked all right to me."

- One of the producers of the PBS production of *Antony and Cleopatra* commented that when the play ends, "Cleopatra is pushing forty and Antony is several years older . . . so there is good reason for cutting down on the romance and the glamour."

Enough? You have not even heard the beginning! I visited Florida several times in researching the retirement and relocation section of the book and, on one trip, while driving to a retirement condominium, I turned on the radio and heard a terse, important announcement:

> . . middle-aged hijacker of a Continental Airlines jet. Ninety passengers escaped through the rear exit. He is still holding seven passengers in first class and FBI agents are talking to the man, who is described as white, middle-aged, between the ages of forty and forty-five.

My immediate reaction was that the announcer must be ten years old!

There is always the reference to chronological age. The generation that proclaimed, "Never trust anyone over thirty!" is now old enough to look around and shout, still more loudly, "Life begins at forty!" Sometimes it is countered by an older person's common sense, as when Gloria Swanson was quoted as saying, "I don't feel like eighty-one—because I don't know how eighty-one feels!" How old, then, is old? What is middle-age?

I think that the theory of *life stages* should be put to rest, to go the way of the Edsel, the Victrola, and the icebox. Those of us who are over forty-five make up a growing, vocal, and perceptive group that is beginning to realize it is not only unfair, but also inaccurate to categorize us in chronological stages, whether they are called passages, seasons, or transitional periods in our lives. Of course, it would make the writing of life-style books more difficult if we did remove the boundaries, but remove them we must. The times are different. Things are just not the same as they were for Otto von Bismarck or, for that matter, during the times that our mothers and fathers were growing up. And, they will never go back to what they were.

Dr. Neugarten has given our historic time a most descriptive name in stating that this is an era of "age-irrelevance." And so it is. First of all, what we are at a specific age is very much dependent upon the society in which we live. It is just as important to think about the era in which we were born. Because the life span in Colonial times was moderately short, our own early American society spawned politicians and diplomats who would have been in college or graduate school were they living in our times. After all, if your projected life span were about forty (if you were lucky), you had darned well better make your mark by the time you were twenty! Had Mozart begun his career at thirty, we would have had little of his music to listen to today.

Though the burgeoning population of middle-aged and elderly people in America is generally attributed to medical advances, that is actually just one of the reasons. The primary cause is an increase in the annual number of births before 1920 and after World War II. Added to that, the dramatic decline of the birth rate after the mid-1960s has substantially contributed to the rise in the median age of the country.

Certainly, medicine has also played a role. Compared to what our grandmothers had to contend with, the minimal death rate of women in childbirth today along with a generally better (if more expensive health care system) has extended the life span of most of us. Thus, the structured life-style of not too many years ago—school, early marriage, immediate children, early aging, and death—has been drawn out to include decades of activity after the children are gone from the family home, resulting in much younger grandparents in many instances—or a great many successful relationships in which there are no children at all. The combination brings a freedom that comes with a society that has also become more affluent than any that have preceded us. This allows us a flexibility of life-style and career selection as never before. As Dr. Neugarten says, no one ever admonishes, "Act your age!" any longer.

I have found students at leading universities who were past the age of eighty, some of them even trying for belated degrees. On the other hand, the mayor of a small Wisconsin city was elected at the tender age of twenty-nine. Each year, over twenty thousand men over the age of fifty choose to become fathers, many of them for the first time, and one of my dearest friends has just become a new father at the age of seventy-two. How nice for the world to discover that our generation is still sexual and lusty! Although Carl Jung was one of the first analytic thinkers to suggest that midlife was the time for maximum potential and personality growth, our generation has borne out his optimism by the greatest surge of career changes and life-style metamorphoses in history. I am not quite sure, however, at just what age Jung considered "midlife." Probably somewhere around thirty!

The problem of "categorizing" has also been neatly handled by Dr. Neugarten. She comments upon the fact that a person need not be young because of chronological age, nor should the word *old* connote a specific number of years. There are, she says, the "young old" as well as the "old old" and it all depends upon your state of mind. Think about your friends—and, indeed, think about some of *their children* and you soon find that some of the "youngest" people that you know are some of the oldest.

But our society has been conditioned to think in easy categories, in neat and inflexible stages. You reach an age, you reach a stage. The Harris survey showed that 5 percent of the American public considers that a person reaches old age before turning fifty! Another 16 percent felt that old age starts before sixty. Soon, we also begin to believe this, and we begin to act "old" before our time. If everyone says so, it surely must be true. They and we have been conditioned to think of physical changes as being the prime causes of our getting old—gray hair, wrinkles, brown spots on the skin.

We soon become the victims of the stereotypes imposed upon us. It is how we *look* that makes us feel old, they say. And as we age, they treat us differently and think differently about us. And *we* believe it. It becomes a self-fulfilling prophecy.

I go into a tiny store to buy a spool of sewing thread, and the man bends to reach beneath the counter. Possibly he is all of forty-five, and I hear him moan, "My back is killing me. I must be getting old!"

I walk uptown and meet an old friend by accident. I have not seen him in twenty years and, frankly, he has not aged badly at all, if I look at the physical signs. (Note that I, too, have commented upon the physical. Like you, I am a victim of ageism!) My friend is sixty-four and he says to me as he pulls off my winter hat and looks at my hair, "My, you've gotten gray!" (Did he expect that I'd gotten gold?) "Well," he sighs sadly, "I guess we're all gettin' old."

I suppose we are, and right now I don't know of any solution to the aging process. I am much more taken with the statement made by a famous racing driver, who at fifty-one is still active, when he stated, "I'm fifty-one in a one-hundred-one-year-old body with a twenty-five-year-old mind!"

I am also warmly reminded of the great Harry Hirschfeld's statement at a testimonial dinner marking his eightieth birthday: "How does it feel to be eighty? Great, when you consider the alternative!"

4 Nonsense, Claptrap, Stereotypes, and Moth-Eaten Myths

It is not aging that is at fault, but rather our attitude towards it.

—Cicero
"De Sevectute"

My dear friend Alex is now in his late seventies—an active traveler, off-Broadway and London producer, art collector, and real-estate executive. Not being busy enough, he is also an active lawyer whose history dates back to the trial of the Scottsboro Boys. Alex tells about meeting a man on a crowded street in New York. Suddenly, out of the throng, the face appeared and Alex just couldn't quite place where they had met before, nor just who the man was. It has happened to all of us—out of context, even a familiar face seems unplaceable. The two men greeted each other and Alex commented, still at a loss, "You know, there are *three* things that happen when you get older. The first thing is that you forget people's names. And—I can't remember the other two!"

I have used the story time and again when I have run into people by accident. It is a superb icebreaker and it always gets a laugh. But, if we analyze it, we realize that we are placing an unfair burden on the process of aging. We do it again and yet again. We are getting older. It is accepted that we must, therefore, begin to forget things. It is the beginning of our own acceptance of "ageism" and it is just as insidious as the processes of racism and sexism. For *we* are the victims.

I am again guilty along with everyone else. I misplace my glasses (a reading crutch that I need almost constantly now that my eyes are—naturally—aging). I blame it on creeping senility. The other night I took a wine glass and placed it somewhere in the house while I idly made notes for this morning's chapter of this book. Some spirit or hobgoblin stole it, though I discovered it several hours later where I had put it in the first place—right alongside my typewriter. I must, obviously, be well into my "twilight years!"

The fact is that, if you were to observe the exact same things among your young friends or your children or grandchildren, you would probably pass these incidents off with a flippant comment that they have "too much on their minds" or they're "too busy" to think clearly. It is exactly this kind of destructive analysis that has plagued women and ethnic minorities in our society. In the corporate world, if a man is a driving, ambitious, single-minded workaholic who is demanding and rigid toward his subordinates, he is destined to become an executive vice president (or even CEO) as a reward for his stellar personality and his efforts. Should a woman exhibit exactly the same type of personality traits, she will become known around the office as "an overbearing, arrogant bitch!"

It is easier to stereotype than to allow for differences. It is easier to do a survey about adolescents who are confined to an institution or older people to nursing homes than it is to probe and analyze the diversity that exists throughout our society. It is easier for the press and for television to choose one vivid, emotional, heartrending example (known as "The Little Girl in the Well Syndrome") than to do an in-depth study of the very real problems of the children and the aged in our society.

Unfortunately, as the myths are published, as the stereotypes are perpetuated by our families, our friends, our employers, our fellow employees, the general public, the media (ah, the media!), and the folklore of aging, a most insidious thing begins to happen to *us*. *We begin to believe them ourselves!* And, in the process, the myth becomes self-fulfilling and self-perpetuating, and we, the victims, then help to sustain both the distorted facts and the nonsense. Well, just what are some of those myths? They begin to crop up as we enter middle age (which to some is still around thirty), and as we pass the point of no return at sixty-five, they increase in quantity, if not in quality. They become ever more destructive to us, to our image of ourselves, and to our functioning in the society. Until now, we have been normal, involved, vital human beings. Age has come upon us. What are we like now?

Well, sir (or madam), just listen to this. We are, without any doubt, rigid and we reject innovation. Only the young (as everyone knows) are flexible and unflappable. We are impatient and cantankerous, of course, and we are moving rather quickly into our "second childhood."

We are all frail and in poor health or, at best, our health is failing rapidly.

Certainly, we are absentminded and slow-witted. Worse, we are a burden to society, to our friends, and to our families. Worst of all, perhaps, is the fact that we are almost totally unproductive in both our personal lives and in the business world. Make way for the young mind, and especially the young body!

Oh—and yes—we are totally unsexual and dispassionate. And middle age is the time when most marriages break up in any case. The end result of all this is that we withdraw, to fade away and quietly disappear from living, unsung and barely remembered. And all this degeneration begins somewhere around the age of forty!

Do I exaggerate? I was in Allentown, Pennsylvania, about two years ago to participate in a seminar about aging. With an hour or so to spare, I wandered across the street from the hotel to browse in a bookshop. The new issue of *Esquire Magazine* caught my eye and the following headlines screamed out at me: HOW A MAN AGES. The subhead read "The Catalog of Decay" and the subsubhead finally gave the real story: "So Many Things Happen as a Man Creeps Past the Age of Thirty." (At least they didn't include women in the article!)

Only in the field of sports can I understand any reference to the aging process beginning in what I consider the early or formative years, since professional tennis or baseball are truly the activities of the very young. Nevertheless, I still must admit that I wince when I read that Tom Seaver has quit at age forty-two or that "the decline of Martina Navratilova has occurred because she has "talked herself into the fact that I am thirty . . . I've been falling apart at the drop of a hat." The most interesting thing about the interview I read was that it was conducted by Ted Tinling, the consultant to women's tennis—who was *seventy-seven* at the time!

The theory of the "big lie" is certainly no revelation to those who have lived as long as we have, especially through the propaganda of so many wars. Say a thing often enough, publish enough articles and books that bring old age down to puberty and everyone will believe it. Say it loudly enough, repeat it often enough, and it will drown out the feeble voice of truth. After all, if a tennis star is at her "sunset" at age thirty, what must *we* be like at forty-five or fifty-five or sixty-five? Soon we, the scapegoats, begin to join the chorus and the fantasy becomes the inevitable reality.

One of the questions asked in the Harris study related to just how the public thought *older* people (no, not over thirty, but over sixty-five) spend *most* of their time. Look at the figures carefully, for some of the estimates were far off the reality.

- *Watching television:* Sixty-seven percent thought that we spend most of our time at the tube. Actually, only 36 percent do that after the age of sixty-five!

- *Sitting and thinking:* Sixty-two percent were convinced that we are posed as a series of Rodin statues, just a-settin' and a-thinkin' and a-whittlin'. The actual figure is 31 percent.

- *Taking a lot of walks:* Only 34 percent thought this, while 25 percent of us actually do spend our time on frequent walks.

- *Sleeping:* Here it was almost 40 percent versus 16 percent in actuality.

The most interesting answer came from 35 percent of those surveyed who thought older people spent most of their time "just doing nothing." I would love to survey some of the young people to whom I've lectured at colleges across the country to find out just how many of them spend a good part of *their* time "doing nothing." Actually, only 15 percent of people over sixty-five claim that "doing nothing" is the main pursuit of the day. That gives us 85 percent who must be doing something! And between the ages of forty-five and sixty-five, *almost all of us* are too busy to do nothing. To make matters worse, the surveys taken among the young about television-viewing habits make us look like shirkers. With most of the kids racking up as much as *seven hours a day,* we older folks are nowhere near holding the Guinness world record.

As you well know, I am not the first author or researcher or sociologist to shout "Bah! Humbug!" to all the nonsense that passes as gospel while masking the truth. The entire Harris study—all 245 pages of it—is devoted to an analysis of aging stereotypes such as image, the media, employment, finances, and expectation versus reality. In their own words, the researchers come to the conclusion that: "The picture drawn in the public's mind of old age and its problems is a gross distortion of what older people say they experience personally."

Most of the popular books I've read on the subject of middle age and old age, however, are frankly depressing. While starting out to disprove the stereotypes, they end up by going along with many of them, from "midlife crisis" to menopausal depression, leading eventually to disintegration and suicidal tendencies. However, in the past ten years or so, some books have begun to take a much more optimistic view of our generation. The titles jump out at me and their themes are upbeat—and it's about time—*Older Is Better,*

Late Bloomers, Looking Fit and Fabulous at Forty Plus. The newest trends in marketing to us as consumers and a reassessment of our vitality and our potentials in books like Dr. Ken Dychtwald's *Age Wave* (Tarcher), with the promising subtitle: *The Challenges and Opportunities of an Aging America.*

One of the most upbeat books on the subject, however, is Alex Comfort's *A Good Age* (Crown), in which he calls the process I've been describing as "sociogenic aging." It is the role that society imposes upon people as they reach a specific chronological age, in spite of all the current talk of age-irrelevance and our own feelings about having reached middle age. If you are sixty-five you must, of course, retire. If you are forty-five you have reached well into midlife, and you must be unemployable or forgetful or unsexual—or all three.

Nina Kenny of the Colonial Penn Group (which insures only older Americans) told me about a newspaper story when I interviewed her for the information in this chapter about older drivers. A gentleman was crossing Market Street in Philadelphia. He had just turned sixty-five and was on his way to a birthday luncheon with his son. Suddenly he felt his son's hand as it took his elbow in a firm grip and guided him across the street. He turned and asked, "What are you doing?" The son's rejoinder was, "Well, you're sixty-five, and I'm helping you across the street." To which the father, somewhat annoyed, retorted, "You didn't help me across the street when I was sixty-four. Why are you helping me at sixty-five?"

It is out of this sea of myths and stereotypes that the problems of aging emerge. And though we may be forty-five or fifty or not yet at our sixty-fifth birthday, it begins to affect us at an early stage. Just look, if you will, at the advertising and note the number of times that the copy mentions "young." It is no wonder that many of our feelings about ourselves begin to reflect society's absurdities, even while we are just entering the road of middle age. If, by chance, we should disagree with what is being said or written in the media, we generally pass it off and say, "Well, I'm an *exception!*"

A very young (thirty-five-year-old, not yet middle-aged) acquaintance of mine was holding forth one evening as only the young can do—secure, rigid, and totally incorrect. (Note, if you will, my own stereotype of the young. Is this known as "youthism?") She claimed that every bad driver she had ever seen was an older person. They held up traffic, did dangerous things, and generally made her life miserable on the highway. I pointed out to her that I thought the accident rate of younger drivers was higher than that of older drivers. Of course, she asked for proof. Soon after that I took the train to Philadelphia to speak with Nina Kenny of Colonial Penn, since insurance companies are not about to take chances on bad risks. There are more than forty million licensed drivers over the age of fifty, and ten million are over the age of sixty-five, she told me. In all, they represent about 30 percent of all the drivers in the country. In spite of what my young friend says, this older driving group is involved in less than 20 percent of the accidents. The under-thirty age group—my young acquaintance's contemporaries—*is responsible for twice as many accidents.*

Most of us older drivers are well aware of our limitations, such as diminished eyesight, or perhaps a small loss of hearing, and, as a result, we compensate for them. Many of us avoid driving at dawn and dusk and, after retirement, the need to drive distances seems to diminish in any case.

I never did bring up the subject again, but the final curtain was lowered about a month afterward in Portland, Oregon, when I heard an early morning call-in show while I was dressing for an appointment. The young emcee (who also must have been about ten years old) asked the question, "Well, what about those old geezers *(sic!)* on the highway?" An Oregon State Trooper called in to answer, "Older people are rarely convicted of speeding, and rarely obliged to take driver training programs." He did suggest, however, that eye exams be made mandatory. So much for another myth.

And, as each of the stereotypes is examined, it evaporates like dew in the sun. There is the myth that middle age is the time when most marriages break up. Before I go any further, did you nod in agreement? Well, it's just not true. The divorce rate is actually highest in teenage marriages, and it gradually decreases and goes steadily downhill through the years.

The middle-aged person who is productive, sexual, affluent, independent, and very strong is not the exception. If I have come to one firm, irrevocable conclusion on this journey, it is that we are *all* exceptions. As mature people, we are a more heterogeneous group than any other in the country. Indeed, it is the *young* who are probably most apt to adopt the habits and protective colorations of conformity. Do you remember the "uniform" when you were in high school? In my generation it was saddle shoes and team sweaters.

It was the young people of the sixties who became the hippies and the flower children because of the sameness of their dress, their language, and their philosophies (not to mention their almost universal white, middle-class backgrounds). In the arena of revolution for the young, there is security in sameness. I must admit, however, that as the eighties came upon us, I looked at the "new" revolution of punk clothing and green Mohawk haircuts and I longed for the return of the flower children.

It is only as we progress from youth to maturity that we begin to dare to be different and act as individuals. How ironic, then, that so much of the country's stereotypical thinking should be directed toward the middle-aged, the aged, and the very process of aging.

The generalizations about aging present a totally negative view of our lives, just as many of the myths portray middle age as a time when we are all to put out to pasture, to gambol on the lawn of the retirement village of our choice. Each as a totality is incorrect, and both are harmful to a fuller understanding of the process and the changes in aging. The list could continue on and on. Older people are all senile. All of them have Alzheimer's disease. Middle-aged people are all politically conservative. Older people really don't want to be with the young, but like to live among themselves. And, of course, "You can't teach an old dog new tricks!"

But, is it changing? That is, after all, what this book is about. And it is what the new books and articles on the subject are all about. Even the popular magazines have begun to join the chorus of protest and reevaluation. Newsweek featured a cover story entitled, "Growing Old, Feeling Young" with the very strong and correct statement atop the article that said, among other things, that "their worst enemy is not nature, but the myths and prejudices about growing old."

Everything in life changes, though not always for the best. Slowly, the myths and the misconceptions are giving way to a more realistic outlook that views aging as a normal event in the life cycle. More important, perhaps, is the beginning of an awareness that the aging population of this country is a significant and valuable natural resource. We are beginning to discover, also, that we do not age in a vacuum, but that all our experiences in life, including our attitudes while still very young, will determine whether we get to the age of fifty or sixty as one of the "young old" or the "old old." Above all, if we have reached this mountaintop in our lives, we are certainly pretty good survivors!

There is one short postscript that has to do with change. It is a delightful one and I'd like to pass it on in concluding this chapter. As I was writing this section of the book, my friend Alex—whose story began the chapter—telephoned to say hello and to chat. I commented upon the coincidental writing of his name right before the call. I reread the story to him, only to hear, "Oh, I've changed my whole approach." I asked what he now said when he met someone whose name he could not recall. He says now:

My memory is not as good as it used to be . . . and it never was!

5 ❀ Is Gerontophobia a Curable Disease?

I had a great aunt who died at the ripe old age of ninety-seven. She went to the hospital at age ninety-two. My mother went there to check up on her and asked how she was doing. The nurse said, "She's a cantankerous old lady. Everytime I go to take her teeth out, she bites me!" My mother said, "No wonder. Those are *her own teeth!*"

—Seminar Participant
AT&T Pioneers Convention,
Montreal, 1985

When I began writing this book, I seriously considered omitting an interview with Maggie Kuhn. I had heard so much about her, had collected many of her articles and statements in my files, had watched her on television, had read about her in the newspapers and magazines, and had even discovered that she had written an introduction to a book dedicated to the good health of older Americans. Falling victim to an author's perversity, I was on the verge of deciding that Maggie and her organization, the Gray Panthers, had been "overdone" and anything that I might add would be extraneous and repetitive. Such a decision would have been a sad mistake and I would have lost both a remarkable interview and an extraordinary personal experience.

"Gerontophobia has reached epidemic proportions. It's a massive social disease!" She said it with conviction, as she says everything that involves her, and that encompasses the process of aging and the distortion of that process in the minds of our society. She went on: "In children, it's a fear of old people—and there's a good deal of evidence that children's books and stories for the little ones begin to infect them with a fear of old people. Old people are presented as witches—troublesome, unpleasant characters. And the little

43

girl on TV says, 'Why Grandma, what are those brown spots on your hands? They're ugly!' and Grandma says, 'Yes, they're ugly, but I'm rubbing them with Porcelana.' Now there's a little kid who obviously loves her grandma, who is reinforcing the self-contempt that Grandma feels. I hate those hands! I hate me! It may be a trivial aspect, but that's self-rejection. It's very deep. And our children reinforce it because they themselves are infected with gerontophobia."

We sat in the living room of the old, rambling, creaky house that had seen better days. It was raining in Philadelphia and I was glad I had made the trip. We laughed each time the electricity in the building went off and then back on again a few moments later. And we sat on wooden, hand-carved, straight-backed chairs for almost two hours and we talked and we laughed and became angry together. The Gray Panthers have since moved to much better quarters, but I will always remember that very special rainy day.

"Think of what gerontophobia does to children and young people," she continued. "Young people infected with it have no future. And middle-aged people are very afraid, if they admit it. It's a Western disease. It's a disease of the advanced countries. We've all got it. The supertechnologically advanced countries, including Japan. We've substituted material values. We've made a God of technology." She sat back. As I mull over those words about eight years later, I realize that this is an area in which *nothing* has changed, and indeed, some things have gotten worse. The attack on Social Security, for example, and about which I shall comment later on, is just another indication that gerontophobia is alive and well today.

How does one describe Maggie Kuhn, who is now entering her eighty-fourth year and is still as active as ever, and in many more areas of our social and political arenas. She is small, slender, with gray hair and a tiny frame, but with a remarkably commanding presence, even today. She's cut down on her travel somewhat and now makes her appearances across the country accompanied by a companion. But she still keeps at it, giving priority to university campuses, "reaching the thinkers and the students who are the future." Their reaction, to say the least, is very very positive.

I remember thinking that I had expected her to arrive at that old house that served as Gray Panther headquarters and come bursting through the door, a firebrand who would rattle the windows and shake the chandeliers. But she walked up the wet path gently, carrying an umbrella, preceded by her young assistant, Cindy Traub, and there was the feeling that I had known her for a very long time. She is poised, beautiful, articulate, intense, and caring—and very impatient with things that don't get done, impatient with people, especially people of *our* age, who don't do anything about improving their situation. She dismisses middle-aged and older people who cry about their plight as "wrinkled babies." She joins those who really care enough to do something, along with the young to fight as Youth and Age in Action, and indeed if you have seen the photos that have appeared both in the daily newspapers and the Gray Panther periodicals, you will note that young and old are always shoulder to shoulder in the marches and the demonstrations.

I shall speak more about the Gray Panthers in a later chapter, for the organization has expanded its philosophy and activism in several important areas, about which Maggie comments today:

> I think we made a very important policy decision. We're not quote lobbying quote for old folks issues. We're working for *societal* issues—and the humanizing and the healing of our society. *Not* for a special privileged group. I've been using the analogy of the tribal elder . . . that tribal elders are concerned about *the tribe* and its survival, not just their old people!

After the interview, I came away with a great sense of "self" and about a week later I sent in my membership check for the Gray Panthers. I have been a member ever since and my latest conversation with Maggie just a few weeks ago only rejuvenated me and reinforced my admiration and love for that wonderful woman.

Possibly all this would matter less if you and I were part of a declining segment, a generation that represented only a small percentage of the American population. But if ever there was a group to whom the census statistics are vital, it is our invisible generation. Older Americans—and that includes us, like it or not—are indeed the fastest growing minority group in the country, as I have already pointed out. The cult of youth may well be on the way out (kicking and screaming, no doubt, and crankily complaining).

But the increase in our numbers is beginning to have a serious effect on our social programs, our economic lives, and our personal view of ourselves; it has already altered our family relationships and our career roles as well as career goals. Finally, and most important, if the portrayals of middle age and the process of aging continue to be exaggerated and distorted negatively, they cannot help but have a deleterious effect upon our young people as well as upon ourselves. Along the line, we are instilling in our sons and daughters—and our grandchildren—a deep-seated fear of growing older.

I said earlier that I am not a Pollyanna (though I have been accused of being just that in my enthusiasm for life and for living). Let us say, then, that I try *not* to be a Pollyanna. We—all of us, the author included—do think about aging. We would be fools if the subject totally slipped from our minds. There are reminders every day of our lives and most of them are amusing incidents, though admittedly we react to them with a start. The view from here is that we think more about the years that are left to us than about how long ago we were born. The police officer on the beat begins to look very young. My cameraman turns to me as I describe an old film just rerun on television and he asks, "Zasu Pitts? Who's Zasu Pitts?" It bothers me enough so that I call him very late one night and tell him to tune in to Channel 4 so that he can see "who's Zasu Pitts!" An entire generation has barely, if ever, heard of Shirley Temple or Chester Morris, or even less likely, my childhood loves, Helen Twelvetrees and Fay Wray. World War II is given five pages (if that) in school history books and the Holocaust is fast disappearing entirely as a subject in school curricula. All of us are aware of the changes. It comes with age.

In the writing of a book, the period of pregnancy, followed by terrible labor pains created by looking at empty pages, and the eventual "unnatural birth" of words on paper can make an author a very difficult person to be with. Not only do we research our books quite formally in quiet library or room settings, but our friends are constantly queried during every social situation. Just a few hours ago, while still in the throes of this chapter, I stopped by to speak with my friend, Ernie (to whom this book is dedicated). He lives near the ocean and we shared a glass of wine with another fishing companion, George DiSipio. Both are "middle-aged" or "older" by any standards, which means that they are somewhere over thirty-five but closer to sixty-five or seventy. We spoke of that first time, that *first* revelation, when we suddenly realized that we were getting older. It is as vivid in everyone's memory as the loss of virginity.

"I think," Ernie recounted, "that it happened twice in the same week. The first time was when someone at work called me, 'sir.'" The second event happened some years back when his teenage children were having a rather noisy party. Ernie, just forty at the time, became annoyed at the shouting and the screaming and the raucous music and came downstairs and demanded that they quiet down. One young man turned and ran across the lawn, brandishing a bottle of beer and uttering loud Indian war whoops. Ernie gave chase and caught him in ten quick steps. The young man, obviously under the influence of alcohol, laughed uproariously and yelled to his friends, "Watch out for *the old guy!* He can run like a jackrabbit!"

We all laughed as I recounted how Gail Sheehy had written that middle age begins in the thirties, bringing forth an expletive from one of the women in the group, whose age is about fifty and who still feels that she has ten years to go before entering midlife. George thought a while, sipping his wine and then quietly told us that he never really thinks about aging except when he realizes that the partners in his law firm, who hired him well over thirty years ago, were the same age then as *he* is now—and he thought of *them* as old men the day of his interview.

I suppose that all this is perfectly normal, perfectly natural, a healthy awareness of the change that is taking place all through our lives, especially as we grow and mature. We have lived through more and have more experience, as well as an innate ability to evaluate what we have gone through and what is yet to come. The examples that most of us give are merely recognition that there *is* a gap between generations. It exists on a cultural level and on a social plane and, certainly, the emotional breach is enormous. I am not at all certain that there is a distance on a financial level, in spite of recent articles telling us just how poor the Baby Boomers are. My observation is that young, middle-class people are, in general, quite affluent. Somehow, they don't seem to have the underlying feeling of financial insecurity that most of our Depression-generation peers carry with them. Some wags have teased that if the younger Baby Boomer or Yuppie has two credit cards, that's all that's needed to survive in today's economic society.

But, on all other levels we may as well face it—we *are* different. It would help some, however, if both age groups tried to understand each other. And herein lies the problem of creeping gerontophobia. The distortions, the misrepresentations, the very folklore have created the myth of "young is good" while "old is bad." Ageism and gerontophobia have created a society in which a wealth of experience has been wasted. The first kneejerk tendency is to give examples of older people who are still active, still doing things, still taking advantage of their experience and vitality to accomplish and achieve. But, what seems to be missing is the understanding that *most* middle-aged people are capable of falling into that category. It is not only the older skydiver, the eighty-year-old marathon runner (a woman, no less), the seventy-five-year-old farmer, or handyman. The talents of older people cut across all professions and it has become more and more common to hear of professionals like Charles Chrichton, who at seventy-seven directed the incredibly popular film, *A Fish Called Wanda,* after having been inactive for over twenty years. My favorite, though, is the recent story of a sixty-five-year-old woman doctor who was a close friend of a Colombian cocaine king and who was dealing in drugs!

And yet, in spite of it all, we keep coming across ironic stories that bring us back to the reality of where society is. During the Mississippi race for US Senator, pitting the veteran John C. Stennis against a man named Haley Barbour, the nation's oldest president, Ronald Reagan, came out for Barbour because government needs "new solutions and fresh, vigorous ideas." The television commercials shouted, "A Senator for the eighties, not a senator *in* his eighties!"

The insidious and destructive societal pressures, the constant barrage of advertising and editorial copy devoted to the young begin to affect us. The pressures from the outside make us begin to doubt ourselves and our image, and the "problems" of aging really begin in earnest. For now, we have become infected with the disease of gerontophobia. Take, for example, the subject of gray hair.

One of the people I interviewed for this book told me that she had discovered her first gray hairs the day she was twenty-three and suddenly, that morning when she looked in her mirror, the world began to change for her. She was becoming middle-aged! How many friends have you known who felt the same thing? Possibly it even happened to you at a tender age. It is not to be passed off lightly, because you (and I?) have just contracted another of the first symptoms of gerontophobia, a dread disease. Why, after all, is gray hair so damned awful? It doesn't change your heartbeat. It shouldn't change your sex life—in fact, it may even proclaim you as a more experienced partner.

The answer is obvious and it is the reason why so many of my female friends in real estate, acting, and executive management have taken to coloring their hair anything but gray. How the society perceives gray has much to do with what our response is to the color in our hair. It was angrily commented upon at a White House Conference on Older Women held in Des Moines. One of the workshops was called, "Images of the Growing Older Female," and the discussion centered upon the differences in how a man and a woman are perceived by society after the gray has begun to take over. One of the comments was that "a man with gray hair is perceived to be sexy, having money and power." To which another woman added, "But a woman with gray hair is perceived as sitting by the fireplace rocking, with a white cap on her head."

If all were well, if gerontophobia were not a social disease, the discovery of a few strands of gray hair would be accepted, as would letting the entire head of hair go gray and natural. And that would be that. But the pressures of society, our families, the media, and ourselves demand that we *do* something about it. Clairol insists that we have a "coloring experience." The family, the children, insist that we look too old, asking us "when do you plan to do something about it?" The slogan, "Does she or doesn't she?" is obviously being answered rather resoundingly with, "She damned well doesn't!" But the arm-twisting continues unabated. I read that Barbara Bush, the wife of the president, receives letters asking her why she doesn't consider a "younger" color. (Punk green, perhaps? Or purple with a Mohawk?) I'm not certain that I approve of the president calling her The Silver Fox, but I admire her stubbornness in doing nothing about her lovely gray hair.

The revolt against all this is happening slowly, against terrible odds (especially from the corporations). Some women are rebelling and letting it "all hang out." In the business world, especially, women who seem to feel more secure and are on the executive level are refusing to color their hair. My wife, Sheryl, saw the first flecks of gray when she was seventeen and she never did anything about it, becoming a beautiful, totally gray-haired woman at the age of thirty-five. The ironic thing about all this is that people still come up to Sheryl on the street or on the bus to ask, "Who colors your hair?" Sarcastically, but with a smile, she answers, "Haven't you heard—it's that new Clairol color, *Going Gray!*"

There are a few other optimistic signs, but only a few. The recent addition to the magazine racks, *Lear's: For Women Who Were Not Born Yesterday*, seems to be doing well. At least we have begun to see the use of "older" models (most with young faces, I might add) in the editorial coverage. I do have some problems with the advertising thrust, though, and I shall speak more about it in chapter 7.

For the rest of us, there are still the problems of job hunting in later life and competing with the young, who have not yet discovered the first telltale flecks when they look in their mirrors in the morning. For out there in the real world, the fears of aging still exist. I have always felt, too, that the range of experience that middle-aged workers have compiled constitutes a very real threat to young managers who are still finding their way. Possibly, however, that is prejudice speaking. But it has been commented upon that one of the reasons that so much shallowness is the norm for television today is the fact that most of the current crop of writers and producers are very young and very inexperienced. Thus, some of the veterans of both New York and Hollywood are having a harder and harder time getting assignments on sitcoms and soap operas, as well as on some of the rare "more serious" shows.

But, it is time that we begin thinking less about what we have lost and what we are losing by entering middle age, and more about who we are and what we are gaining in new freedoms during these years. Attitudes must change— and that goes for both the young and the middle-aged. In the next chapter I will discuss just how we can begin setting out to change them and just who (and what) our targets are in order for us to achieve that change. There is no doubt that gerontophobia lives. But, given the proper treatment, it is not fatal and, indeed, it can be cured!

6 ❀ The Middle-Age "Hit List"

Life'd not be worth livin' if we didn't keep our inimies.

—Finley Peter Dunne
Mr. Dooley in Peace and in War

W e're stuck with a situation of self-fulfilling prophecies . . . granted that we are our own worst enemies, our next worst enemies are our families— and our physicians! Certainly, that's plenty of enemies to have!"

I laughed. The telephone conversation to Portland, Maine, had gone on for well over half an hour at that point and it was destined for still another thirty minutes. The vitality emanating over the line was the best thing that had happened to me that day. Though my original reason for telephoning Marty Knowlton was to learn more about how he founded Elderhostel (chapter 19), he and I were soon caught up in the conversation of middle-aged peers who were probing deeply to find out just who we are; covering the common ground of experience, laughing at ourselves and at the society in which we live, discussing our future plans in teaching, writing, traveling.

Most of all, I was charmed by the idea of Marty's list of "enemies." It made me feel almost a part of a previous presidential administration that was supposed to have kept its secret "hit list." The only difference, I suppose, was that the president's men had not put *themselves* at the top of *their* list.

Ever since Dr. Robert N. Butler of the National Institute on Aging (and who has since established the chair in geriatrics at the Mt. Sinai School of Medicine) coined the word, "ageism," it has become more and more evident that many of the middle-aged and elderly are *themselves* as prejudiced as any younger group of people. It stands to reason, does it not, that if we have learned all our lives to have a negative attitude towards aging, we will carry that same attitude into our later years?

Over these past few years, I have studied with interest the polls taken on the subject of aging and it has struck me rather forcefully that not only do the young have their myths and prejudices and folklore (most of it incorrect) about the process of growing older, but so do many of us, *but only about others!* In other words, when questioned about our attitudes about quality of life, about feelings, about vitality, we answer that *we're* quite OK. But, it is the *others* of our generation who suffer from everything from senility to financial disaster. *We* are the exceptions.

And so, when I spoke to Marty, I must admit that I was a bit startled when he spoke of the family as one of our enemies. The *family?* The family as an enemy? The sacrosanct, American, true-red-white-and-blue family?

Marty roared, "*Families?* Well, God, how old are you?" At the time, I was fifty-seven. "Well, you're old enough! I'm sixty. Suppose you and I, in the event that we were free—that we had no wife, were widowed or divorced— suppose we started to go out and began dating a woman. Suppose we decided to stay away for the weekend!"

I contemplated the situation and muttererd some innocuous remark while Marty continued and the telephone shook: "*Why, our families would be outraged!*"

I nodded and he went on, warming up as the AT&T clock ticked away. "Oh God, the kids really set a terrible standard of conformity. I use that because it's a rather striking example. You may have a daughter or a son who's living with someone, living without bothering to get married, and *you* decide to go off for a weekend with a person of *your* age. God God! Children in particular seem to get quite outraged at parents who fail to conform. Now, mind you, they don't *want* you to be sick, they don't *want* you to show signs of mental aberration, but they behave as though that's *exactly* how they *do* think of you!"

By the time Marty had finished that portion of his tirade, I began to resent the children we'd never had. How dare they think that way? He was right; he was very right! Having taken care of our kids quite properly, we proceeded to the next enemy on the list, *our physicians.*

This is a terribly difficult and complex area for someone of my background to treat. Like you, I was brought up in the era of house calls and the adulation of the family physician as a minor (or major) god. When my dear mother spoke of "the Specialist," there was a feeling that we were to face East and genuflect. The subject is so complex, in fact, that I shall devote the greater part of a later chapter to problems of health, the doctor, and the responsibility that we all have for our own health. But, still retaining a part of my heritage of guilt, I envision a fantasy in which my family doctor (whom I loved, but who has now retired, leaving me to the vicissitudes of the cruel world) is saying to me, "If *I* am your enemy, as you proclaim in your book, then *you* are *my* enemy—and I will not treat you for the terminal illness with which you are afflicted!" In spite of this, I grit my teeth and push onward.

From a very pragmatic view, however, I wonder why we expect our physicians to feel any different from the other elements of our society. If ageism affects even the aging, why should it not affect the doctors? They live with us too. Why should we expect more from them than we do from ourselves? Perhaps because we cannot bear to shatter the idols to whom we look when we need help.

"Yes, but if you could just get doctors to say that this is a disease, but it just happens to be with an older person," Marty went on, warming to this new subject, "if you could do that, you'd have taken a mile-long stride. But, in fact, what the doctor says is, 'This is an older person and there's not much we can do for an older person anyway.' You still have a formidable number of physicians who frequently use the diagnosis of 'senescence.'"

I am reminded of the story told again and again, in various forms, of the old gentleman who visited his doctor complaining of a deep pain in his shoulder. "What can you expect?" the doctor says. "You're ninety-seven years old." The elderly gentleman retorts, rather haughtily, "My *other* shoulder is ninety-seven years old too, and *it* doesn't hurt!" I found the story again in Alex Comfort's *A Good Age* (with a 104-year-old knee) and it was told to me two weeks later by my friend Rudy (with a ninety-five-year-old foot). You can pass it on with whatever part of the anatomy you wish. It makes an excellent point. Possibly the worst part is that we who are getting older also use it about *ourselves* when something begins to ache.

There is no doubt about it. The aging population feels that it is being "ripped off" by the medical profession, and to a great extent it is. Marty Knowlton suggested that, when I visit the Elderhostels next summer, I speak with the elderly students at the noon meal. He guaranteed that the subject of health and medicine would come up, "and you will hear expressed what can only be described as a *hatred* for doctors, a terribly bitter hatred. 'Nobody cares about the aging; the doctors don't like them.' And I think our grounds for dislike of the medical profession are very well perceived, indeed." (I did visit and they did bear him out.)

Since that conversation, I have thought long and hard about my own experiences and those of my immediate family, most of whom are even much older than I. Is it an overstatement to label the doctors our "enemies?" I think about these past few years and the appalling exploitation by the medical profession in places such as Florida, where the elderly population continues to grow. I think about the overdosing of drugs and I think perhaps *I* am paranoid, until I come across an article in a national publication like *Newsweek*, entitled, "Overdosing the Elderly." Story after story about iatrogenesis and nosocomial infections in hospitals (more on that later), the growth of consumer organizations that are fighting back, such as the People's Medical Society (and still more on that later), and I realize that I am not alone—and I am not paranoid—and I make note of the hit list: The Medical Profession.

Marty Knowlton and I ended our phone conversation some 30 minutes later, promising to contact each other if our busy schedules permitted. My notepad would be deciphered later in the quiet of my office, alone with my typewriter—my illegible scrawl eventually decoded to read, "Three enemies: self, family, physician." There simply had to be more, even though Marty felt that three were really quite enough.

In the months that followed, I began to suspect that my "hit list" was incomplete. Somehow, I felt sure that there must be other "enemies" of the aging. I mulled over the three on the list, "self, family, physician," then I penciled in one more: "the corporation."

The list was filling out and I felt like Edward G. Robinson as "Little Caesar," deciding who was next. (Thank goodness we are all old enough to remember Edward G. Robinson!)

It is not only that the American corporation is youth-oriented. The hidden slogans, "Make way for the young ones coming up and give them a chance," and "Step aside, retire, you've played your role," are actually very practical prejudices. The corporation can ostensibly justify catering to the young while rejecting or casting aside the older worker. It has nothing to do with an older worker's lack of efficiency, as we shall see later on. It is another of the pragmatic realities brought forth by the accountants and comptrollers. It's more economical! It costs less!

I think, however, that before I discuss corporations and my feelings about them, as well as discussing their inclusion on my "hit list," there are several important points from which we must begin. First off, there are corporations in America that are paragons of loyalty, integrity, and even paternalism in its best sense. I think first of the Cummins Engine Corporation in Columbus, Indiana, a family-run organization that has been cited over and over as the classic model of conscientiousness as it refers to their working people. In recent years, the family has been deeply involved in preventing the takeover of the company by outsiders, even though they might have benefited greatly. Their reasoning was that they owed their employees the loyalty that they, the workers, had given them for so many years.

The second point is almost in contrast with the first, indeed almost a contradiction. We must always remember that the corporation is—as a friend describes it—an "economic machine." Put simply, it exists to make a profit. Thus, all the unfortunate and, indeed, unfair things that seem to happen are a direct result of just that rule of thumb. And the people who run the corporations must live by that rule. For the corporation is merely a reflection of those people, good or bad, competent or deficient, skillful or bungling. They may not *intend* to create the traumas of which I write, but these things happen to us at times nonetheless. So, if we look carefully at this "economic machine," we begin to understand why some of these things are being done to us.

Primarily, the young worker or the employee just starting out receives less pay than someone with seniority. The additional expenses borne by the corporation are minimal when someone is under twenty-five, rather than over fifty. Health insurance, pension funds, the disability insurance costs are all lower for the young employee than for the older one.

It was borne out for me quite forcefully when I started my small corporation (now ten years old) and we grew large enough for us to hire our first outside employee. I filled out the necessary papers, filed the forms with the federal government and the state, discussed the plan with my insurance agent, pension advisor, and my accountant. The fact that this young woman was eminently qualified for the job, had just the right amount of experience (much of it with me in a past company), spoke five languages, and could handle a film crew anywhere in the world appeared to make no difference. The key question always seemed to be, "How old is she?" And the reaction to my answer was, "Great! She's young enough to make the additional expenses minimal."

Multiply this, if you will, by the ten or fifty thousand people in a large company. The total can be substantial. The result is always the same—the old must make way for the young. For example, a new pension plan is not vested until four or five years after a worker begins the job. It is possible that the entire sum put into that plan will be returned to the company if the worker leaves before that time. In dealing with the fifty-year-old, early retirement is a good way for the corporation to become much leaner. Thus, in these past years we have seen, more and more often, the pressures for retirement of people still in their fifties. "Leave now and get a large settlement or stay on and we can promise nothing but your vested pension next year." There have also been companies that have gone into bankruptcy, with some pension funds being wiped out—the older worker again being the one to suffer. Just recently, I heard of yet another case, a man who had worked for twenty-seven years at his job, being declared "nonessential" after all that time, and forcibly retired.

For years, too, the corporations of the country were the leaders in the fight against some sort of national health care, especially toward older workers. "Socialism" and much worse has been leveled by the attacks mounted through the American Medical Association and the Fortune 500. Suddenly, as we enter the nineties, a new cry is being heard—from whom? From the corporations, of course, from CEOs like Lee Iacocca. We hear the executives who have been so strident and single-minded in their condemnation of a national health policy now demanding that the government do something about *their* mounting health insurance costs. I look with wonder and with awe as they have now begun to join forces with Ralph Nader and with organizations like the Gray Panthers!

There is yet another way in which some corporations play the villain, and I think it is tightly tied to the problems of ageism in the company. In all the years of dealing with America's top companies and in reading both the news and business sections of newspapers and magazines, I have seldom seen an acceptance of responsibility for the human, physical problems created by a manufacturing processer or a corporate philosophy. Blanket denial is the typical response to the accusation of being a bad corporate citizen.

Certainly, not all corporations are guilty of this, and many for which I have produced films in these past forty years are very much concerned with the environment, the inner city, and the rights of minorities. Their public image is also their private one, and for that they are to be congratulated. It is always good to read of a company like Ben & Jerry's (ice cream) in Vermont, who contribute 7 percent of their profits to charitable causes.

But, when we read of a defective product being recalled, it is generally at the urging of the government or Ralph Nader or some active consumer group in Washington. I keep waiting for someone to take responsibility for the problems of lung cancer and heart disease that have been placed at the doorstep of the tobacco industry. I was saddened this past year to hear of the retirement of the surgeon general, Dr. C. Everett Koop, for in the past eight years he has done more to point the finger of guilt at the cigarette than any other government agency. And what, I ask, is the answer by the industry? "Not proven" the executive says, holding a lighted cigarette in his or her hand.

I wonder when a concerned corporate citizen will step up and genuinely respond to the Love Canals, the PCB dumping, and the poisons that are polluting and killing our rivers and our lakes. The answer that "at the time our company did it, it was the state of the art" somehow doesn't seem good enough. The cancer in the asbestos industry, the brown lung of the cotton mills, the black lung of the mines, the unsafe machines on the assembly lines and on the farms, are all a part of the picture.

Were you—or I—completely satisfied with the attitudes after the Bhopal disaster in India? What about the Exxon oil spill in Alaska? For years, the company had assured us that any emergency could be and would be taken care of with dispatch. Indeed, did our "environmental" president even bother to fly to the distant state to witness what is described as one of the worst environmental disasters ever to befall our wildlife and our ecology? At our own small island, we can no longer eat the striped bass because of the PCBs dumped into their spawning grounds by major corporations. Where are the people who will take responsibility?

The answer to all this is exactly the same as the answer to ageism, and it characterizes much of American industry. It is more economical to deny that it exists. To admit blame is to be forced to pay. If these are our good corporate citizens, why should we expect them to treat their workers any differently, and especially the middle-aged workers who are beginning to cost them more money? Why should the employee be any different than the environment? The appalling thing to me, in addition, is that these same executive denials are made by people just like *us*, who live in our communities, who have families just as vulnerable to the poisons in our atmosphere and our workplace, and who can "put on another hat" when they enter their offices. I have never been able to understand that.

If it will help at all, you can be sure of two things. First of all, it is much worse in many óther countries. There are cities I have visited all over the world where the smog and the smoke and the carcinogens seem to enter your hotel room once you awaken in the morning and open the window to greet the hazy sun, fighting its way through the gloom. In Zagreb, Yugoslavia, the industrial smoke is almost impenetrable and much worse than the awful smog of the Los Angeles valley. Athens, Greece, has gone from azure, clear sky to impossible inversions in only twenty-five years and companies are being offered tax advantages if they will but move a hundred miles from the lovely city. Unfortunately, this is the only world we have.

The second point is that it seems to be getting worse. The country has been moving more and more toward a laissez-faire attitude in terms of the business community. For the past two administrations and now, well into this one, corporations have been subject to much less government interference from the EPA and from OSHA and the other regulatory commissions.

The bright light on the horizon, hopefully, is that President Bush has indicated that he would like to reverse the trend and has taken steps toward controlling acid rain and improving the environment. For a while, though, I was convinced that the path we were taking was finally to let the corporations police themselves! If that had happened, you can forget the way that Pittsburgh looked before the new industrial laws were instituted. If we had let the corporations police themselves, we might approximate the situation by comparing it to the Ku Klux Klan investigating a lynching in Alabama in 1933!

Once again, I looked at my list: "self, family, physician, corporation." One more to go—another member of the hit list bent on making us invisible. But, just because it is last on the list, don't ever think that it is, therefore, least. Let me introduce you to a not-very-good friend of ours, and possibly one of the more dangerous of our "enemies": the media.

7 The Medium Is the Mirror

Thou art unseen, but yet I hear thy shrill delight.

—Percy Bysshe Shelley
"To a Skylark"

I will admit right at the start that it is sometimes too easy to condemn the press, radio, movies, or television for our invisibility. For too many generations, the media have been condemned for all manner of social, economic, and sexual ills. In my mother's time, her mother condemned the "dime novel" for instilling hopeless romantic dreams in a young girl's head. The era of yellow journalism, still with us today in many of our newspapers and magazines, has been cited as spreading crime and violence through the reportage and glorification of the convulsions that wrack a changing society. Indeed, it is the media that are the first *victims* when a society is in turmoil or something needs to be hidden by a government in power. South Africa is a prime example. The media were the first to be blacked out during the huge Chinese upheavals in the summer of 1989. It is no wonder, for the media wield enormous power.

Recently, our library books have again become the targets of the wrath of parents who hold the publishing industry responsible for the absence of worthwhile values in their children, for sexual promiscuity, smoking marijuana, using crack, for abortion, rape, and lack of ambition, as well as a less-than-intense involvement with God and flag. I read with horror of a Midwest group that was taking books off the shelves of the local libraries because they were spreading the heresy of "humanism" (whatever is meant by that) as well as birth control and other distortions too numerous to mention. One of the books that I grew up with, *The Catcher in the Rye*, is no longer there. *Brave*

New World has been banished, along with *Animal Farm*. Thousands of kids are now missing the wonderful world of Holden Caulfield, along with the fantasy-reality of some of the world's best writers.

You may be certain that if the society is sick, the media will be blamed for spreading the plague, whether it be through television, advertising, motion pictures, or the books we read. And once attacked, the contemporary media have a tendency to bury their heads rather than fight back as once they used to. Witness the history of *Satanic Verses* and the death threats against Salman Rushdie, the booksellers, and the publishers.

Of course, much of what we *choose* to read is rubbish and most of what we watch on television is neutral. Most of what the magazines print is shallow. Every sizable city in the country boasts a daily newspaper whose best attribute is that it is just thick enough and wide enough to wrap the morning trash for collection or to pick up after the family dog. But I tread very lightly in one important area when I speak of the media as an enemy of aging.

I do not believe in censorship. I do not believe that we should muzzle any part of the media. I am fully aware that the rights of the parents of whom I speak are as sacrosanct as my own—*but only in making themselves heard and felt,* and not in any way impinging upon my choice of what I read or what I view or how I think. "Your freedom ends where my nose begins," Voltaire said, and I mutter a loud, "Amen!" And when someone says to me, as they have no doubt, to you, "But you have to draw the line somewhere," I can only answer, *"Your line or my line?"* Who is to draw the line?

The media, with all the warts and flaws of any institution run by human beings, may be no more guilty of perpetuating the myths and stereotypes of aging than other segments of our society. Indeed, is it fair to blame *all* our problems on just one element that mirrors what all of us seem to think about ourselves?

One of the most interesting conclusions of the Harris study was that, generally speaking, the public is *not* critical of the way the media portray the people of our generations. The media themselves point to this conclusion when faced with complaints. They tell us that they merely report and reflect the stereotypes and myths that are *already* a part of the public image. Certainly a possibility. But does that relieve the media of *all* responsibility for the prevailing impression? Am I being unfair when I declare the media responsible in large part for distorting our image? Am I unfair when I designate them as an integral part of my hit list? Not by a long shot!

This is a society based upon a strong media presence. A majority of our citizens cannot remember the era before television. Because of our high literacy rate, newspapers, magazines, and books play an important role in the dissemination not only of facts, but of pseudofacts and myths as well. An institution so pervasive and so powerful as the American media cannot be allowed to excuse itself with, "We're only a mirror. We give the public what it wants."

Ironically, the middle-aged—our generation—run the media. (And those in charge are, by happenstance, almost all men.) With more and more of the outlets—both print and electronic—now being controlled by a handful of media barons, the outcome will probably be even more ominous in terms of how we are represented. Though I was raised in a much more naive era, when we expected some good to come from the people in power, I see that it is only pressure brought by large segments of the marketplace that gets their attention.

It is no different in the political arena, with the media feeding on the handouts of the politicians in power. And thus, we naively expected aging presidents and legislators to have some compassion for an aging population. But, beginning in 1977, when the notorious "notch effect" reduced benefits for people born in 1917, we then suffered through eight years of an administration that, to say the least, was indifferent, if not downright hostile. Our basic source of income in our later years can be saved only through the hue and cry of what the politicians derogatorily call, "special interest groups," namely *us*.

Television: The Distorted Image

My television set is still an old, decrepit, black-and-white model dating from about 1954 (though I have recently acquired a new color set for use in my videotape work). I see no reason to change the original set; it still works. I do not feel a need for color, as my father obviously did when he got his first color set. I entered the room to exclaim, "Dad, the baseball diamond is all blue!" Barely turning around to answer, he retorted, "So what! It's in *color!*" The only time I see color television over the air or on cable is in hotel rooms in distant cities while dressing for the day. In those early morning hours, as I watch for what passes as intellectual discussion by uninformed Hollywood actors and actresses who have only the barest acquaintance with the material they are presenting, I vow again to retain my black-and-white set until it self-destructs. Besides, even though it is an old model, it still has one of the remote control units, so when I do get angry, I can simply shoot a beam at it and shut it off completely. It gives me an unmatched sense of power!

I mention all this to put this chapter into its proper perspective. It is not, by any stretch of the imagination, an objective view of television. It is, rather, a selective compilation of the things that relate only to us—the middle-aged and the aging in our population. I leave the overall analyses to those who spend more time than I do in front of the set.

Back in the forties, when I was a young television director, I gave a speech to a group of men at a local social club. In awesome tones I informed them that we had "over 100,000 television sets in the United States and the next year the number might very well double!" I smile now as I write this, for the statistics have long since arrived at amazing totals.

As of late 1986, 98 percent of all households in the United States had television sets, with 92 percent owning color TV. That does not include those in bars, lounges, airports, hospitals, or portable TV sets. When I first wrote *Second Spring* I commented upon the fact (with a large exclamation point) that there were 700 stations broadcasting television shows, without including cable. Today, about eight years later, almost 1,700 stations broadcast television, and about 3,700 cable systems are in operation! And none of this even begins to touch the nearly 50,000 nonbroadcast television users in corporations, public service sectors, and teleconferencing networks. Even as I write these figures, they are probably going out of date, and new technologies to tempt us and seduce us and propagandize us are arriving every day, from the VCR, now in 50 percent of all American homes, to HDTV (High Definition Television), with Japan just going on the air even as I write. (And the cost of a basic receiver at $60,000!) The bottom line—as always—is money.

In his marvelous little book, *Television and the Aging Audience* (University of Southern California Press), Dr. Richard H. Davis of the Ethel Percy Andrus Gerontology Center defined television as "pop art . . . aimed toward the masses. Further, it is mass-produced by profit-minded entrepreneurs solely for the gratification of a paying mass audience. . . . Television, which is supposed to be free and operating in the 'interest, convenience, and necessity of the people' is actually the servant of the merchandisers."

Maybe we older people are a viable and growing market. Maybe we do represent the majority of prime-time viewers. But that is not the deciding factor. It is *how* the marketer thinks of his audience that eventually determines the programming, casting, image, or myth to be broadcast and perpetuated. Some time ago the brilliant *New York Times* columnist Russell

Baker began his weekly satire with the statement that "the faces of television newswomen are never wrinkled." He went on to explain that he did not include the *men,* such as Walter Cronkite. Their faces, he wrote, "always seem to have arrived fresh from the presser two seconds ahead of the camera." Imagine your reactions if one evening, on prime-time network news, a woman in her sixties appeared, delivering the anchor spot commentary for one of the major stations in your city. No more Rather, Cronkite, Chancellor, Safer—but an attractive, gray-haired, articulate, intelligent older woman! Possibly you would nod and say, "Who'd believe the news coming from a little old lady who could be your grandmother?"

In fact, not only is the suggestion fantasy, but the exact opposite seems to be happening on television. (Barbara Walters is always used as the *exception.* Tomorrow, perhaps, we will have yet another.) The aging population, if you were to believe that flickering purveyor of misinformation and trivialization, is a *vanishing* breed. Look only at the dramatic shows on television, those great "slice-of-life" hours that communicate the shallowness of our lives when the schedule is not busy with "T and A" ("tits and ass" in TV's charming executive vernacular—more modestly known as "jiggle shows"); only 3 percent of the major characters on the shows are old.

- *Old women* account for less than 1 percent of the major characters on these shows.

- *Older black women* are generally depicted only as victims or as corpses.

Considering that over 12 percent of our population has hit the sixty-five-year mark, the figures—to say the least—certainly don't reflect "real life." I have noticed, however, that some shows, such as cooking shows, do feature people whom we might call "older," and possibly their appearance has to do with their years of experience in the field of food. Pierre Franey, Madeleine Kamen (not to mention the wonderful pioneer, Julia Child) now hold forth where youth once trod. But in the field of TV news, in sitcom, in soap operas, in drama, the older person—and particularly the older female—is seldom seen. A few years back, a TV anchor in Kansas City, Missouri, lost her job at the age of thirty-seven because, "My boss told me I was too old, too unattractive and not deferential enough to men." As she described it so well, "For a man, wrinkles are credibility, for a woman disqualification." All this at age thirty-seven!

I would be as breathless as a Madonna-fan teenager if I had been the first to discover all this. There have been incredibly deep and reflective studies of the problems of television and its portrayal of the middle-aged and aging. Not only is the study by Dr. Davis a complete and well-structured report on the problem, but the Media Watch of the Gray Panthers, the White House Mini-Media Conference, and Dr. George Gerbner, Dean of the University of Pennsylvania's Annenberg School of Communications (and his staff) have all issued complete and damning in-depth studies on the imbalance of ages on television, and the destructive role that stereotyping plays in programming.

Dr. Gerbner sampled 1,365 programs in his original report, involving almost 17,000 characters, covering television plays, movies, cartoons, situation comedies, and crime-action shows. Immediately, he found that *more than half* the TV population was between the ages of twenty-five and forty-five. The only statistic that makes me feel we are not alone is that the under-eighteen group, who make up about 30 percent of our population, are represented by 8 percent of the fictional characters.

- Between forty and sixty-five, the *men* more or less hold their own.

- Aging men begin to represent power, political clout, and sophisticated, gray-haired affluence. Frequently in prime time, the aging man is represented as a despicable villain, but be grateful for the little things—at least he *is* represented.

In direct contrast to what actually happens in our society, where the women begin to outnumber the men, television gives us exactly the opposite picture.

- The middle aged woman begins to disappear from the screen as she turns the corner at forty or forty-five.

A note from Dr. Gerbner tells me that there should be a new, updated report coming out about the time that this book is being published. I am most anxious to see if there has been any change at all over these past few years. For, if there is extreme justification in crying out against a state of invisibility, the woman of our generation must certainly have an inside track. She begins to disappear very much as though the antenna had been turned on the wrong axis and away from the beamed signal. And no amount of adjusting of the dials will ever bring her back.

Dr. Davis explained it only too well. "Society's regard for an individual appears to be in direct ratio to his contribution to the gross national product. . . . Individual appeal (sometimes confused with worth) is measured on a value scale of attractiveness. The best women are beautiful and young. The best men are virile and young . . . in TV, however, men become more powerful as they grow older. They control the money." And here, of course, television does mirror our society, does it not?

But it is not only the "disappearing act" that disturbs the researchers and the sociologists. Even worse than the disturbing statistics is *the way* in which television represents the aging portion of our population. The Annenberg report states, "More older characters are treated with disrespect than are the characters in any other age group. About 70 percent of older men and more than 80 percent of older women are not held in high esteem or treated courteously, a very different pattern of treatment than that found for younger characters. A much larger proportion of older characters than younger characters are portrayed as eccentric or foolish. A greater proportion of older women than older men—two-thirds compared to about half—are presented as lacking common sense, acting silly, or being eccentric. This male-female distinction is not salient in other age groups."

There is an interesting and ironic twist to the presentation of the aging man on television, however. It is true that the role of our male age group is frequently associated with power. But before you explode with pride, read on, sir. The Annenberg report also concluded that "Old men have the highest ratio of fatal vicitimization among all male age groups. Old men in television drama, especially when in a major, prime-time, serious role, are more likely to be evil than any other age group. Evil must have power to be credible. But in a world of happy endings, evil must also perish—hence the high ratio of old men who are killed."

There is an interesting exception to all this, though it does not take place during prime-time hours. On the daytime radio and television serials—the soap operas—younger characters are frequently depicted more negatively than older characters. The latter are often the sympathetic friends, older business people, even older women. The younger ones seem to do nothing but get into some sort of trouble, depending upon what is currently "in" at that moment—abortion, pregnancy, rape, AIDS, crack, or stealing someone else's spouse.

If we turn to the area of television news and documentaries, the coverage is even more strongly unbalanced, since most of the reporting is concerned with the elderly *poor*. What follows from that is a picture even more distorted—the institutionalization of the elderly, the retired couples on welfare, the unemployed, the homeless, the destitute. Economic problems, poor health, loneliness. The decrepit, the unloved, the unwanted, the hungry, and the suicidal. No matter what demographics exist to prove the contrary, this is our television picture of the aging.

It is no wonder that, according to both the Harris study and the Annenberg report, the more people watch television—and especially the younger generations, who average as much as *twenty-two hours a week*— the more they tend to perceive old people in generally negative and unfavorable terms. "Those who watch more television believe that people (especially women) become old earlier in life," concludes the Harris study.

What is the reason for all this? Money? Sure. The young audiences to whom television caters? Of course. But, in the past few years, I have become aware of yet another factor that seems to be one of the major explanations for the perpetuation of myths about aging, and that is the rapidly lowering age scale of both the executives and the writers who feed us this daily pap. Follow the logic if you will. If there is a deep-seated prejudice in this country about aging, and if our young people are infected with it early in life, does it not stand to reason that they will continue to perpetuate those stereotypes as they take over the management and control of the airwaves? Thus, in following that logic, we find that the *writers* of television programming are getting younger and younger—but even more importantly—the *older* writers are being squeezed out of the business.

Article after article, collected in my files during these past years, speak to the fact that producers discriminate against writers over forty years old—as well as against women and minorities. (Heaven help the woman or minority person who is also over forty!) Young executives have actually stated that they just don't believe that older writers can entice a teenage audience. Experience doesn't count. Craft no longer counts. As always, in America, youth alone seems to count. In an excellent article in *CINETEX Report* (April 1989) Steven J. Fisher commented, "Youth has no bearing on creativity and, in fact, may explain a certain shallowness in television and film today due to inexperience."

He also quoted Stephen Lord, whose writing credits include *The Loretta Young Show* (remember Loretta Young?) and several feature films. Lord feels that, "I know I am definitely a better writer today than twenty years ago because (1) I know more, (2) I understand more, (3) I have had relationships that I didn't dream existed when I was younger, (4) I can more easily identify with my characters, (5) I know most of the cliché plots and avoid them, (6) my craft has improved greatly."

Is anybody listening? Indeed, is there any hope? The damage has been done for so many years that even the public seems to see nothing wrong with both the image being presented on television or the fact that there is blatant age-related bias against the most experienced people in the field. In turn, the networks and the cable systems raise their halo-crowned, antenna-shaped heads and innocently say, "Why are you picking on *us?*"

Every once in a while, in addition to the more mature hosts of cooking shows, the television screen does give us a picture of the middle-aged audience with a show specifically designed for our group. For a few years, the Public Broadcasting System produced a program called *Over Easy*, devoted entirely to the issues, concerns, and challenges of older Americans. And, for the past seven years or so, my friend Jean Phillips has been host of a similar cable program called *Prime Time.* But it is a small dent in the system and somehow I find myself comparing it to the years of pointing to Jackie Robinson and Ralph Bunche as examples of racial equality in America. There are dozens of children's shows on television, cartoons directed toward a young audience through the Saturday morning programming (along with the most violent toy commercials—"no batteries included"), and we are expected to rejoice when, every once in a while, we are given a show of our own. And what a time slot it gets in most places. For a while, *Over Easy* was broadcast at 7:00 A.M. on *Sunday* in my area! It's hardly a time when I would be awake watching television!

But, even when we are "given" our own shows, we find that the networks— convinced that old age starts at forty—will offer a mistress of ceremonies who is the glamorous daughter of a famous movie star, as one program did. She was half the age of the audience for whom the show was intended. All the commercials on that particular show were oriented toward the young—*not one* included a representative of the middle-aged or older viewer. And this one was televised at 7:30 on a Saturday night. Now, if you've read this far, you certainly know that on Saturday night we all sit home and long for our younger days of carefree weekends on the town. I do not know if the program is still being aired, and I frankly do not care.

At the White House Conference there was a slight note of hope in another area, though it was just as quickly dashed. After commenting upon the fact that broadcast television has rarely acknowledged the existence of senior citizens, much less their needs, a suggestion was made that "cable TV can change all that. In many communities 'public access' channels have been set aside for programs produced by local groups. However, only about a tenth of all cable systems have public access channels, and only a small fraction of these carry programming by and for seniors."

Again, the bottom line is money. After making the first optimistic statement, the report concluded: "As channel time increases in value, nonprofit programs may be bumped off." Coming from a very tough New York neighborhood, I loved the last two words, "bumped off." They could not have been more succinct or more appropriate.

Advertising and Commercials: "We Pause Now for Thirty Seconds of Youth"

Now that I have passed my sixty-fifth birthday, I am allowed by society to be eccentric, an incurable curmudgeon. Nay, society *demands* that I be eccentric if I am to fit into the mold. Society will, therefore, be happy to know that I am, indeed, quite idiosyncratic. I talk back to commercials.

I talk back to television commercials. I talk back to radio commercials. I even talk back to newspaper advertising that strikes me as being stereotypical. I am currently spending my mornings talking back to an absolutely appalling commercial for a local bank that features the most obnoxious child in the world along with his father. And I once spent almost six months talking back to an executive who did commercials for his Fortune 500 corporation and was busy trying to get me to write to my congressman to complain that the tax laws were unfair to big business!

Interestingly enough, I have observed the end result of all this talking back. Not a damn thing seems to happen to change the advertising industry.

If television and its programming are on the hit list of the aging group of Americans, then the advertising community must certainly be at the head of the class. For some years I was involved in the production of television commercials. I moved away from them because of the frustration of working with advertising people. Much of the copy, the design, the marketing approach, and the supervision of advertising (and thus in the TV-commercial world) is done by the young "geniuses" of the industry. After a visit to one of the leading agencies in the country, I was struck once more by the fact that the advertising copy is not only *directed* toward the "Pepsi Generation," it's also *written* by them. Even when the agencies do target the older audiences, they seem to flounder and miscarry. As Richard H. Davis of the Andrus Gerontology Center put it, "Advertisers who have their copy prepared by youthful creative geniuses may fail to sell to an older audience they wish to target because of inappropriate techniques employed by those individuals, who do not truly understand that the currently fashionable advertising methods may turn away older audience."

What are those attitudes? Advertisers are convinced that such things as brand preference and buying habits are well formed by the time we are in our thirties and that they don't change very much as we enter our forties and fifties—and certainly not past sixty.

There has been a recent "discovery" of our true market and our potential strength, mostly due to the work of people like Ken Dychtwald (*Age Wave*), who has been telling both corporations and the public that they're missing a bet by not looking more closely at us as an affluent group of consumers. But even then, there are two major categories in which we seem to predominate— not the fast automobiles, or the luxurious travel destinations, or the food products new to the marketplace, but denture cleaners, little liver pills, laxatives, pantyhose with tummy control tops (all necessary for that gradual physical breakdown), life insurance, Medicare supplements, and *coin collecting* (the latter to keep us busy during the hours when we are not sleeping or watching television).

The second area is one in which you don't have to tune in very long to find the catchword for television advertising (and to a great extent, the ads in newspapers and magazines). It has five letters that spell *young,* and it is ubiquitous and frequently disturbing. It is not only the beauty products that promise a "different, younger look," or "younger-looking skin," for even in their feeble attempts to change, the copywriters manage to trip over their typewriters. I watched a commercial for Camay and heard the phrase, "for a beautiful complexion *at any age!*" I looked up, startled. Where was the word, *young?* Was the advertising world changing at last? The women shown first were between the ages of twenty and thirty. The woman shown finally on the screen did look quite attractive, and the announcer intoned, "See how lovely she looks at forty-one!" The end. Life begins at forty, and ends at forty-one? And so does beauty? Of course, I talked back to the commercial, but to no avail. The deluge continues.

An ad for another product features *a child,* possibly about six months old, and we read that "Little Emily is in the process of getting facial lines." And then, a short time later, we see another child, only fourteen days old, and again we are warned that "she's already developing facial wrinkles." A cos- metic surgeon tells us that he can "recapture your youthful image" and all it takes is breast enlargement, breast reduction, nose and chin reprofiling, face and neck lifting, eyelid correction, abdominal tightening, lipo-suction, or the latest methods of cellulite removal. We are promised youthful eyes. Youthful skin. Youthful buttocks. We have become an Oil of Olay Society!

No matter what the category, though, advertisers favor youthful women to sell the products. On the other hand, they consider age to be an asset in men. The celebrity, of course, is age-irrelevant, since reputation and instant recognizability are factors in choosing the spokesperson. In the world of "voice-overs"—the off-camera actors who sell the product without being seen on the screen—men are chosen between 80 and 90 percent of the time. The advertising industry claims that the choices are based upon "substantial market research and the testing of specific commercials" before they are put on the air.

Now let us look at the *way* in which older people are shown, if they appear at all. As a character in a television commercial increases in age, that character's *physical activity* decreases in direct proportion, and his health problems increase at a rapid rate. In a study done some years back, researchers found that 3.2 percent of the characters between the ages of thirty and forty experienced some sort of health problem, from headaches to minor arthritis to muscle pain due to physical activities. However, as the characters entered their sixties (and up to seventy), almost 35 percent were complainers of ill health. In the real world, the study concluded, people between the ages of sixty and seventy do not experience ten times the number of health problems of any other age group.

The youth culture makes itself still more evident in the implied promise of most commercials and advertising—sexual conquest. In every such commercial ever screened by a researcher—and there have been many—the high degree of sexuality involves young and attractive actors. It holds true for television—it holds true for newspapers and for magazines. But I have, lo and behold, found one glorious, shining exception!

In going through my local newspaper just the other day, I came across an ad for *New Choices for the Best Years*, a magazine that once carried the title of *50 Plus*. On the left page was a photo of a couple who were about sixty and the caption read: "At age fifty-nine, this is how Irv and Lillian Beck look." On the right page, the caption read: "But this is how they feel" and the photo showed a couple of indeterminate young age (possibly thirty or so) heavily necking in the back seat of a car! Hallelujah! The copy, for the first time that I can remember, told it like it is:

The way people look at fifty-nine is no indication of how they feel. . . . We know these people not only have more money to spend, but more time to spend it. Which is precisely what they do. On everything from vocations to vacations. And even those who've retired from work, have not retired from life.

No aches. No pains. No liver pills. No dentures. Their radio commercials—to which I do not talk back because they are so funny—also cover the aging group of Americans who travel rather than sit at home and watch television. *Modern Maturity* magazine has also taken the same tack by featuring older people who are quite "normal" by society's young standards.

But, for the most part, you might just look at the advertising that fills the pages of our magazines and newspapers. Just look at the promises of Bermuda and Nassau and all the outer and inner islands. Look carefully at the photographs that accompany the advertising copy. All young. All impossibly attractive. All sexy. *We* older folks are probably back at the hotel sleeping again, or watching Bermudian television. The trend is even evident in publications that say that they are geared to the middle-aged consumer (or the older person), such as *Lear's*. Even here, the thrust of the advertising is in staying young, though I notice that more and more upscale products such as sleek automobiles and diamonds are beginning to fill the pages in the search for the new affluent consumer group that we have become.

The advertising world is guilty of creating a society in which we must project a certain image of ourselves when we reach a particular age. We are the victims of a society and an industry that perpetuates the distorted thinking of that society by telling us when we are to grow old, and if we have grown old, that we have less social value, less economic worth, less feeling of *self*-worth unless we take steps to go backwards and to become young. Advertising and the commercial messages, ever present in our vast media, are amplifiers of all these contorted precepts. The images that they present begin to have the power of commandments. And it is no wonder that the older viewer or reader becomes angry and filled with anxiety.

Interestingly enough, the television commercial field is one place where the pressures we can bring to bear have begun to show some slight effect. The portrayal of older persons as characters has improved somewhat, and more and more messages are being directed toward the middle-aged and the elderly. This can probably be attributed to the fact that individuals and organizations have mounted strong protests about "ageism," and also to the Rip Van Winkles of the ad world who have suddenly awakened to discover a brand-new market. Instead of the "Fountain of Youth," they have belatedly located the

"Affluence of Age." Both subjects will be covered in later chapters. But for now, it is time to wander over to our bookshelves and see how well (or poorly) we fare between the covers.

Our Popular Prose: Balderdash on the Bookshelves

I arrived at New York's Pennsylvania Station on a rainy morning, too early for the train. It is, unfortunately, my destiny to remain a "Type A" personality, one who can never be late for an appointment or a train or plane departure, and one who is impatient with those who are perpetually tardy. Born of a "hyper" mother and nurtured in the field of communications, "on time" translates more easily for me as "too early," while arriving late would probably mean being right on time! But my penchant for promptness allows me ample opportunity to wander, to observe, to lose myself in the surroundings of a new neighborhood while waiting for the designated hour. It was just such a morning and the train to Philadelphia for my meeting with Maggie Kuhn was still more than two hours away. I wandered into a bookshop, though I have never found a book I wanted to buy in an airline terminal or railroad station bookstore. But I do like to wander through them and I revel in looking at the pictures on the covers.

I had become intensely aware by this time of our invisibility and our false images on television and in the world of advertising. I had not realized until then, however, that the problem would extend even into my beloved books. The bookshop, so crowded with easy-to-read, pass-the-time-on-Amtrak paperbacks, was to offer still another view of the youth culture and the invisibility of both middle age and the older generations.

As usual, the books in the paperback "sex" section were turned face out so that browsers could not only read the titles, but also could be tempted by the nubile flesh of the half-dressed girls and women who graced the jackets along with the faceless, young, athletic men. And, in case any of us had missed the point of sexuality being only for those under thirty, the titles helped set the record straight. *So Young a Bride* next to *Young Girl for Sale* and *Sexy Young Playmate*. A few books down the row, I found *A Bride So Young* and I wondered how much it differed from *So Young a Bride*.

But these "young" titles are also accompanied by those marvelous words that tempt us with the story inside (such as it is): *Desire, Lust, Ecstasy, Promise, Pleasure, Nymph* (or *Nymphet*), *Passion, Horny,* and *Turning On.* I would have loved it all as a kid. But, having had my fill of vicarious book-cover sex and not seeing anyone on the cover that I knew or recognized, I moved on to the romantic novels, published for yet another trade by firms like Harlequin.

But even here, nothing much was different. The words changed somewhat. Instead of *Lust*, I read *Magic* and *Snowflake* and *Flame* and *Stars* and *Moonlight* and *Love* and *Paradise*. The jackets still flaunted the lovers, though more fully clothed, yet all of them were *young*. I began to wonder. Where are *we*? Where are the aging faces on the covers of the books? I finally found out.

Walking past the ever-growing proliferation of books about Wall Street and how to make money, leveraged buyouts, and real-estate killings, I finally found us. We are on the *biographies!* We have lived long enough to get our pictures on the covers only if we achieve something. There *we* were, in all our famous glory—not as half-clothed nymphs cavorting in a *Playboy* or *Penthouse* bedroom, or standing near a misty castle with Heathcliff coming through the gloom, but in sections of serious reading. Isaac Asimov, Lillian Hellman, Phil Donahue, Albert Einstein, Joan Crawford, Jacob Javits, Luciano Pavarotti, Henry Kissinger, George Burns, Bill Moyers, Jackie Kennedy, and Samuel Goldwyn, to name but a few.

It was time to hurry so I could be early at the gate. On my way out of the shop, two books caught my eye. The first was called *Forever Young* by Dr. Stuart Berger and it promised right on the cover that it was about "Keeping Your Bones Young and Making Your Brain Younger," and the second was back at the paperback sex section and I wondered how I had missed it the first time through. I laughed as the book seemed to leer right back at me as I read the title: *She Liked Them Old.* I mentally thumbed my nose at it and made my way into the cavernous terminal.

The arena of literature and the editorial content of our magazines is but a carbon copy, an instant replay, of the other segments of the media, especially when it comes to the aging. The invisibility and the stereotyping that permeate the television industry and the field of advertising are just as rampant in books, especially in the literature written for children and young adults, an age when opinions and sensibilities are developed that will be carried through life.

The Council on Interracial Books for Children has been studying the problem and analyzing children's print media for more than twenty years, and though their first target was racism and the stereotyping of blacks and other minorities, they began to uncover a vast array of other stereotypes: about women, about disabled people, about working people—and about the aging.

Acknowledging that the traditional fairy tales and classic children's book presented older people as witches, goblins, and ogres, the council also found that the major problem with contemporary children's books was the same as in the other media: the invisibility of older people on their pages. Older people, especially sane, useful, active, articulate, sensible, experienced older people, just do not exist. In the late seventies, they conducted a study of some seven hundred picture books and found that *almost six hundred* contained no older characters at all!

The pattern I've been writing about begins to make itself felt again. First invisibility and then less-than-adequate treatment of the characters who do appear. It doesn't change when the literature given to our children is analyzed. Older characters, if they show up at all in *Jane's Trip to the Zoo*, are generally referred to as "old" or "little" (or "little old") or "ancient." I wonder how my friend Alex would feel—all dignified six feet, three of him, a vital man in his late seventies—if I were to refer to him as "little old Alex"!

Older characters in children's books also do very little of interest, it seems. They appear as janitors, shopkeepers, elderly grandparents who sit in rocking chairs, Grandpa whittling on a piece of wood, Grandma smiling—just smiling. They are seldom, if ever, still working in professional careers (except for an occasional kindly "little old" doctor) or in vital, competitive activities. How does a youngster reconcile all of this with *you* as a grandparent, if you are one? If children are fed the image of the grandmother who stays in her kitchen baking pies, except when she sits on her rocker on the porch, how on earth can they accept the actual grandparent who has just come back from a day of creative work or playing golf or jogging, and is dressing to go out to dinner with friends?

Their own grandfather, if he tried to whittle, might cut his fingers badly, since his job does not require that he know how to handle a knife. And their grandmother, in this day and age, may well be (and probably is) a chic, attractive woman in her late forties or early fifties, and possibly (probably) still active as a lawyer or shop owner. I smiled when I read an article some years back stating that everyone accepted the fact that Lillian Carter, Jimmy Carter's mother, was indeed a grandmother (and a great-great grandmother). But Mr. and Mrs. Jimmy Carter are *also* grandparents. So if the children can only think of the rocking chair, how do they reconcile Miss Lillian's flying off to India to visit the people with whom she worked in the Peace Corps when she was in her sixties? Indeed, how do they reconcile Grandfather Jimmy Carter now working physically in the rebuilding of Homestead properties in the inner cities as a part of a program to help the poor and the homeless?

Studies of adolescent literature show very much the same pattern, with older characters never in the mainstream of the plots, but merely bit players on the edges—shadow puppets who play out roles unrelated to real life. They are quiet, self-sufficient, never causing any trouble, never "making waves"—underdeveloped people, not so much totally invisible as unimportant. Interestingly enough, the studies of the early literature for adolescents show very much the same patterns of bias, so ageism is not a newly discovered, contemporary phenomenon. It is the awareness of it that is changing.

Ageism is, of course, omnipresent and our awareness of it is a step forward in trying to change the patterns. Sociologists have found the infestation in every area of the print media. An analysis of more than two thousand cartoons from a wide range of magazines showed that even in this medium (or *especially* in this medium), the elderly are treated negatively if at all. Older people appeared only 1.5 percent of the time in the cartoons in women's magazines, yet I would wager that more than half the readership of those publications is in *our* age group. In the cartoons that did use older characters, most of the themes dealt with sexual or mental dysfunction, political and social conservatism, or elders as the butt of a joke or prank.

But even if a cartoon did admit that an elderly person might have sexual feelings, for example, the physical form of that character was totally negative. From time to time *Playboy* magazine used to feature a sexually oriented, nymphomaniacal elder named Granny. But her physical appearance thwarted the men whom she approached—sagging breasts, large stomach, very thin legs. In one of the *Playboy* cartoons, Granny stands naked near a group of Western stagecoach bandits and the caption read: "Honest, lady, we don't *want* to rape anyone!" In my trips to my local barbershop, I have not seen the cartoon in the stack of dog-eared back issues that keep us amused while waiting our turn to be shorn. Perhaps a combination of the middle-aged and the feminists forced the cartoon out of the magazine.

But *Playboy* and *Penthouse* are not the only guilty ones. In the studies done on cartoons, the standard magazines, the family magazines were just as culpable in their own way—*Better Homes and Gardens, Ladies' Home Journal,* the *New Yorker, Reader's Digest,* and the *Saturday Evening Post,* to name but a few.

And are there exceptions? Certainly, there are. There always are exceptions and my current favorite is the one done by the talented cartoonist, Bulbul. An obviously older couple is face-to-face with a younger couple, whose demeanor shows their shock at the words spoken by the elderly, gray-haired lady, "No son, Charles and I are not just friends . . . we're lovers."

"Hooray for Hollywood": Two Four-star Movie Reviews

There is an interesting thought that occurs when you begin to do research on the media in relation to the subject of aging. Everything written about it in the past still goes on day by day. There's no need to spend weeks in the public library scouring the literature of ancient Roman poets. The phenomenon is a living, breathing perversion of our society, and in each day's newspapers, magazines, television programs, and advertising, the research grows and the monster feeds upon itself to become larger and more apparent. The research collected piece by piece over these years since the first edition of this book was published might well be a mirror image of the original material that filled the files eight years back.

As things change, nothing changes, it seems. The motion-picture industry is a good example. It is a varied business, and some serious films are made by intelligent and well-meaning producers and directors. Though the "pop" movies proliferate for our subteens and teenagers and the sequels pour out of the funnel to play to youngsters who see the same film eight or nine or ten times, and then repeat the performance at *Rocky VI, Star Wars X*, and the *Return of the Return*, the small art houses that are left and some independent production companies occasionally try to present a "slice of life." But when Hollywood gets hold of the subject matter for a stereotypical story line, no one can outdo the masters of popular poppycock.

My neighborhood once had one of those motion-picture theaters where, for half the price of the uptown cinemas, the local population could see double-feature cult movies, reruns, classics, and the newly released bombs that have had their three-week run and are doomed to oblivion or to hidden screenings for film students such as I. It has since been torn down, the victim of real-estate "gentrification" in our neighborhood, to be replaced by a shopping complex that has two chain boutiques, three fast-food outlets and a video store, where customers can now rent the same awful movies.

During its last weeks, they played a film that I could not resist. The marquee screamed out at me, *Middle Age Crazy!* How could I possibly pass it by, since by that time I was thoroughly steeped in the subject of my writing. I had never heard of the film before. I might hope, after seeing it that beautiful, sunny day when one should have been in the park, that I might never hear of it again. Hollywood did not disappoint me. If ever there was a film that reflected America's self-hate about getting older, it's *Middle Age Crazy*. I wondered, first of all, just what age they might be showing as middle age. They told me right at the beginning.

Bobby Lee (played by Bruce Dern) is celebrating a birthday with his family. It is a difficult time, we find, because he is about to pass a milestone and enter middle age. Bobby Lee is leaving thirty-nine and turning forty. How awful! What a trauma! The entire film is based upon the premise that Bobby Lee is having a middle-age crisis of huge proportions.

"Forty," one of the characters states. "That's when the shit hits the fan. That's what happens when you hit forty. You start dreamin' about all those sweet little things you should have been puttin' it to when you were young."

Bobby Lee's wife, Sue Ann (Ann-Margret)—the film takes place in Texas so everyone has two first names—tries to keep him confident, happy, and sexually fulfilled, but his mind strays, followed by his "aging" body. At a graduation ceremony for his son (so the boy can leave home to go to college, thus also giving them an empty-nest syndrome) Bobby Lee sees himself making the valedictorian address to the students and their relatives. In his imagination, wearing a cap and gown, he delivers a tirade of self-deprecation denoting the future for which the graduates are destined. "You don't wanna be the future. Give 'em back their silly damn hats and stay eighteen for the rest of your lives!! The future sucks! You wanna see the future? Look up there at your parents with their big asses and drooping tits! That's the future!" ("T and A" again!)

Well, now Bobby Lee does get some good advice from others in the film, including Sue Ann and his father, who gives him the next big kick in the trousers as an "aging" man. Grandfather, who is sixty-four, advises Bobby Lee, "There's nothin' that makes you feel old like lyin' in a motel and listenin' to someone in the next room screwin'."

In the next scenes Bobby Lee "runs away from home" on business, has an affair with a Dallas Cowboys cheerleader, changes his Oldsmobile for a Porsche and his business suit for cowboy boots and jeans. The sound track blasts out a rock song that warns us, "He's middle-aged crazy, tryin' to prove he still can!" (Sonny Throckmorton, Phonogram, Inc., New York).

There was one marvelous sequence in the film when Bobby Lee decides to throw over his business and his wife for the cheerleader. Abe Titus, the tycoon who uses Bobby's construction company, is angry over the hero's not showing up for a meeting (since he is ensconced in bed with the cheerleader). Bobby tells him, "I'm not walkin' out. I'm just takin' stock. For all I care, you can take everything and shove it up your conglomerate!" Mentally, I applauded, while busily scrawling notes in the darkened theater.

For those readers who follow things like this to their conclusion, let it be said that Sue Ann has her own affair; Bobby Lee comes home after being rejected by Ms. Dallas Cowboy. He finds the cheerleader in bed with another man, and she reminds him that in *her* generation there are "no strings attached." Of course, the movie was made before the AIDS epidemic! Bobby Lee ends up in a California hot tub with his wife, Sue Ann. Meanwhile the track stridently screams at us once again. "He's middle aged crazy. Tryin' to prove he still can." The camera pulls back slowly and ends on his Porsche, which he has vowed to trade in for another Oldsmobile.

Update: A Brief Review of "Cocoon"

Since that time, there have been one or two notable attempts by Hollywood to give exception to the pattern of ageism and stereotyping. It may well be the tokenism to which I referred as the "Jackie Robinson Syndrome," but I suppose we all should be glad for the little things given to us by California production companies. I did not see *On Golden Pond*, for which Henry Fonda received an Academy Award. I do understand that it was a remarkable portrait of an aging man who struggled valiantly with the physical limitations of his years.

However, I did see *Cocoon*, the film that is always pointed out to me as a breakaway from Hollywood casting. And, indeed it was. With Don Ameche, Hume Cronyn, Jessica Tandy, Wilford Brimley, Gwen Verdon, and Maureen Stapleton, the videotape box promised me that "this time youth is not wasted on the young."

I enjoyed it while I watched it, mostly because of the superb performances of the cast. And then—and then, I had my doubts and I realized that once again we had been exploited. Looking at *Cocoon* carefully, the film was not about people who were old. It was about a *science-fiction story* that happened to cast people who were old. Follow me, if you will:

- It takes place in a nursing home, given that there is a part of it that caters to people who are still active. There are male nurses at the desk; people need passes to leave. When I mentioned to a young (forty-five-year-old) friend, that I thought the film perpetuated the myth that all older people were in nursing facilities, he retorted, "Well, isn't that where everyone that age is?"

- It indicated rather strongly that the only time that older people are vital enough to go out and have a good time, to dance, eat, laugh—and even more importantly, to want sexual relations—is for them to find a "fountain of youth" (the swimming pool with the cocoons), so that they are re-vitalized enough to think "young" again.

Over all, I felt that *Cocoon*, in its way, was just as exploitive and dangerous to the perpetuation of stereotypes as *Middle Age Crazy*. Possibly it is even more exploitive because it is so well cast and so well produced. When we had finished viewing the videotape, I turned to my wife, Sheryl, and asked what she thought. She smiled and said, "*E. T.* with seniors!"

No matter what we do, the media will never be perfect, for none of us are paragons, nor perfect role models for our peers or for the coming generations. Neither are we the only special-interest group to take the media to task for the omissions and the perpetuation of stereotypes. The women in our society have rightly fought the problem, as have the ethnic minorities, and especially a young, talented black filmmaker named Spike Lee who is not afraid to confront the blatant racism of our country head-on. Even big business, long the sacred cow of our democracy, has begun to criticize the media.

One of the largest of the Fortune 500 companies took an ad on the op-ed page of the *New York Times* to complain that the redeeming social values of big business, if any, are not evident on prime-time television. They complained about the characterization of businessmen just as we have about aging. Two out of three businessmen on television (with no count of businesswomen) are portrayed as greedy, foolish, or criminal, and half the business they do involves illegal acts. Sound familiar? Television is not only antiaging. It is also antibusiness. And all this with the Wall Street scandals that followed the publication of that article by just a few short years. Without doubt, the business community will continue to fight the image.

And so, then, should we. The first step is awareness. Never underestimate the power of the media to mold opinion and to make us doubt even ourselves. The issue was brilliantly summed up when the ex-governor of New York, Malcolm Wilson, was once asked about the public image versus the private man in the case of Nelson Rockefeller. "In today's world the truth is irrelevant," he said. "It's the perception, and the perception comes from the exposure people have to the media."

PART II

So
Who Are We,
Anyway?

Now that we know so many things we are *not,* it is time to move on to discover some of the things that we *are.* For we are a unique generation in a very special kind of society, having shared experiences so alien to the other generations that surround us.

Not only do the younger people justifiably profess ignorance when we mention the names of our former movie idols or a part of the history through which we have lived, but they are also insulated by age from those encounters that shaped our lives, from the Great Depression through the Big Apple and Lindy Hop dance crazes, World War II, and the Holocaust.

In the same way, we are different from the generations that preceded *us,* and it was we who could not fathom *their* involvement with World War I, Prohibition, and the Black Bottom. Given the changes that take place so rapidly, no one who follows us will ever be quite the same as *we* are, for that is the measure of a changing and dynamic humanity, and it is neither bad nor good. It just *is.*

8 We Can't All Be Chinese

Youth, the curse of the young, the worship of the old.

—Fortune cookie served to the
author in a Chinese restaurant

When the going gets tough, when the awareness overtakes us that life is not always fair, when children talk back to their elders (us), and when the newspaper headlines vex us with changes that are violent and unsettling, we can always remind ourselves that the Chinese treat *their* patriarchs with veneration and respect. It is comforting to know that somewhere we elders are treated well, with the deference and adoration we so richly deserve!

It is, perhaps, our own sensitivity toward the personal process of aging that makes us turn toward other cultures and how they treat their aged. I have used the example of the Chinese time and again, even as I have read in the daily newspapers of youth gangs that roam the streets of Chinatown in New York and San Francisco, of the extortion and the murders, and of families that are fast disintegrating in the crowded tenements of Hong Kong. I persist even when I read of the turmoil and the upheaval and the violent revolution of the youth against the Chinese government in Beijing. I suppose it is comforting to think that it may be better somewhere else; it was always easier at some other time.

And thus I read with a perverse sense of understanding when Colin M. Turnbull wrote in *The Mountain People* (Touchstone-Simon & Schuster) of the treatment of the older people by the members of the Ik tribe in Kenya. He wrote of an old man taunted by the children of the village, slapped in the face, and knocked over to the accompaniment of laughter and glee. For the Ik, the terrifying treatment of members of the tribe by one another was the result of upending a basically mobile society of hunters and forcing them to become farmers. I wonder what *our* reasons are? And how do other cultures really treat their elders?

One thing is certain. In most societies, especially the primitive ones, and at most other times in historical anthropology, the elder was a rare species indeed. Just survival into old age took superhuman effort and a good share of luck. In Elizabethan England, for example, it took the birth of about *nine* children to guarantee that there would be one or possibly two survivors past the age of fifty. Disease, the pestilence of the Black Plague and smallpox, wiped out a large segment of the population that had survived an appallingly high infant-mortality rate. Diet was inadequate (when not poisonous) and wars completed the job that disease had left undone. Even today there are fetid slums around the world where three out of five children die before the age of five. Given such a ratio, old age might be considered as starting at about eighteen!

Thus, not only were the elders few in earlier history (as well as in many developing countries today), but those few survivors carried with them, in turn, the knowledge for survival of the entire culture or tribe. Even among the Australian aborigines today, it is the middle-aged men who teach both the boys and the girls of the tribes the crafts, the husbandry, the camp customs, and the tribal lore and rituals. Thus, the aging members of the group have a prestige and are given a reverence that cannot be equaled in our own society.

The outback of Australia is a hostile, waterless, sun-seared desert, so unbearable that I have seen an aborigine stand all day in the shade of a solitary rock, moving with the shadow as the sun traveled overhead, waiting for a passing kangaroo. Should the game appear, the hunter had but one chance to bring it down. I was taught to throw a boomerang by a middle-aged aborigine, but I have never hit anything with it in my life. Unskilled in the primitive ways, I would burn up or starve in the outback.

In such a society, the middle-aged men maintain an authority conferred upon them solely because of their age and thus their experience. They are relentless in their discipline of the entire community and in the maintenance of tribal law. It is an elder who is always the leader of the group, knowing more and having met more of life's hard experiences than any other member. At the tribal sessions, it is again the older men who participate while the young men do not join in at all. It is, of course, a male society, and the women do not have the same high status when they enter middle age.

As far back as Babylon and ancient Greece, and even among the Hebrew tribes, it was always the elders, those few survivors, who created a personal gerontocracy, and it was they who most frequently became the prime bene-ficiaries of the social order. They were the ones who handed down the tribal laws with the admonishment that they were divinely inspired and thus must be followed as they dictated. Ruling councils were, of course, made up only of elders. Even so, I doubt very much that anyone actually *liked* the idea of growing old.

There is an ancient Japanese poem that says it well. Obviously the poet was not overjoyed with the idea of aging. It was written about A.D. 905:

> If only when one heard
> That Old Age was coming
> One could bolt the door,
> Answer, "Not at home,"
> And refuse to meet him!

(Donald Keene, ed., *Anthology of Japanese Literature*, translated by Arthur Walley, New York: Grove Press, 1955)

About seventeen years ago I set out to produce a television special called *Celebration* and it starred the late Lorne Greene. It was to be a celebration of *all* stages (*sic!*) of man's life through five major periods: Birth, Childhood, Adolescence, as well as Betrothal, Marriage, and Old Age. Note if you will that I totally eliminated an entire generation—*us!* At that time I had also become a victim of the myth that we all disappear at the age of forty or forty-five, to rest on our plateau and to reappear when we are ancient. We filmed in fifteen countries during a single year, including Australia, Turkey, Venezuela, Hong Kong, and Kenya. It was my first strong involvement with the idea that there might, indeed, be significant similarities in the various cultures as well as strongly defined differences.

The aborigines, as I've mentioned, do pass through five very well defined stages of life: childhood, adolescence (the initiation period), early manhood and marriage, the maturity and authority of middle age and the spirit world of old age. In other tribes, such as the Giriama and the Masai of Kenya, the woman's role in middle age is that of a teacher of the young. She initiates her daughters into womanhood, teaches them about childbirth, knows the reme-dies for stomachaches, and how to cure the rashes on the baby's skin; she instructs on teething, herbal medicine, and other remedies passed on by her own mother. For the men of the Masai, however, there is a specific ritual designed to help the warrior shed one role and enter into another capacity in the tribe.

It took many months of preparation and planning before we could get permission to film the Masai ceremonies, and we traveled about a hundred miles outside of Nairobi into the Rift Valley to find our contacts and to be introduced. Then we spent most of the day being shown the encampment, surrounded by thorn-tree fences, stepping gingerly over the droppings of the cows that live right in the center of the compound, and politely refusing the gourds offered us. We had been informed that the honey-milk drink was fermented with cow urine and that the teeth must be gritted while drinking so that the flies do not get into the mouth.

The ceremony we filmed is called "passing the fence." When a Masai becomes an elder, he loses his rank as a warrior. Needless to say, the Japanese poem that I have quoted might just as well refer to the Masai, since no warrior likes to give up his role in order to become an elder, even though the new rank will make him highly respected. The ceremony is in no way connected with the chronological age of the warrior. His time comes when the last of his sons reaches the age of initiation.

For four days the candidate remains isolated from the rest of the tribe while food is brought to him by his wives; only an emergency in the compound or in the prized herd of cows will allow him to leave. Another companion of his during the four days is the honey-wine fermented drink that is present at all Masai ceremonies from the naming of a baby at the age of one to the marriage celebration.

After his stay in the dung-covered hut, the man dons his warrior dress for the last time—the headdress of ostrich feathers, the cape of vulture feathers, and the ankle rings of monkey skins. Armed with his war club, knife, spear, and painted shield, he is ready for his midlife crisis.

The other elders wait for him in his home, still another mud hut topped with cow dung, and the gourds of wine are brought right along with him. The elders chant, "Become an old man. Go, become an old man." And the warrior shouts back at them, "I shall not! I shall not become an old man. No, I shall not!" The fifth time the elders repeat their demand, however, the warrior, now meek and obliging, crosses over into another stage of the Masai culture when he softly replies, "I will go then. I will become an old man."

He changes clothing, the warrior's proud adornments left to his sons, and he replaces it with the long, ankle-length dress of the elder. No longer the lion hunter, no longer the fighter and protector of the nomadic village, he is now known as "the father of Gundai," or whatever the name of his son is. For the village, it is an excuse to celebrate with endless gourds of intoxicating honey-milk wine (with flies).

Perhaps our own concepts of the roles of the aged come directly from the rituals of the ancient tribes. Among the Masai the elder "retires" into a life quite different from that of the man he was before. He does not move to the Masai version of Florida or Arizona, but he does a lot of sitting. From that moment on, sitting around the compound all day and smoking their pipes, the elders have a continual conversation about the village, the supernatural, and the current problems. They hear the war stories of the retired soldiers. They give advice freely to the young people of the compound, and they mediate and hold councils to see that the ancient Masai ways are continued and the customs are left unchanged. Most of all, they are respected by everyone in the village; I was told that they even become more kindly and friendly to strangers as well as to their own families.

Of course, the treatment of the elder and the entrance into middle life and old age vary from culture to culture, but the fact is that most of the traditional ones are based upon a thinning out of the tribe due to early accident, disease, or living conditions. We may well long for the adulation given to the Navajo elder or the Polynesian father and mother (until they came to Hawaii and had to fight desperately to retain their culture), or be wistful about the treatment of aging relatives by the ancient Chinese. But the fact is that no other culture in history has ever had the sheer numbers of older people that we now have and will have increasingly into the twenty-first century. In addition, no other culture has had, along with its aging poor, so large a percentage that is fairly well off financially. So, we are not like the Masai, we are not the *exceptional* survivors who have entered middle life and old age. Thus our society requires that we look differently at the role of aging.

Our placement in chronologic history cannot change. We cannot, and do not, live in another time, and we cannot change the era in which we are growing older. We would not change our geographic home for the outback in order to be venerated as an aborigine elder, and the affluent, industrial society places us in a totally different role from that of our nomadic cow-herder brothers in Kenya. It takes years of learning and the assimilation of both spiritual and practical knowledge for a tribal medicine man to be accepted and respected by the community. But our doctors graduate from medical school and begin their practice at the age of twenty-seven. Lawyers go from school into jobs that pay salaries that were distant dreams to us and to our parents. Financial geniuses are frequently barely thirty or possibly forty years of age. There was a time when an apprenticeship of five or ten years was

required before a young craftsperson or professional entered the world of
responsible work. It is no longer true today.

Of course, there was also a time when the American household was
maintained by the extended family unit and, not being Chinese or Polynesian, we begin to fall back on our idealized memories of the Norman Rockwell
view of aging, as immortalized on so many covers of the *Saturday Evening Post*.
Whatever happened to the kindly family doctor (who made house calls); the
elderly smiling (always smiling) grandmother who took the turkey out of the
oven at Thanksgiving; the friendly, ruddy-cheeked general-store keeper with
the penny candies behind his glass counter; the primly proper schoolteacher,
stern but loving; and the irresistible family dog?

Where, indeed, are the "good old days" that we long for when we find that
life changes around us too quickly for us to catch our breaths? Where are the
days of yore, when we selectively remember only the good things that
happened and a euphoric mist overtakes us to make us long for the stuff of
memorabilia? The Broadway shows come back: *42nd Street*, *Anything Goes*,
and *Brigadoon*. Those were the days! Or—be honest—were they?

I wonder how many of us would go back to the labor-intensive days of the
last century. The reason Grandmother was shown taking the turkey out of the
oven was that she rarely left the kitchen. After hauling the water, bathing the
kids, preparing breakfast for Grandfather and the brood, sewing, cleaning,
washing the clothes, and cooking, it's an absolute wonder that she even had
the energy to smile for the Norman Rockwell cover! My father would not have
gone back to World War I, I am certain, even though his only stories about
that time did not include the three wounds he suffered, but only the good
times that he had had with his youthful comrades. When he told us his sagas,
the lice-ridden, rat-infested, horrifying trenches never existed.

There was a delightful book I picked up some time back. It was written by
Otto C. Bettman and it was called, *The Good Old Days They Were Terrible*
(paperback, Random House) and he forcefully reminds those of us with
selective memories that the food eaten by our grandfathers was apt to be
ruined by spoilage; street crime was just as rampant as it is today (with the
one exception of the drug epidemic); and diseases such as malaria, diph-
theria, and intestinal infections took an awful toll of children and adults.
Ocean travel for our forebears was in the stinking holds of ships, the steerage
in which my own grandparents traveled to this country; and on city streets,
the horsecars created a tangle of traffic in dust, mud, and manure.

In the Arab cultures there is prevalent an interesting indifference to age.

Even the youngest child is referred to as "less than one," while the "elderly" may be forty, fifty, sixty, or more. Precise measurements are not critical to their society and, unlike our Western culture, there is no tyranny of time and punctuality. Why, then, in this day and age, must we chose *a time* to become old? New freedoms have been given to us as well as to the youth of our country.

We no longer have to hurry "to make our mark" by the time we are thirty, even though so many younger people feel impelled to do exactly that. As the life span increases and the era of age-irrelevance grows around us, we can take advantage of a second chance and even a third. Our affluence has made us, like the elders of history, a gerontocracy. We control the media, the political arena, the economic structure of America. When, then, have we succumbed to the myth that it is the time to retire from living? Those of my readers who have reached middle age, by whatever definition you choose, are still "pups" in today's society.

The fact again is that by believing all that is told us, we have abdicated the power of our gerontocracy. We forget that the young, who have left our homes in *their* search for freedom, have also left us *our* freedom in the process. If the society is more mobile now, and the young leave home not to go down the street to work but to go to San Francisco or Paris to "find themselves" (while we may very well be paying the air fare to get them there), they also leave *us* unfettered. If they can travel to get away, *we* can travel for pleasure.

It is time that we surfaced. We may not all be Chinese, but we do not need to be. We do not need the veneration of the young in order to reject our own tribal ceremony, our own rituals that proclaim the coming of age—retirement, withdrawal, invisibility, a halt in our forward movement.

Last night, while reading about the tribal laws of the Navajo, I had a whimsical dream about our own ritual of aging. The last of our children have been initiated into adulthood and are "doing their own thing." I dress in my finest warrior clothing and, carrying my attaché case and business cards, I enter the hut where I am to change my role in our society. I am to become an elder.

However, instead of the other elders being there to judge me and give me commands, as with my brothers in the Masai, all who sit cross-legged on water beds and knapsacks are young. They are dressed in their own warrior clothing: designer jeans and T-shirts. Their hair is cut in Mohawk shape and dyed green or else they are bald, women and men. Their T-shirts, on closer inspection, proclaim tribal ritual incantations, sayings from the supernatural

and writings of the soothsayers of their generation: "We're the Pepsi Generation," "Woodstock Still Lives," "Sun Your Buns in Venice, California," and
"Nuclear War??!! There Goes My Career!"

The leader is a very young girl, barely fifteen, who is half sixties hippie and
half eighties Punk, and her T-shirt reads, NOW THAT I KNOW EVERYTHING,
WHAT DO I DO? She intones as I enter the hut, "Go. Become an older person."
Behind her, the chorus murmurs, "To Florida. To Arizona," and somewhere
in the dim half-light of the hut a squeaky voice repeats, "But send money.
Send money." Five times the young girl gives her command, "Go. Become an
older peson," and four times I answer, "No, I shall not!" The fifth time,
however, tired of all the repetition, as she utters the magic words, "Go,
become an older person," I draw myself up to my full height, my feathers
flapping, my monkey skins shining, and I retort, "Go screw thyself." And
with that, I stomp angrily out of the hut.

9 "Twenty-Three Skiddoo," "Oh, You Kid!," and Other Useful Phrases: The Language of Us

High thoughts must have high language

—Aristophanes
The Frogs

Some time ago, I was one of several guest speakers at a conference in New York. I look forward to these appearances, mostly because I am an inveterate ham who likes to hold forth in front of a captive audience, and partially because I always have a perverse expectation that the luncheon will be a gourmet feast. Of course, I am always disappointed in the hotel fare, generally finding it a cross between an airline meal and a fast-food takeout, though served on elegant china. Nevertheless, I remain optimistic in the face of countless culinary disasters and hours of boring speeches (no doubt including my own).

This particular session dealt with a variety of subjects, including travel, advertising, and communications. The key speaker was a young (about thirty-five) business consultant and, having had my first glass of wine, I sat back expecting to hear a new approach to corporate communications. It didn't take long, possibly a few paragraphs of introduction, and three or four slides, for me to realize with no small feeling of inadequacy that *I did not understand a word he was saying!* This expert on communications was simply not communicating.

Surreptitiously I looked around, thinking that it was I who was lost and that everyone else had just not yet had a glass of wine to dull the senses. I met the eyes of a table partner and he shrugged. I knew I was not alone. Another slide flashed on the screen, the words illuminated in red and green:

The disaggregation of a corporation into Natural Businesses is a prerequisite to Strategic Analysis and Formulation.

My table partner rolled his eyes skyward, we quietly toasted one another with our glasses of wine, and downed the drink quickly, the better to ignore what was happening.

We grew up, you and I, in an era of straight talk. When my mother said, "Finish your dinner and do your homework," there was absolutely no doubt in my mind what she meant. The great and the near great, as well as our families, said exactly what they meant—nothing more, nothing less. Franklin D. Roosevelt told us that we "have nothing to fear but fear itself" and I understood every word. Winston Churchill reported to the British people in the dark days of June 1940, and he said, quite simply, "The news from France is very bad." No gibberish, no gobbledygook. "Bad" meant "*bad.*" The British understood. Compare this, if you will, with the pronouncements of our current crop of politicians and business executives.

How many of us understood when the crisis at Three Mile Island occurred and someone in the Nuclear Regulatory Commission reported that it was a "failure mode that had never been studied"? Think, if you will, of the panic that might have occurred had Churchill reported the news from France in "high-tech" jargon! As a child, I once had a "failure mode" with my first two-wheeler. My father, poor unsophisticated person that he was, called it an *accident.*

There is no doubt in my mind that one of the greatest areas indicative of the generation gap is that of language. As the new technologies have begun to permeate every sector of our society, the virulence of slipshod and deliberately vague abstractions has infected our everyday speech, our schools, our advertising, our business and medical communities and our person-to-person communications, from interoffice memos to business letters that answer consumer complaints.

In an article in the *New York Times,* Professor David Ehrenfeld of Rutgers University rightly called it "this pestilence of indirect language." And we, the generations who grew up with straight talk, whose mothers and fathers called it an "icebox" even after it became electric, begin to think that it's *our* fault (once again) that we are understanding less of what is being said to us.

The Colonial Penn Group once ran a series of delightful ads—all of them directed to our generation. One of them, in particular, caught my fancy. It was titled "Do Old People Talk Funny?" and the copy read, in part:

> We've contended for a long time that young people can and should learn a lot from their elders. Nowhere is this more evident than in language. We think it was George Bernard Shaw who once said that England and America were two great countries divided by the same language. Today, that division has extended to the generations in this country, and probably in England too. It is our view that, as a rule, older people speak more plainly, clearly, and coherently than the younger generation.

There is a universal quality in the new, ultramodern speech. As it becomes more complex, it says less and less. It becomes more abstract, more cleverly phrased, more vague. It is much harder work to be precise. Bertram Gross called it, "Triplespeak," a system whereby the establishment purveys myths to the public.

On its simplest level, "accelerated obsolescence" becomes "product design and engineering" and, as there becomes more of a need to obfuscate and cover, the Reagan MX missile is known as "The Peacekeeper" and capital punishment is made less obnoxious by calling the hangman an "execution technician." If we become too explicit in what we mean, it becomes dangerous, and Dr. Ehrenfeld and Mr. Gross both place a large part of the blame for the new speech patterns at the doorstep of a bureaucracy with too much to hide.

Our generation went to school, we rode in elevators, and some of our grandparents grew up on the farm. In what Richard Mitchell (*Less Than Words Can Say*, Little, Brown & Co.) called "The Principle of Unnecessary Specification," the little red schoolhouse had become "a venue for learning systems served by a professional infrastructure." We no longer ride an elevator, at least not by technical standards. When I recently visited a friend in a tall apartment building, I got to the fifteenth floor in an "integrated, single-module, vertical transportation system" operated by "an integrated, single-module, transportation system operations engineer"! And the "farm" has given way to "a macroagricultural environment." No wonder the young people are leaving them to go to the big city (or "urban infrastructure")!

Am I exaggerating? Look around you. Unrented real estate is now termed *negative absorption*. A recent item told me that a new nightclub had done away with bouncers. They now call them "Ejection Executives." A recent airplane trip told me, via the loudspeaker, "Your breakfast modules will be coming down the aisle." At the airport, in order to change planes, the same disembodied voice informed the passengers that we were to be put on a "people mover" to get to the next terminal. Nowhere do we find anything that is "new and improved." Everything is "state-of-the-art." We have state-of-the-art plumbing, security systems, technology, state-of-the-art comfort zones, entertainment, and even a new cruise missile that has been heralded as "state-of-the-art devastation"! As someone so rightly said, *state-of-the-art* does not say that the product or system *works*, but only that it has been taken as far as it can go—so far.

We no longer live our lives. We "function." One of my books won what I might have called "second prize" when I was in a "professional learning infrastructure." However, the new society thinks that I might be terribly disappointed at being second, so the award reads, "First Runner-Up." I no longer live in an apartment. I have "created my own space." And when I borrowed a wheelbarrow to move some equipment, Russell Baker reminded me in his column that what I had actually used was a "single-wheeled Inertial Powered Freight Transportation Vehicle."

I find it ubiquitous, I find it overwhelming, and I find it hilariously funny. Remember, this is an era where schoolteachers remind us that their students do not know the meaning of the word, *clockwise* because they all have digital watches. There was a time when I might have looked for a job and the Help Wanted columns would have listed occupations such as "nurse" or "historian" or "sales manager." Some of these archaic job descriptions still exist, of course, but the Help Wanted page becomes evermore complicated with the times in which we live. In the Help Wanted columns of our Sunday newspaper, I found an ad that read, "Engineers—Software/Hardware, *We Speak Your Language.*" I realized again, just as I did at the luncheon meeting, that not only did they *not* speak *my* language, they were not speaking the language of millions of our generation. There were jobs in "biomass" research, "waferfab" engineering, and "microprocessing," one of them requiring knowledge of "MRP theory, MRP software (MAC-PAC, MAPIC, COMSERV-AMAPS), and System 34."

Arlington County, Virginia, advertised for an "Urban Revitalization Facilitator" and United Technologies was looking for a professional interested in "shipboard sensor correlation with AN/SYS automatic detection and tracking systems." It transcends the technologies, however, for I think that all of us can understand and accept the fact that these new technical breakthroughs require new language to describe their functions and their purpose, as well as their operation. But, when the society as a whole begins to adopt "Triplespeak," I get a bit uncomfortable. When the cities dub the people who pick up our garbage every day "sanitation engineers," or the reason I go to the bank is to "access my money"—somehow, I feel it is no longer *my* language.

I am certainly not against technological achievement. I am not against the progress made in electronics or aerospace. I was certainly willing to give up my Victrola for the latest product in my newspaper ads: a "Sonic Holography including a time-delay system with controllable reverberation mix and SL-7 Linear Tracking Turntable, an Autocorrelator system, and a peak-unlimited downward expander." It even has an on-off switch!

But, since "newspeak" is everywhere, when we begin to use our common, ordinary, straightforward language, it is *we* who are accused of "talking funny." In a previous administration, a presidential press secretary, caught in a lie, called his previous statements "inoperative." The perfectly acceptable, old-fashioned term, "togetherness" had become "integrated familial tendencies." The simple, forceful, descriptive word "now" had evolved into "at this point in time." Can you just imagine our mothers and fathers saying to us when we were children, "You'd better clean up your room and I mean *at this point in time!*"

Oh, our generation is not entirely innocent by any means. Along the way, many of our peers have contracted the disease of tortured syntax and modern malapropism. Presidents Reagan and Bush, both strong advocates of not raising taxes ("read my lips") have called them by every other name but the unmentionable (T-A-X). The current euphemism is "supplement" as in the new Medicare "premium." Tax? Of course not!

I was sorry when Alexander Haig left the Reagan administration as secretary of state, for he gave the Washington press corps a field day with what then became known as "Haigese," an almost totally obtuse language. Many of his utterances have become classics. "Theological isolation of a functional objective" is but one. "When we find ourselves in a dialectic fashion at one end of the spectrum" is another "Haigism."

There is a classic example of how the language has changed around us, created by the transformations in the relationships of young people in our society. Years ago, there were intimate relationships developed by the young, many of them were quite innocent by today's standards. The dated language of so many years ago just doesn't hold up for today's social couplings, especially when it is no longer "his place" or "her place" but "their place."

And so, the language of an earlier time, descriptive in its simplicity, has given way to confusion and abstraction again. The Colonial Penn ad, "Do Old People Talk Funny?" told a part of the story:

Not too long ago, an attractive young lady of impeccable breeding and unusually good manners made passing reference to a social engagement involving one of her "beaus." Her contemporaries in the group looked a little puzzled. Older people present smiled benignly. It was unusual to hear such a young lady use such an old-fashioned word.

Later, the younger adults attempted to pinpoint her meaning. Did "beau" mean lover, intimate friend, special companion, roommate, casual acquaintance, or what? They thought it was a funny word to use. The older people thought the word was perfect. It said enough about the relationship. It didn't say too much or tell people more than they wanted, or had a right, to know.

If you have children who have left home and have taken on the new colorations of cohabitation without marriage, of noncommitment, do you now find it difficult to introduce them to your friends—not because they live together, but because the relationship defies a specific description in today's popular language? "I would like to introduce you to my son and his 'significant other,'" or "Meet my daughter and her roommate, George," or "my son and his spouse equivalent." (It is even more complex when the other special person happens to be of the same sex.) A famous conductor was reputed to have had a longtime "intimate companion," while a young friend of mine honestly admitted to living with his friend in "sinful cohabitation."

Strangely enough, it is the bureaucrats, so guilty of doubletalk themselves, who have finally come up with a solution to this problem. The Bureau of Census has invented a word that is quite descriptively accurate. Your son's or daughter's live-in partner is merely called a *posslq*—or, in explicit language for us older folks, "person of opposite sex sharing living quarters." And there you are—"I'd like you to meet my son and his posslq." The trend may take us back to the simple words again, however, since the prevalence of AIDS has created a new move toward permanent relationships and marriage. It would simplify things considerably if this is true.

There is one segment of society in which the new "high-tech" word brokers are having some trouble, however. That group is *us*. They just don't know what to label us and they have been trying desperately to categorize our generations in "newspeak." So far their efforts have been feeble failures. *Middle-aged* is too simple a description, and it now seems to cover everything from age thirty up to and including sixty. The words *aging* and *elder* belong to our descriptive language more than theirs. We are, indeed, a challenge to them. They've tried *senior citizen* and they've tried to tell us that we are entering our *harvest years* or our *golden years* and that we are getting riper, grayer, or more mature.

Unfortunately, these attempts pale when compared with the descriptions they can come up with for schools, job designations, elevators, the old family farm, and the space shuttle program. I wait with great anticipation to see what the young technicians and technical wizards come up with that will, once and for all, put us into our semantic places while still reflecting their feelings about those of us who are getting older. And, with the Baby Boom generation fast approaching middle age, they had better think carefully about what they are going to call *themselves*.

There is no doubt that it will come. One day we will open a newspaper or a magazine and find references to ourselves among all the words that are poisoning direct communication and honesty. We will know it's about us because the article will deal with the "Primogenital Humanoids Commencing Obsolescence."

Who said, "You can't teach an old dog new tricks" (or—a venerable canine topical prestidigitation!)?

10 ✸ It Is Just Possible That "Midlife Crisis" Ain't

> In the middle of the journey of our life, I came to myself within a dark wood where the straight way was lost.
>
> —Dante
> *Divine Comedy, Inferno*

I must have been about eight years old when I first became aware of that terribly threatening word, *crisis*. In the hushed tones that my mother reserved for matters of grave importance, or for subjects not fit for "the children," she worriedly explained to my father that my three-year-old brother, ill with pneumonia, was "at the crisis." Mind you it was not *a* crisis. It was *the* crisis, when either the fever, reaching its peak, would drop precipitously, or the patient would be in desperate straits. That illness was, indeed, a true crisis for my younger brother and just possibly it was also a crisis for me—a wrenching, helpless emotional experience that stays with me today.

Well, *the* crisis passed and the fever broke. My brother survived beautifully, even before the discovery of penicillin. And—if I can believe the literature, the media and the articles that appear daily—he and I have survived at least two hundred other crises in our lives in order to reach middle age and prepare ourselves for the worst crisis yet to come.

The problem I have is that, given the penchant of Americans and our media to use this word for every change, every stage of progression through life, I fear that I was probably not even able to recognize my midlife crisis when it descended upon me and then passed into history. I don't even know if I had one! After all, we live in a crisis society, and *mine* may well have been lost among all the other crises that I managed to live through and survive. My reading in the past few years leads me to believe that we have a crisis in currency, in health care, in our marriages, in our child-rearing habits, in the kitchen (as well as in the bedroom); a crisis in loving, being loved, and in being unloved. We have lived through a missile crisis, and the most recent newspaper informs us that "*NATO, at the age of forty, is suffering a midlife crisis.*"

Our children have been deprogrammed out of religious cults by a process called "crisis counseling." I found that my own beloved industry, motion pictures, was also being plagued by the disease as I read an article called "The Real Crisis in American Films" (as distinguished from the counterfeit crisis). This very morning the newspapers tell me that New York is in the midst of several crises all at one time: vagrant and homeless crises, our continuing drug crisis, a crisis in which our entire infrastructure is collapsing (bridges, roadways, transit), and a judicial crisis in which court cases are backing up as far as the eye can see.

It stands to reason, then, that *we* were next in line to be noticed. Dr. Bernice Neugarten, with her marvelously fresh view of middle age and aging, wrote in *Prime Time* magazine ("Must Everything Be a Midlife Crisis?" February 1980):

> The media have discovered adulthood. Gail Sheehy's *Passages*, Roger Gould's *Transformations*, and a dozen other popular books have all accorded adulthood the treatment of high drama, drawing from Erik Ericson's writings, George Vaillant's *Adaptation to Life*, Daniel Levinson's *The Seasons of a Man's Life*, and other studies. Journalists and psychologists make the news by describing a "midlife crisis" as if it were the critical turning point between joy and despair, enthusiasm and resignation, mental health and illness. People worry about their midlife crises, apologize if they don't seem to be handling them properly, and fret if they aren't having one.

A popular stand-up comic recommends that, if you are not having your midlife crisis on schedule, you go immediately to a camp in the Catskill Mountains where experts will induce one for you. The *Wall Street Journal* publishes a cartoon depicting a large group of weeping adults in a living room as the hostess explains, "I thought they'd hit it off. They're all going through their midlife crises." A game appears in the marketplace to further perpetuate the stage of life: THE MIDLIFE CRISIS GAME. "Can you survive your middle years without cracking up, breaking up, or going broke? This hilarious game of strategy by Gameworks will test your ability during those sensitive years." Along with it, the catalog also offers a MIDLIFE CRISIS SURVIVAL KIT, which "provides all the ingredients for surviving your Midlife Crisis, with a midlife survival test, exercise gym, portable carbon dioxide inhaler and a life-style patching system."

Soon after the original publication of this book, I received a gag birthday card from two of my favorite people, who wrote that "this card would be in grossly bad taste for anyone else of your chronological age" and it showed a drawing of a man who, I assume, was trying to look "young" with running shoes, bright green shorts, while carrying a rolled-up newspaper turned to the Obituary page. He was hysterically running on a treadmill marked "The Beginning" and "The End" and the large headline read: "How to Know When You've Entered the Mid-Life Crisis." I won't bore you with all the ways one can tell, but here are just a few examples that littered the card:

- When you read the obituaries before the sports page.

- When the treadmill you chose to run, runs faster than you choose to.

- When all your thrills are vicarious.

- When your fantasy turns to women half your age and sports cars twice your budget.

- When your favorite TV show is sponsored by a "tired blood" product.

The bookshelves remind us, if other segments of the media have failed (though they sure have tried): *The Gray Itch* (The male metapause syndrome), *Women of a Certain Age* (The midlife search for self), *The Male Mid-Life Crisis* (Fresh starts after forty), *The Forty-to-Sixty-Year-Old Male* (A guide for men and the women in their lives . . . to see them through the crises of Male Middle Years), *The Wonderful Crisis of Middle Age*. After an afternoon in my local bookstore, I became so depressed that I wanted to purchase another book called *Exit House: Choosing Suicide as an Alternative*.

It is a trap, and again we are the victims if we believe everything we read and hear about ourselves. It all seems so logical to us. If the changes through which we have lived are described as *crises*, it makes it easier to accept the fact that we do constantly change, that life is complex, unpredictable, and a frequently illogical series of events that do not necessarily take place at predetermined intervals in time. We begin to use the term *midlife crisis* too often as a *reason* for our change in direction or in our thinking. We find it quite logical to hear that talented Hollywood director Paul Mazursky has said that, at age fifty-two, he was battling midlife crisis and that, "I reached the point at thirty-two years old when I wasn't working very much and I was heading for middle age."

Certainly there are some crises that are apt to happen more often at certain ages than at others. For example, we are more likely to suffer the death of a parent (or a peer) as we grow older, and Daniel Levinson's "settling down" is more apt to include first marriage and children at twenty-five rather than at fifty-five. Yet 25 percent of all *second marriages* take place after the age of fifty! Are not *both* crises examples of *normal* change, normal growth, a normal life cycle? The crises of our lives for the most part are as age-irrelevant as the entire society. And though Levinson also declares that "it is not possible to get through middle adulthood (forty-five–sixty) without having at least a moderate crisis," he does indeed specify critical periods in the lives of subjects in their twenties and thirties. I suggest, then, that too much is being made of our midlife crisis, whether or not we have encountered one so far, or we are too old and might well have passed one by unseen and unnoticed. The crisis, the event, the change, the transitions, the pointing of the fickle finger of fate has less relevance to age than we care to admit in this era of categorizing and putting our lives into neat, well-defined little packages. Look at this list of crises, add your own if you like, and tell me at what age they occur:

- The loss of a job.

- Divorce and legal custody of the children.

- Death of a peer, a spouse, a parent, or a child.

- Change of career.

- Failure or rejection of some significance—the actor who is constantly rejected, the professor refused tenure, the student applying for a particular college.

- Severe illness—a young woman who spent three months in the hospital during her freshman year at college because she was allergic to penicillin.

- Catastrophic illness—the breadwinner suddenly found to be ill with cancer, and not covered by major medical insurance (just as 38 million other people in this country).

- Violence: rape, mugging, murder. Or devastating accident: a plane crash, a falling object, an auto or bus collision.

• Extended unemployment—the hapless, unskilled black or Hispanic or the mother who wants to return to the workforce but cannot find a job.

Except for a very few, they are all age-irrelevant crises. As young people, we thought that these crises in our lives were totally insoluble. The rebellion of a teenage generation, such as what happened here in the sixties and in China in this past year, are *crises* for them and for us. Drugs and adolescent suicide, teenage pregnancy, are also crises in the contemporary catalog of social problems. We may make light of the crises of the young, but if we think back to our own high-school days, the first signs of acne before the senior prom were as serious to us then as the empty nest, menopause, or limited retirement income is to us now. One writer even listed "orthodontia" as a crisis of the young!

It cannot take but an instant for the reader to think back to the trauma and the horror of the death of a young peer. I had spent four years in the army during World War II, and I suppose it was to be expected that one might hear of a friend lost in action or of another friend killed in an airplane accident over Texas while on a training flight—a death especially ironic, since he had survived seventy-five bombing missions over Germany! But it was wartime and horror stories competed with one another for our attention. Death was a constant companion of life and so many were perishing that the death of a single person paled among so many. It was true of Korea. It was true of Vietnam.

But, not too many years later, when I was thirty-one, my best friend, Midge, died of cancer. She was only one year older than I, and pregnant at the time. It was Christmas when I got the news and, though I had seen her waste away during the previous year, I could not accept the fact that death would be the end result, certainly not in someone so close, so vital, so gentle, and so very bright. I cried for most of the day and took my car and rode uptown to visit her husband, roundly cursed by taxi drivers for my erratic behavior on the road. And each Christmas, even to this day, depression sets in and it suddenly occurs to me that I am still torn; that I still miss her so many years later.

Of course it was a crisis. And many have occurred since then. I am stating as strongly as I can that crises can come at *any* time and that they are not predictable, like preordained transitions that take place at a particular stage. Neither am I stating that crises do *not* occur during midlife. I am merely making a semantic demand that we call a crisis a crisis when it is, indeed, a crisis, while resisting the temptation to label each wind of change a hurricane. As my friend Frankie says, "They don't even let you have one bad day. Just try to have one bad day and they call it a crisis."

I was speaking to a middle-aged friend about her feelings at this time in her life, and the description of a friend of hers is a case in point:

> This is a woman who is, first of all, very heavy, so she's got a lot of physical things against her. About four or five years ago when her husband, a brilliant engineer, moved out to live with his younger secretary, she didn't have any money problems. She even started college, finished it, and went on for her degree in business administration. She was, effectively alone, and she got kind of used to that.
>
> Then her husband contracted cancer and he came home to her to die! He died within a month. She actually took him in when he came back. She was furious at him, but she took him in. He left her well off, with about a quarter of a million dollars.

I asked what had happened to his young secretary.

> I don't know. I suppose she gave him up when he contracted cancer. It was quite a scene—a heavy afternoon when my friend and I went to clear out the apartment that her husband shared with his secretary. Well, it now turns out that my friend's lawyer has absconded with most of the money her husband left her. Within the year, her father died of cancer and a brother who lived in the Caribbean area died of a brain hemorrhage, leaving her without any support system at all. All within a year. What would you call this?

Well, I would call it *a crisis!* But the example cannot be used to proclaim the coming of middle-age crisis for an entire generation. There is no common pattern of change, nor is there a consistency of life-style, adult conflict, or entrance and exit through ridgidly fixed stages. Gail Sheehy labels her ten-year passages, for example, as "The Trying Twenties" or "Passage to the Thirties," and Levinson says of a writer in his early thirties that "by this time . . . *it was late to develop his talents*" (italics mine). Dr. Neugarten answers these authors by stating, first of all, that the media coverage of middle age is based upon too little evidence (Levinson on only forty *men* and Vaillant on ninety-five Harvard grads). She adds:

> Choices and dilemmas do not sprout forth at ten-year intervals and decisions are not made and then left behind as if they were merely beads on a chain.
>
> It was reasonable to describe life as a set of discrete stages when most people followed the same rules, when major events occurred at predictable ages. People

have long been able to tell the "right age" for marriage, the first child, the last child, career achievement, retirement, death. In the last two decades, however, chronological age has moved out of synch with these marking events. Our biological time clocks have changed.

She explains further that the onset of puberty is earlier than it has ever been, menopause arrives later for women, there are new life-styles in work and career orientation, and people are living into old age as healthier, more active adults. When the children leave home, the parents now find the freedom to pursue a range of new activities and an expansion of their vital life style.

The theory of "age-irrelevance", of course, is not without its detractors. In spite of a society that is changing around them, some sociologists and other scholars are throwing up their hands in horror at the very thought that we may be entering a new era of aging. Using the term "life-span specialists" (a contemporary designation that might well have gone into the previous chapter), they proclaim that the social order will be destroyed if we do not have age norms as an "anchor."

One sociologist even goes so far as to state that an age-irrelevant society is a rudderless one. A gerontologist terms the theory preposterous. If, as still another gerontologist contends, age-irrelevancy will encourage the old to try to stay young, thereby denying them the dignity of old age, I must ask if *dignity* is a private monopoly of the elderly.

It is terribly unfair to our generations to characterize our problems and crises as indicative of our *age* rather than pointing out that much of what we experience during the middle years is quite normal and very much to be expected. The Chinese, in all their wisdom, seem to have found the truth again, for the Chinese word for crisis is composed of two characters—one signifies danger; the other represents *opportunity*.

It is seldom a crisis when the children leave home, and it is perfectly normal when three generations of family members are living their own active and fulfilling lives. As we age, we begin to plan for retirement, accepting the fact that we will (or will not) give up our work to pursue other activities. And though we try not to dwell on it, the aged do accept death as a part of life.

Some time ago, psychologist Douglas Bray and his collegue Ann Howard did a twenty-year study of more than four hundred employees of the Bell System. It dealt with career success and life satisfaction of middle-aged managers, and one of its most interesting conclusions was that only 22 percent of the subjects were undergoing what might be considered a midlife crisis. This means that the great majority were *not*.

The authors of the report are not without a sense of humor. Since so much attention was being paid to crisis in middle life by psychologists, psychiatrists, and sociologists, they came to the conclusion that "the middle-aged male was threatening to replace the white rat and the college sophomore as the dominant research subject in psychology."

Up to this point you have probably noticed an overwhelming balance in favor of the *men* of our age group. Though they offer various forms of apology for omitting more than half the population, researchers and authors have, until this time, concerned themselves almost wholly with men. Daniel Levinson did not have the funds to pursue a thorough and balanced study of both sexes in *The Seasons of a Man's Life*. Vallaint studied *male* Harvard grads because there were only male Harvard grads at that time. When Bray and Howard began their research with Bell System middle-level managers, well over twenty years ago, almost all (if not all) in that category were, of course, men.

The reports reflect both the attitudes and the demographics of our society—male-oriented, the woman at home taking care of the kids. If a woman played any role in the job market, she was generally paid less than men (and still is, in most cases); she was not eligible for equal pension rights, she sublimated her professional choice to the geographic location of her husband's job, and the potential of top management was denied her (and still is, for the most part). Because she started her career late in life, after the kids had gone, she was at a disadvantage during her entry into the corporate world, almost like running the marathon and told that she had to start one hour after the race had begun. To top it off, she was always expected to look "young."

Are women, then, not allowed to have their midlife crises, even in fantasy? If, as the studies show, women have more stressful life experiences than men, if differences between *the sexes* are more significant than differences between the young and old of each sex in terms of economics, emotional stress, and society's demands—not to mention fulfillment—then it stands to reason that women, too, should be entitled to feel the "panic" of middle age.

Dr. Neugarten calls it "the psychology of timing" and indeed it is. Widowhood at an early age, or sudden widowhood at any age, can be a critical shock, followed by a painful readjustment in a society that demeans widows and singles them out for unequal treatment and loss of status. Nevertheless, as we age, there is a more realistic, underlying perception that widowhood may well happen in our sixties or seventies. Looking around us, we know that many of our friends have been recently widowed. Death, then, may come as a shock, certainly, but the term *crisis* may well not apply.

But it is in the area of woman's sexuality that the male-dominated society has created the most myths, though many of them are being challenged and broken down one by one. It is not only that *women* are changing so much. It is possibly that the *society* is being made aware that much of what we have heard and read is pure fantasy. Researchers (bless them) are even discovering that the Victorian woman actually *enjoyed* sex, though her demeanor and the contemporary attitudes denied everything.

We know, of course, that women are hysterical. Even my mother perpetuated that myth. After all, the word *hysterectomy* comes from the Greek word *hystera* (uterus). Even your doctor probably believes it! The myths have built up through the centuries and women (as well as men) have had their own strong self-doubts, feeling that if society keeps saying it, it must be true. We all try to live up to other people's expectations, and in this area we are no different than when we were twenty years old. Which brings me, in turn, to the climacteric, or menopause, the female "midlife crisis."

I remember my grandmother, then my mother, whispering about "change of life." The flushes, the end of fertility, femininity, sexuality, attractiveness, and vitality. In other words, the end. The worst possible thing that could happen as a woman grew older.

There is no doubt that hormonal changes take place, and with them many psychological ones, but if we believe the women who have written on the subject and the interviews conducted with hundreds of women, the onset of the climacteric is but another event in the gradual pattern of the female adult. The past ten years or so has also witnessed an increase in the number of menopause clinics around the country, where women who do find that the changes are rather severe can go for help. It is, in a sense, an escape from the doctor who passes it all off with, "It's all in your head. If you stop thinking about it, it will go away. I'd suggest you get a job or a hobby and forget about it, my dear!"

Most important of all, perhaps, is the discovery that menopause just can't be defined either by averages or by myths. More and more articles are beginning to appear that define both the realities and the myths of menopause, and it is the latter that are as damaging to women as the "midlife crisis" is to men. Keep in mind that medical literature usually is based upon studies of disease. As a result, we just cannot generalize from the findings to include a majority of the population. Certainly, some 75 percent of all women who reach menopause experience disturbances or discomfort ranging from dry skin and hair, hot flashes and insomnia up to changes in the nervous system, vaginal dryness, bone loss, and even incontinence. However, only a very small percentage visit their doctors for treatment. In a survey conducted by Dr. Neugarten, with one hundred normal women between the ages of forty-three and fifty-three, only 4 percent of the women stated that menopause was their major concern. Over 50 percent, however, declared that "losing your husband" would be their greatest worry.

In addition, over 65 percent maintained that there was no change in their sexuality after menopause. And even many of those who thought that there was a change felt that sexual relations had become more pleasurable, because *the fear of pregnancy was no longer there.*

I was appearing on a call-in radio show in Chicago and the subject of midlife crisis and menopause came up. After a short discussion with the host of the show, a call came in and an irate woman berated me quite heatedly. "What do *you* know about it?" she angrily asked. "You're a man!" I tried to answer as best I could, explaining that it was research, discussion, observation, and that I also had done films on breast feeding and immunology for the Quechua Indians in Ecuador, and even if I wasn't very good at it, I did know something about it!

A moment later, another caller contacted the station. This time it was a woman, and she quickly defended this guilt-ridden author against the charge of being a man and not understanding. "I'll tell you how I handle it," she said. "I get a few flushes—sure I do. But I just wipe the sweat off my forehead and go on with my life!"

A great number of writers have zeroed in on another phenomenon—the "male menopause"—but even here the symptoms of depression and fatigue and the reassessment of life-style, job, and family generally have their roots in psychological and job-oriented situations rather than in hormonal changes. This, too, as life expectancy increases, is a normal effect. The term *male menopause* will stay with us, however, because it makes for another gold mine of articles in popular magazines.

It is normal and quite natural to ask questions as we progress in our lives. It is a reasonable query, "Why me?" when life seems to strike us out. But most of what we experience is all a part of normality, a natural result of change and growth. My friend Carol, over luncheon one afternoon, put it well:

Why is it that you expect at some time in your life that everything will go smoothly? You will have a status, finances will be secure, and your personal life will smooth out. Why do you expect that it will happen—but it doesn't?

Jonathan Swift might have answered her by saying, "There is nothing in this world constant, but inconstancy." I feel that part of living is solving problems, that there must be some challenge in order to create change. As Gail Sheehy put it so well in *Passages,* "If we don't change, we don't grow. If we don't grow, we are not really living."

What we too often call "crisis" is merely growth.

11 ❀ The Empty Nest, the Bulging Nest, and the Boomerang Syndrome

I'll tell you my definition of freedom: The children all have jobs, they've moved away, and the dog dies!

—Seminar Participant
AT&T Pioneers Convention,
Montreal, 1985

Imagine, if you will, another time. You are about to leave your parents' home, possibly forever. It is a very special time in your life and in theirs, for you are the last of the children to make your way into the world. Possibly you have gotten married, or you are leaving home to do what passed for "your own thing" in that more naive era. Or perhaps it is just the four years of college that lie ahead. Whatever the reason, the secure nest will soon be empty, except for two adults who have had little time alone together through their twenty or thirty years of marriage.

You are gone and the first visitor to knock on the door of the little house, the sounds filling the now-empty rooms, is a sociologist who is taking a survey on what has been discovered as a *new* crisis in middle life, "the empty-nest syndrome." Breathlessly he or she asks, "How do you feel about your last child leaving home?"

Think for a moment about how that question might have been taken by your parents, and especially your mother. For more than twenty years, she has been conditioned to accept marriage, homemaking, and the rearing of her children as the main function and purpose of her life. To be called a "good

107

mother" is the accolade that she accepts most easily, while sublimating all her frustrations, her dreams, her personal goals. When you left her home, she certainly felt that she might miss you somewhat, since she rather liked you as a person. But deep down, under all the platitudes and the social acceptance of the role model, she has begun to feel a sense of relief and a freedom from bondage. The researcher asks the question again: "How do you feel?"

If she answers truthfully and tells not only of her sadness, but of her relief and the newly found sense of joy bubbling up somewhere in her psyche, she is admitting that she was not that good a mother after all, or worse, that she did not love you. How could she possibly even imply that to a stranger? The guilt would be too much to bear afterward. Therefore, she tells the sociologist what she thinks she *should* say. After all, this was not a time when women gave vent to their honest feelings, nor a time when a more liberated society accepts such feelings. In the atmosphere of our parents' generation, your mother would be encouraged to dissemble, to bury the feelings of freedom while giving vent to the sense of despair and loneliness that accompanied your going out the door. She would promptly be marked down by the researcher as having a chronic and classic case of "empty-nest syndrome."

This is not, by any means, farfetched, for out of the distorted studies of the generations right through the 1950s has come one of the most damaging myths about middle age. It is, probably, even more a lie than a myth and it has been especially demeaning and destructive to women in particular.

I wonder why it took so long to discover that women might welcome the end of mothering and see it as a time of liberation. The contemporary surveys, conducted now that people are not afraid to speak their inner feelings, have begun to find that women do *not* suffer unduly when the nest empties and the fledglings have flown off. In one study of 160 middle-aged women with an average age of forty-six, Lillian Rubin of the Institute for the Study of Social Change (University of California at Berkeley) found that only *one* was suffering from the classic symptoms of the empty-nest syndrome! Many were, indeed, ambivalent about their feelings, but almost all greeted the event with a strong sense of relief.

If anything, it is the *fathers* who are more vulnerable to the change in family status, especially those who feel neglected by their wives or who have worked long and tiring hours in pursuit of status and career. Thinking that they can at last spend some more time with the growing children, they find instead that the home situation has radically changed. The stereo no longer blares the records of Public Enemy, Funky Worm, or Big Daddy Kane. They have been replaced by the wife's collection of Bach and Vivaldi. How many *fathers* of our generation have insisted, for reasons of their own, that their children attend a college close to home, while the mothers deeply felt that school on the North Slope of Alaska might be a good educational beginning?

My friend Dee wrote me a long, deeply personal letter. It was his answer to my questions about this strange malady, so much a part of the crisis literature. "In previous generations, people tended to act the way they were expected to act," he wrote. "People of middle age were supposed to act in a particular way. So they did. Consider the European widow dressed in black. She looks old and ugly and plain and alone and stalwart and not full of joy. She probably became like that because everyone wanted it that way. Her children would be ashamed and concerned and grieved if she didn't. Today, most people in America have a lot of options. We can choose *where* we want to be, and we do. And with whom. It's not just an economic choice. There's also a big change in *perception*. People don't have to look old. Or act old. Or think poor."

Friends like Dee have been important to me in this search for a true picture of this stage in our lives. Having no children of my own, I was particularly interested to find out how *they* felt about the empty nest, since all of them were losing children to the cruel world or their offspring had already sprung. How could I know, after all, that the earlier studies were not correct and the newer ones were equally falacious or inaccurate? No child of mine had ever left the house, never to return. Dee's children had been gone only a short time when he wrote again.

"We had a baby ten-and-a-half months after the wedding, so we are now, for the first time, going to be 'just a couple.' It's not good, or bad. Just different from all we've known together. We've been excited and anticipatory about the empty nest. . . . We've just begun to experience our new roles. So far, we are going out a lot more—perhaps three nights a week. Eleanor has already changed her reading habits. She always read a lot, almost every day since our marriage. But in the past she read Regency romances, history stuff, and other escapist literature. In recent weeks, however, she has been reading a series of classics like Jane Austen and she has begun Barbara Tuchman's *A Distant Mirror*. Somehow this suggests to me that she has enough stamina or emotion or leftover intelligence to invest, by choice, in something of substance. This, after years of reading only for relaxation and escape."

This was about eight years ago. The update is even more fascinating. Soon afterward, Dee left his substantial position as a vice president with a large soft drink company and returned to his first love, teaching. He has been a professor at the University of Tennessee for all these years and the new freedom now allows him to take a visiting professorship in Lisbon, Portugal, every summer, where he teaches a marketing course at the university (in English).

There are marvelous stories about newly liberated parents changing the entire decor of the house after the children have left. One couple turned the children's wing into an office and hobby shop, much to the chagrin of their progeny when they returned for the holidays, to find that they had been dispossessed in the name of liberation. Another reported with relief that she can now sit in the living room and have a conversation with another adult without having a teenager sitting and glaring at them. If the loss is a trauma, it is only transient as new life-styles begin to emerge and new options materialize. Here are some examples that surfaced during my interviews with friends.

Time for quiet, candle-lit dinners at home or in a restaurant, alone or with friends. Time to enjoy two in a house with more time for self-indulgence. Time to say good-bye to the youth collectives that camped in the living room or the friends who tagged along each time the children came home with some newly discovered "best friend." Time, too, to welcome the kids when they come home for Christmas and to admit that it's a joy to see them again. Time to pursue the hobby that always seemed to elude you. Time to go back to school. Time to play tennis because you want to rather than because it serves as an escape from the responsibilities of the children. Time to listen to the travel ads and do something about them. Time to think quietly. Time to be what you always thought you might become. Time to be yourself.

My friend Dee wrote, "I'm glad for the new times. I don't feel 'Is that all there is?' It's just the *past* in a process so gradual that it never occurred in one moment of time. When the boys call long distance, it's nice. But it's not wonderful. It's not like those warm-all-over TV commercials for long-distance telephone. I find that days go by when I don't think of them at all. Eleanor acknowledges the same experience, even though she is involved more in sending packages and forwarding their mail to them.

"Our kids are nice. I like them. I'm pleased with them. Each is different from his parents and different from what I thought he was or would grow up to be. I'm glad I did it. I'm pleased I don't have to do it any more!"

On a walk through our island, I came across a dear friend who was working in her garden. She is on the edge of the empty nest. Her daughter will soon be going away to college. And the mother is already beginning to suffer from the empty-nest syndrome, quite in contrast to Dee and Eleanor. "At certain times," she said, "I talk a good game and I say, 'I can't wait for her to go'—but by the time she's gone, I'll miss her. I don't know what it will be like. . . ." She paused and flipped her feelings 180 degrees: "I'm looking forward to it, though. I'm looking forward to being my own person. I'm looking forward to not having to come home to cook dinner. I'm looking forward to having much more mobility, to traveling with my husband on business."

Once again, her mood shifted and she looked up from her garden, determined to be the pragmatist, and she smiled. "I guarantee that when it comes to the holidays, my *neighbor's* daughter will come home and mine won't." I asked her if that disturbed her and her eyes sparkled. "Of course it does," she retorted, *"Who's going to help me cook?"*

The Bulging Nest

If we have settled the "crisis" of the empty nest, you may be certain that something will quickly replace it. Times have changed so rapidly that it is no longer required that we deny our sense of freedom when the children leave. In fact, many of us admit to anxiously awaiting their exit. *What happens if they don't want to go?* What happens if we buy them an airline ticket to Alaska if we live in New York; New York if we live in Alaska, pack their clothing, open the front door—and they won't leave home? *This* is a crisis!

There may be many reasons for the situation, not the least of which are the high cost of housing, the slow climb up the economic ladder for children just entering the job market—or just plain convenience. The Federal Department of Education conducted a study in 1987 that showed that almost 30 *percent* of all college undergraduates are still living with their parents. Again, there may be very real economic reasons, but some of the answers given by live-at-home students transcended the money aspect. Most of them cited good food, sleep, privacy, and *having laundry done* as benefits over dorm life at college.

At the very least, the arrangement requires a delicate juggling act between parents who had expected the children to leave, and children who in no way are planning to depart. Some parents love it. Others hate it with a vengeance. Ann Landers, the columnist, once advised a parent signed "Hopefully Desperate" to "throw the bum out" when a letter was written to her describing the plight of one family. The mother wrote of a twenty-two-year-old son whom she had tried to evict without success. The young man was in debt, paid nothing for his room and board, lived like a vagrant, kept his room like a pigsty, stole from his father and brothers, and, to top it off, wrote rubber checks. To make matters even worse, the mother complained, "All I can do is refuse to accept his collect calls. But mostly he doesn't call collect. *He is here!"*

Ms. Landers answered the plea with a citation of US and Canadian law that allows a parent to institute a civil or criminal suit for *trespassing* once the child has reached majority. A friend of mine, not so hostile as that toward her twenty-five-year-old son, wailed about the *bulging* nest in her own home. Things were just too comfortable there for the young man ever to consider leaving. The nest would not only *not* be empty, but it seemed destined to be distended forever.

My friend claimed that she had tried everything. "Every night," she said, "I move his bed closer and closer to the front door. But he doesn't take the hint!" I, myself, have sent her the item written by Ann Landers, but other than that, this is one time that I mentally give thanks for not having had any children! I seriously wonder if I, as a father, would have had the courage to "throw the bum out!"

The Boomerang Syndrome, or the Refilled Nest

It comes with a knock on the door or a long-distance telephone call (collect). The life in San Francisco is not quite what it was supposed to be. "Doing your own thing" required sharing the apartment with California's best cockroaches. The trip through Europe to "find himself" included losing his cash to a pickpocket, misplacing his airline ticket, and deciding that he might want to bring his sleeping bag and his new sleeping companion back to your house "for a while."

Or on a more serious note, the economics of the world is too much for the young, newly marrieds to handle, especially since the baby was born and they'd like to save some money to buy a new house at today's astronomical prices. One young couple, interviewed by a reporter, just couldn't save enough unless they gave up their large apartment that had an artist's studio for the wife, dinner out four times a week, and the personal computer just purchased by the husband. So they went "home" to live with their parents until they could straighten out their finances! Someone has dubbed the movement "Parenthood II."

Though there may be very real problems, a great part of the *boomerang* trend is that the expectations of our younger people are dashed rather easily, it seems. They were brought up (by us) in an era of affluence, with minimal problems of growth and the high hopes that accompany our catering to a generation that "deserved" everything and was rightly labeled with the word, *"Me"* followed by the very derogatory contemporary designation: *Yuppie*. The very fact that slight and shallow magazines such as *Self* are such huge successes is a tribute to the thinking of the children now reentering the nest in ever-increasing numbers, unable to cope not only with the economics of the world, but with the unfinished business of their emotional growth.

I am not pointing to our generation as paragons of balance, by any means. In our day, when we finally left home we expected much much less. We settled on a job, any kind of job, even if it were menial and tedious. Perhaps that was a flaw in our personalities. But we expected to struggle and we expected to build our lives bit by bit. We expected, at first, to possibly share a room with one or two or four others, until finally we were able to find peace and quiet in a place of our own.

The personal computer (or the equivalent at that time) came after the marriage, after the kids, after the career—if it came at all. But the important thing about this new boomerang syndrome is that it strongly tells us that there is no statute of limitations on parenting—no less the beginning of Parenthood II. You have emptied the nest. Your freedom—your richly deserved freedom—is yours at last, and suddenly you are once again parents, but with extreme differences this time around. The problem has been growing so substantially that articles and books are now being devoted entirely to the subject. When I first coined the phrase, *Boomerang Syndrome*, I did not expect to see so many studies following close behind, including a new book in 1989 called *Boomerang Kids* (J. Stegall, J. Okimoto, Pocket Books).

Not only is it possible that you are now having to deal with the care of your own aged parents, but also with the return of the children you thought had finally gone. And while they were gone, they developed their own life-styles and habits, sometimes affected by the partner with whom they had chosen to live (whether at their house or yours). The returning son is discouraged with the job market, the daughter is just taking up "temporary residence" in your home. The dinners you served when they were growing up are not quite right now, because "you don't know anything about nutrition," and your son George is now a vegetarian. Alice's boyfriend didn't give a damn whether or not she made the bed or cleaned up when they were together in their apartment, but for some reason *you* seem to care. You actually get to like her boyfriend (or new husband) better than you ever liked her (for he has moved right in with her, of course). The problem of a son or daughter returning to a home where there has been a remarriage or divorce is even more severe. The return, for whatever reason, may turn the home into a battleground. And privacy is lost on both sides.

There is no doubt that solutions have to be worked out. And other than turning the welcome mat upside down when they arrive, both sides have to adjust. Some parents totally avoid having to face the boomerang by giving up the spacious, four-bedroom house and moving into a small downtown apartment without a guest room, just as soon as the children leave home for the first time. In addition, there is an invisible, but strongly worded sign over the front door that reads, "No Sleeping Bags Allowed."

Others have divided the house into separate living quarters with several common rooms. Still others have begun to achieve some success in this new extended family situation by making use of its positive aspects and the unexpected benefits that can go along with the difficulties. However, my own feeling, after speaking to families who have had to readjust their lives, and after reading many reports on this growing phenomenon, is that the advantages are heavily weighted in favor of the young (again).

The economic regrouping and the feeling of inability to cope is strongest in our children and, if they come home to live with us, it is *we* who are helping *them* to adjust to *their* vicissitudes of life. For them it is a chance to "find themselves" yet again, to change direction, or to pursue a new career, frequently at much less financial cost. If they are a couple and they have children, it is they who benefit from our free baby-sitting and it is they who can now save for the dream home that we, as parents, struggled to acquire on our own some years back.

For us, there is the possibility renewed feeling of being needed again, for whatever pragmatic reasons. Possibly there is also a challenge and a sense of rejuvenation in the new living arrangements.

But all sides report that it is not easy. For those of us who have welcomed the empty nest, only to find that it is filled once again, the emotional shock can be severe and the sense of anger that we feel is quite natural. It may be difficult, if not impossible, to turn down the request of a child to return home again, but if it happens, the "ground rules" should be laid down firmly and at once. It is, after all, *your* home to which they are coming back. The chores of cleaning up after dinner, taking out the garbage, or walking the dog late at night in the rain (particularly if the dog belongs to the child) should be clearly designated or the situation will disintegrate into chaos. You, in turn, may want to think about your demands that your grown daughter be back in the house before midnight, now that she is turning thirty. It takes maturity of outlook on both sides to make it work.

Psychiatrists, sociologists, and marriage counselors are watching the phenomenon closely to see how it all turns out. Anything that replaces the myth of the empty nest will be welcome, even the truism that "parenting never ends."

A Brief Postscript

There is a new extreme surfacing in the family relationships of our generations and, though I smiled when I first heard of it, I am not so sure that it is not a good idea. It is called "benevolent disinheritance." Many parents feel that they have amply provided for their offspring during the twenty or thirty years that it took to raise them, nurture them, send them through college, and provide loans for their first business ventures or their first homes. Their children are financially secure, do not need their help any longer, and are quite independent.

As a result, there is a growing trend to cut the children out of the last will and testament. A large number of children have been out of contact with their parents for years. In many cases, no close relationship even exists outside of blood. On the other hand, in their later lives, the parents discover that friends and neighbors are more in need of their money than their children are. Thus the disinheritance, and the accompanying outcry of the children left at poverty's door along with their personal computers. It is the same shriek of pain that we sometimes hear from our children if we remarry when we are widowed or divorced. Many presume that the new spouse is obviously out only for the money that is rightfully theirs.

We are, of course, entitled to lead our own lives, whether in our empty nests or with our own "posslq," at whatever stage of our growth and regardless of the complaints of our children. We are entitled to do as we please, go where we please, and live where we please. We are also entitled to do with our savings and our pensions exactly what we please. And so the idea of "benevolent disinheritance" strikes a chord in my perverse sense of humor. This, in turn, reminds me of a famous George M. Cohan song, "Always Leave Them Laughing When You Say Goodbye!"

12 The Sexy Sexagenarian: Everything We Wanted to Know About Sex, We Knew a Long Time Ago

JEALOUS MAN, NINETY-THREE, BATTERS WIFE, EIGHTY-SIX

Sun Biu, ninety-three, dragged his wife, eighty-six, out of bed and stomped on her chest because he thought she was having a love affair.

—*Japan Times*
Tokyo

The New York taxi driver, always the philosopher of unsolicited trivia, made his way slowly through the crawl of midtown traffic. I sat back, resigned to a long trip, sorry that I had not walked the short distance, while he droned on, covering the present administration in Washington, the long past mayoralty of John Lindsay, the influx of undesirables and Yuppies into the city, and finally, the current news story being covered with the thoroughness of World War II. If you remember, a famous diet doctor had been shot four times by his paramour and the murder trial was yielding ample subject matter for feminists, people on diets, the millions who had read his book, and New York taxi drivers. For most of the stop-and-go trip I barely listened to his monologue, but one comment made me sit up and take heed, for I was, naturally, right in the middle of my research for this book.

"What the hell," he screamed over the blaring din of horns. "He was no angel. He was screwing everything that moved. I don't even know how he could do it. *He was seventy years old!*"

Not too many weeks after the incident, for which the doctor's paramour went to jail for a long term, I was deciding whether to attack what follows with humor, wit, and sarcasm—or with the anger that I had begun to feel at the perception of older people as asexual, nonsexual, or sexually extinguished, much like *Tyrannosaurus Rex*. Some contemporary friends and I were discussing a woman of about fifty-two. And once again I heard it and wondered why I had not been aware of it before—even among our peer groups.

The woman's daughter (she was twenty-six) was complaining because her mother had rented a summer house with some younger people and had become a "swinger." The daughter, of course, was distraught. Her mother, in her words, had gone into her *second childhood*. My contemporaries seemed to agree. The woman's mother was not *acting her age*.

Indeed, when you read the little news item that opens this chapter, what was *your* reaction? Did you smile, shake your head, laugh out loud? Disbelieve? Or did you, quite possibly, wonder why the item was even published at all? So, what is so damned unusual about an eighty-six-year-old woman going off and having a fling? (I doubt that the latter was your reaction.)

The prejudices and preconceptions about middle-aged and older people falling in love, or actually making love, was further borne out for me at the AT&T Pioneer's Convention in Montreal told the seminar the following story:

> My mother is eighty-seven and has been in a retirement home for five years. She has been married five times and she has outlived all of her husbands. She met a boyfriend about five months ago who also lives in a retirement home. She told me recently, "I would like to invite Don over." I said, "Well, why don't you?" She said, "People might talk!"

And these are people well *past* middle age. What, then, is the problem with *our* generations? The Roman sage Publilius Syrus wrote, "It is natural for a young man to love, but a crime for an old one." It took some centuries for an answer to be written (in 1972) by Simone de Beauvoir, and it was long overdue:

> If old people show the same desires, the same feelings, the same requirements as the young, the world looks upon them with disgust; in them, love and jealousy seem revolting or absurd, sexuality repulsive.

Where does this denial come from? Why the distorted perception of older people as asexual? Worst of all, why have *we* accepted another of the myths and stereotypes that cast us in the roles of the unimportant, the unfeeling, the insignificant? The reasons are complex, but if we examine them one by one, they become a fascinating study in how the absurd can become accepted as pure gospel.

Can you, even now, picture your parents having intercourse? If there is one generational truism that overlaps the era in which we were born, it is the inability of almost any young person to imagine his or her parents, or anyone else over forty-five, making love. It has not changed, even today, and not too long ago a young woman I know asked her mother, with a tinge of annoyance, "Why do you and Daddy close the door when you go into your bedroom? What do you do in there?" Her mother drew herself up to her full five feet, one inch, and responded, "The same thing that you and your boyfriend do when *you* close *your* door!"

It is as incomprehensible for that contemporary young woman to think of *her* parents making love as it was for us—and for our grandparents when they were young men and women. We were conceived through some act of sterile acrobatics, perhaps, and then it stopped. The interesting thing is that, until recently, no one even bothered to *ask* us if we continued our sexual interests after the birth of the children. As we got older, it became even more unusual for anyone to care. Dr. Alex Comfort observed that the sex surveys did not even include older people. The reason was that "everyone *knew* they had none, and they were assumed to have none, because nobody asked."

This was further borne out in a delightful article in the *New York Times* by June Wilson. In searching through the bookstores for the literature on geriatric sex, she could find nothing, even copies of Alex Comfort's book. One bookstore manager explained that it was discontinued because "it didn't move."

Although the times have changed in terms of sexual attitudes, many perceptions have remained exactly where they were fifty years ago. Recalling that *we* could not envision our parents and grandparents having intercourse, how interesting it is to note that our children are also unable to close that same emotional gap. And *they* are supposed to be liberated. We were retarded by comparison. Or were we?

At seventeen, I—like millions of my male contemporaries—was in a constant state of anticipatory tumescence. Little did I know that the girls of our generation were also sexual beings. The categories of girls were, of course, designated by our parents: good girls, fast girls, and bad girls. Since all the girls in our neighborhood were good girls, the perpetual ache in the loins was never to be sated by them. However, always the optimist and the fantasist, each of us carried a rolled-up condom in the small pocket of our wallets, where a permanent ridge formed and the protection lay there "just in case" we should get lucky and find one of those fast girls from another borough. The rubber lay there so long, in fact, that should we ever have had need for it, it probably would have disintegrated into a little puff of dust as we took it out of its hiding place! Nevertheless, the youths of our day retained their optimism.

William Styron in his book *Sophie's Choice* writes of a typical situation in those more naive days when his hero meets a girl from Brooklyn and, each time they are together, the sexual tension builds, only to have her pull back from the act of intercourse at the very last moment. It was true. It was, unfortunately—hilariously—devastatingly true. If we young men were lucky enough to meet a moderately "fast" girl, the ceremony of sexual petting took place through an array of medieval armor: brassiere fasteners and hooks, snaps, buttons, zippers, garters, and girdles. And if we were fortunate enough to finally make our way to the bare flesh that lay between girdle and stocking top, a firm hand usually reached out to stop us and a voice came from the darkness in a combination of worldliness and naiveté: *"What are you doing?!"* Somehow I could never figure out just why she didn't know what I was doing?

I never met one of those bad girls. If I wanted to change the contraceptive in my wallet just in case I did, I was always unlucky enough to find, upon walking into the drugstore, a woman clerk behind the counter. Muttering something about needing some toothpaste, I would purchase what I really did not need and shuffle out of the store, knowing that the protection that lay in my back pocket "just in case" would have to do for another year or two. It did have one side benefit: I never ran out of toothpaste.

Of course the times have changed—and interestingly enough—have changed yet again. First came the huge wave of sexual liberation and freedom to "do your own thing" without guilt and in total abandon. This lasted for a while, and then the condom made its return—because of herpes—because of AIDS, and once again the nineties, ironically, the druggist does a land-office business in the department that was once devoted solely to contraception and now is a barrier to a dread disease. Ironically, too, about 40 percent of the US condom market (currently about 300 million dollars a year) is due to the purchase of the item by *women*. What a change from the old days of the hidden cache behind the counter.

Now the corner druggist keeps his display of contraceptives right out on the counter. They are advertised in magazines, on bus posters, their use trumpeted on television (with certain mid-Victorian prudish limitations): "Trojan: for Feeling in Love," and what a choice there is today! Trojan-enz, Trojan Ribbed, Trojan Plus, Ramses Intercept, Conceptrol Shields, Conceptrol

Supreme, Fourex Natural Skins, Cavalier, and with fanfare, "Stud 100: World-Famous Delay Spray for Men."

Did we, then, as we entered middle age, miss all the sexual liberation and freedom? Do we envy now the ever-complaining younger people that sex is no longer easy and uncomplicated and "why did AIDS have to happen to *our* generation?" Were we born too soon to enjoy being able to shop for our contraceptives openly and without the furtive forays into the drugstore that had the same clandestine feeling as making a cocaine deal today? But, weren't there many other things that more than adequately took the place of the sexual "freedom" and the "cold sex" and the "dangerous sex" that we read about now? Can we discard or minimize our feelings about commitment and caring, and was it so bad to "fall in love" so often? Were we wrong to demand that our displays of sexual affection be made in private? We were, of course, different from the younger generations today, but so were our parents different from us. And, again ironically, since the advent of AIDS, young couples once again seem to be turning to monogamy and commitment.

As I walked along the beach last summer, while the bathers dodged the strong waves of the Atlantic, a young couple lay near the dune line, their lower torsos barely covered with a jacket. Oblivious to the passersby, they were obviously having their own personal intercourse, the rhythms rising in telltale tension, her legs jumping like a rag doll's as he made love to her from behind. As I passed them I laughed, but certainly not because of what they were doing. I remembered reading a lecture that Margaret Mead had delivered to a class of college women. "There's nothing that you do that we didn't do," she said, "only we didn't do it in front of the dean!"

But it does not stop. It does not, by any means, stop. The erotic relationships and sexual couplings may change, but there is no reason that they should terminate at some particular age. Our children and grandchildren may express the thought that we are finished with sex, but the obscenity occurs when *we* begin to believe them and we perpetuate the same myths. Over and over again, in the contemporary surveys that have been conducted among middle-aged and elderly people, the theory is reinforced by our own contemporaries, but when asked if *they* like sex, the retort is, generally, "Yes, but I'm an exception."

There are over sixty million "exceptions" in the country today, and it is becoming more evident to everyone that continuing sexual desire in middle and old age is not scandalous; that erotic relationships need not be kept clandestine; that this remarkable, earthy pleasure continues through our fifties, sixties, seventies, and well into our eighties. The perpetual tumescence of the male may be gone, but other changes take its place.

In the words of Dr. Ruby Benjamin, a sex therapist with both a practical view of sex and a marvelous sense of humor, "Sexuality is more than the genital organs, the reproductive system, and the act of intercourse. It includes one's concept, partner choice, and patterns of interpersonal communication. The sex act is only one connection with sexuality. Aging can make the older person view sex as intimate communication in its best sense: tenderness, companionship, touching, caressing, the feelings of being needed and wanted and the ability to give pleasure to another person and receive it in return. All these are expressions of sexuality. The sensuous part of sexuality is as important, if not more important, then the sex act itself as we grow older."

In the article that I mentioned earlier, June Wilson put it beautifully when she wrote: " 'The second language of sex' suggests the possibility of renewing love every day. It involves playfulness, as well as passion, and talking, laughing, teasing, sharing secrets, reminiscing, telling jokes, making plans, confessing fears, uncertainties, crying—in and out of the warmth of the bed, in privacy and companionship. It need not always involve sex at all."

In a study by Andrew Barclay, a psychologist, he reported in the journal *Medical Aspects of Human Sexuality* that even the sexual fantasies change with age. These fantasies, much like the sex drive, do not disappear, but their focus seems to dwell on a *wider variety* of sexual pleasures. He wrote, "It (the sex drive) may be thought of as a river which is narrow at its source, rushing noisily through the rapids, but spreading out, slowing down, and meandering more as it approaches an outlet.

We tend to find more things pleasurable as we age; we become less dependent upon sexual intercourse or genital contact as the sole expression of our sexuality."

The body changes, of course. Orgasm may take longer to achieve and may, in fact, occur only once in several acts of intercourse. In men, the erection may also take longer when compared to that of the young studs mentioned earlier, and it will certainly take more time between acts of intercourse for the erection to appear again. In women, the capacity for orgasm may also be slowed, though not terminated, by the aging process. The vagina may thin out and be less lubricated and elastic. But, as Dr. Benjamin says, "*all* physical responses are slowed as we age."

The most important thing for us to remember, however, is that, if there is a diminution of male sexual prowess and female responsiveness in the process of aging, it is usually due more to psychological rather than to biological reasons—boredom or preoccupation with the problems of family, the job, the financial situation; severe fatigue, or concerns about health, such as a recent heart attack.

The medical profession, as usual, has done little to counter the "bad press" that sex for the aging has received in our society. In direct contrast with many medical reports, a study by the National Institute on Aging showed that healthy older men maintain their production of sex hormones at levels found in younger men. In a further investigation, their scientists found that older men continue to ejaculate the same number of sperm as their young counterparts, though the proportion of immature sperm increases with age. Statisticians can, of course, point to the more than twenty thousand men who become fathers after the age of fifty, and I would like to add one of my dearest friends, who did so well into his seventies.

But physicians, to no one's surprise, are sometimes as ill-informed and as subject to the myths of sex and aging as the general public. Dr. Benjamin says, "Some physicians and other health professionals, through sheer ignorance, can pass along destructive attitudes when they become aware of the sex problems of older people. Some men and women look to their doctors for permission to express their own sexuality for recreational purposes but, in fact, get the doctor's own personal, puritanical answers. In one study, 39 percent of the physicians questioned said that any woman over fifty should not *have* unfulfilled sexual needs. One would hardly expect an older woman to express her sexual desires and needs to one of *them!*"

Possibly we are throwing off the yoke, however burdened we have been with society's (and our own) view of ourselves as nonsexual hermits after the age of fifty. Much of the psychological impotence in men is caused by the self-destructive view that it is inevitable that it will happen—and so it does.

For women, the self-image perpetuated by our youth culture can cause anxiety in those who feel that physical beauty is a fundamental requirement for sexual gratification. As Dr. Benjamin says, "I wonder when those cute little freckles of youth become those ugly age spots of the older woman . . . older women, each of us, need to begin to command respect and admiration—not in spite of being older but because of it. Sexual image and self-image are at stake. We need to develop our own standards, not to compete with younger women."

About ten years ago it all began to surface, slowly at first but in an ever-increasing flow of articles, research studies, and news reports. Somehow, with wide-eyed wonder, the reporters, many of them young, began to write of retirement communities in Florida and Arizona and California where older people were discovered holding hands, dancing together, dating, kissing in public, and even becoming engaged and getting married again. This, in direct contrast to *Cocoon*, where it took a "fountain of youth" to bring out all these human emotions in older people.

For those who did not want to marry, sometimes because of Social Security benefits that would be reduced, there were "nonmarriages of convenience," very much like those of their children and grandchildren. And instead of the stories being published as "exceptions," the flow began to increase and they are a remarkable object lesson both to our children and to those of us who think that "acting our age" is equated with giving up the pleasures of sex, whatever its form. A women whom I interviewed told me that she had never enjoyed sex until she married for the second time. She was married for the second time at the age of seventy!

More than 225,000 readers responded when "Dear Abby" asked in her column whether women over fifty enjoyed sex. Over 50 percent were enthusiastic in answering yes!

My uncle Jack remarried for the second time at the age of eighty-nine, his bride a mere snip of a lass at eighty-two. Luckily the wedding was conducted in a cathedral in deference to the faith of the bride, and the church, not to be put off by stereotypes and myths, had my uncle sign a paper agreeing that the *children* would be brought up in the Catholic faith!

It is even happening in the hallowed halls of the nursing homes and the retirement residences, where society once refused to believe that older people have any feelings at all. On a visit to one such home I was invited to luncheon by the staff psychologist. One by one, the elderly came down to their midday meal. A seventy-five-year-old woman in a wheelchair was pointed out to me and the man who pushed her toward the dining room was identified to me as her lover—not her friend, not her companion, but her lover. He put her to bed every night, helped her to dress and undress, and spent his leisure hours talking to her and holding her hand. Years ago they both would have been expelled, for everyone knew that at seventy-five it was impossible to have a lover. But, today, there is a glimmer of a gradually changing attitude on the part of the patients and the administrators, both of whom no longer deny the need to touch, to hold, and to have sex if they want to. I can only hope that it becomes more universally true as administrative executives continue to become more enlightened. Unfortunately, the attitudes I have described are not yet universally accepted.

If all this is taking place at the age of seventy and older, why are we denying sexuality to the generation still in their forties or fifties and sixties? It took me many years to discover and to admit to myself that my own mother was a sexual person, though she played the role of the twenties flapper right to her death and would never admit publicly what I am about to relate.

She traveled to Tulsa to visit my brother and his family and on the plane she met a young woman doctor who was flying to meet her "special person."

When my mother telephoned from Oklahoma, she said in her best sotto voce tones, reserved for matters of personal and private import, "I was dying to ask her where she was going to stay when she got there." I told her that the young woman would probably stay with her boyfriend. "Not her," retorted my mother, "she was a good girl!" (There we go again—a *good* girl.) What my mother never admitted, however, was the fact that *she* had lived with my stepfather for *nine years* before they finally got married!

So sex lives! Dr. Benjamin even reports that there is evidence that sexual activity serves as therapy for arthritis sufferers "by increasing the adrenal-gland output of cortisone, thus alleviating the symptoms." However, she laughingly adds that she does not therefore advocate that, if you are suffering from arthritis, you grab the first partner you see and have sex for "medicinal purposes."

When it comes down to the image of ourselves as middle-aged and older people, our sexuality, and the fact that we are generations who are finding new opportunities in all areas of our lives, you might think about one thing. If you should weaken and cast a wistful, slightly envious eye at the younger generations and their sexuality, lack of commitment, and the so-called *freedom* of their life-styles, keep in mind that it has also brought with it a thousand other dissatisfactions and problems. As they probe their own myths and stereotypes, trying to live up to what society thinks they are, it becomes more and more evident that the trade-offs are not as glorious as they would like us to believe. What they seem to have gained in physical freedom they are fast beginning to lose through the warnings and the fears that accompany AIDS. Article after article in the popular magazines comment upon and make suggestions about just who brings up the subject of condoms first—and what if "he" won't use one? (The classic male response seems to be, "It's like taking a shower with a raincoat on.") Along with this loss of physical freedom, there has also been a loss in emotional depth.

Just like us, the young are in a constant state of change, of discovery, of deep, sometimes very disturbed personal soul-searching. Though they think of *us* as asexual, they are also drawing back, more and more frequently, from the contacts that have no depth and from relationships that involve no long-term or permanent commitment. It was with a bit of wry chagrin and a smile of sympathy that I read a review of a new book written *for the young* by Dr. Gabrielle Brown. Finally, it was time to take a good hard look at the end of an era of sexual freedom. The book was titled, *The New Celibacy*.

13 In the Image of God

Doctors are whippersnappers
in ironed white coats

Who spy up your rectum and look
down your throats

And press you and poke you with
sterilized tools

And stab at solutions that pacify fools.

I used to revere them and do what
they said

Till I learned what they learned on was
already dead.

—Gilda Radner
New England Journal of Medicine*

I have always been amazed at the speed at which humor travels, and just as astonished at the endurance of some jokes, first told to me as a teenager and then recounted some forty years later by the child of a friend, who then tells it as newfound gospel. If the humor has in it a basic truth or an element of hostility, it seems to spread even faster. Societies have been known to survive because of their sense of humor, their stories frequently hiding the deep conflicts of their political, economic, or social lives.

*Used with permission. *New England Journal of Medicine*, vol. 319, p. 1358. Copyright 1988, Massachusetts Medical Society.

There is a long line in front of the Pearly Gates, as St. Peter checks the credentials of all who are to enter Heaven. The wait seems interminable, but since time is no longer of the essence, it doesn't seem to matter, until those assembled see a man in a white jacket, a stethoscope around his neck, walk briskly around the waiting crowd, past St.Peter and through the gates. An angry murmur arises, mutterings of "Who does he think he is?" St. Peter holds up his hands to calm them, saying, "Oh, that's God. He thinks he's a doctor!"

Not too long after hearing that joke for the fourth time, I was on a crowded airplane from Los Angeles to New York. The movie, which I half-watched and whose title I have since forgotten, starred Frank Sinatra and Faye Dunaway. Somewhere in the middle of the picture, poor Faye Dunaway is lying on her deathbed. Sinatra, unhappy with the treatment she is receiving, grabs her doctor by the lapels and angrily hurls him against the wall. The reaction in the plane was astounding. Three hundred people applauded and shrieked approval! The only ones who did not join in were those not watching the movie—unless they might have been doctors and their families.

What has happened to our gods? What, indeed, has happened to the benign, understanding, omniscient, omnipotent doctor of medicine? Was the doctor, in fact, *ever* a figure to be idolized? Or is it possible that *we* are, once again, as guilty of stereotyping an entire group, just as they are in passing us off as "getting older, so what can you expect?" Have *we* perpetuated the myths about the doctor and did the doctor, in turn, begin believing all that gratifying public relations material he kept reading about himself or herself? The folk hero. The steady-handed, sharp-eyed surgeon. The kindly *Saturday Evening Post* family physician. Commands given in the knowing tones of a U-boat captain. Follow the orders and you will live happily ever after. The image of the doctor as god has, rightfully, become tarnished.

For those of us in our middle lives (or older), medicine and the attitudes of our physicians play an even more important role in our well-being than they ever have before. It is quite true that chronic diseases increase as we age, though the incidence of acute conditions actually drops. Nutrition becomes more important to us—or at least it should. We—and our doctors—tend to turn more frequently to drugs as a panacea. Surgery soars at an alarming rate, most of it unnecessary, it seems. The prevailing attitude of the medical profession is that nothing can be done to cure many of our miseries because we are aging. And to add to that problem, recent studies have indicated rather strongly that the medical profession makes many of its decisions on the *chronological* age of a patient rather than the actual physical health. As the perception of the aged as patients continues this way, the older generations are not even being given the *fundamental* care afforded the young. On their own, many doctors are performing a "medical triage," deciding among themselves which patients will get the best that medicine has to offer and which shall not.

Finally, consider the appalling rigidity of the American Medical Association toward much of what is new or innovative. Soon it becomes clear that the doctor and the hospital can actually be a threat to us as we age—that is, unless we know the nature of our problems and some of the solutions that have been discovered, and unless *we* take an active role in our health care.

So it is high time that we take a harder look at our beloved family doctors and their surgical friends. It is time to return to an important member of the "middle-age hit list."

More Myths, More Stereotypes

A medical publication, *Pediatric News*, published an article some time ago commenting upon the fact that "physicians behave differently toward a patient depending upon the patient's race, sex, age, and personal appearance." The article went on to suggest that doctors look more carefully at their attitudes to make certain that *everyone* receives "courteous and empathetic care."

But doctors are, after all, people, so why should we expect them to feel any different when the prejudice toward the aging of our society is found on every level, even among *ourselves?* Unfortunately, the field of medicine is not insulated in some magical way from the rest of our imperfect world, so it is not surprising that the doctor also develops a demeaning, superficial, false, stereotypical view of aging. In a survey taken by the American College of Physicians, one-third of the doctors asked thought that a seventy-five-year-old woman had five years or less to live. Actually, the demographics tell us that if a woman turns seventy-five today, she can expect to live to age eighty-seven. Added to that, two million women in the United States are over eighty-five, the fastest-growing segment of our population. If we are not aware of it, why should our doctors be?

Even in their own medical journals, the physicians of today are subjected to a constant barrage of media stereotypes. One survey analyzed 151 drug advertisements that appeared in the journal *Geriatrics* over a period of twenty years. Though as time passed, the number of women in the ads increased and a more positive view of the elderly began to emerge, a large number of the ads portrayed the older adult as either sad, ill, incompetent, or withdrawn. In addition, over 30 percent of the headlines in the ads showed the elderly as negative.

Add to this the fact that there are about sixty-five thousand trained *pediatricians* in the country, and somewhere around four hundred trained *geriatricians!* In over 125 medical schools, only about 30 are seriously committed to the study of aging and geriatric medicine. A bright sign on the horizon is that there is a growing cadre of gerontological nurses and nurse educators. But, if we look at the training and the thrust of the curricula in the medical schools, we begin to understand the diagnosis given by our favorite family doctor, "Well, you're getting older, what can you expect?" Or the all-encompassing catchword explanation, *senescence.*

The myths of aging are so pervasive that we begin to believe—and our doctors share our view—that as we grow older *all of us* complain about our health, worry exclusively about our physical condition, and visit the doctor's office with a severe case of hypochondria at the slightest sign of malaise. Of course, there are some who do just that, but the National Institute on Aging issued a report that said, in part, "While it is true that certain health problems do increase with age, there is no evidence that health complaints are disproportionate among older people. . . . Specifically, older people report more problems with the sensory, cardiovascular, and genitourinary systems. This is not surprising, since these systems are known to be more susceptible to disease and disability with increasing age." The report concluded that the proportion of people who might be considered hypochondriacal is no higher among the middle-aged and aged than it is among the young!

We have been so conditioned by society that we take it for granted that we will have aches and pains as we reach middle age. And so do our doctors. We accept the myth that we will deteriorate rapidly after the age of fifty (or thirty?) and the mind will disintegrate into irreversible senility, forcing us to live in a shadow world of depression and confusion. As for our doctors, too many of them believe that too. It is true that our *speed* of response declines as we age, but it has been proven time and time again that most older people maintain a normal level of vigorous mental capacity right up to their deaths at eighty-five or ninety. Alex Comfort points out that less than 1 *percent* of all people become senile—a smaller percentage than that of young people who go insane!

One of the most appalling responses of the medical profession is to label, automatically, the symptoms of confusion, depression, memory loss, or deteriorating judgment as "senility" or "senescence," just because the patient is getting older. These signs may very well be caused by dozens of other *treatable* diseases, by improper nutrition, or *by the very drugs being prescribed by one's physician,* as we shall see later on. But, if in any of these cases, if you should question your doctor about diagnosis (or God forbid, *mis*diagnosis), prognosis or treatment, the response frequently resembles that given a child who asks a precocious question—a mixture of amusement and disdain. If so, it may be time to find a new family doctor!

Intervention—Not Prevention

There is a temptation to offer a small apology when modern medicine is taken to task. I was brought up in the era of reverence toward the family doctor, and my own physician up until this year when he sadly retired, Dr. Bob Levin, is a classic and shining exception to everything negative that I feel and that I write about on this subject. In dealing with the average doctor, each criticism that I make is countered with a request for the name of the medical school that I attended. After all, if I am not an MD, how can I even begin to know how to phrase my questions, much less criticize Hippocrates and his fellow travelers?

My wife once asked our former family physician just what the side effects would be for a drug that he had prescribed for my aging mother-in-law. His answer was, "It's better you shouldn't know!"

I think it is time for modern medicine to agree that we have a *right* to know, a right to be involved in monitoring our own health and well-being. Doctors are aware that more and more of us are questioning, probing, and exploring new approaches. We are terribly disturbed at the reaction we get from the stubborn kingdom that derives so much of its power from our own trust, so often misplaced. Too many of us have "horror" stories about medical care— just bring the subject up at your next dinner party and you'll see what I mean. It is no wonder that we have begun to question more deeply, to ask for answers long denied to us, to demand that we be *heard*.

Just a few years back, the People's Medical Society was formed, with the express purpose of making us heard and felt, to give us a voice in the treatment of our minds and bodies, to make us active *consumers* as well as patients. The small membership fee is well worth while. (Write to: People's Medical Society, 462 Walnut Street, Allentown, PA 18102)

Some years back I watched an early morning television program in Los Angeles, and was fascinated by an interview with Dr. Robert Mendelsohn, author of *Confessions of a Medical Heretic* (Contemporary Books) and a work that came out just a few years before he died, *Male Practice: How Doctors Manipulate Women* (Contemporary Books). Impressed by the man and his thinking, I immediately read the latter book and then telephoned him at his office in Illinois. If he felt so strongly about the mistreatment of women by gynecologists, obstetricians, and general practitioners, was there a parallel in medicine for the aging? After all, he mentioned that almost seventy thousand hysterectomies were performed in the United States each year and that *not more than one in five could even be considered clinically necessary!* It seemed to be a classic case involving more than half of our generation: being a woman and aging at the same time. He told me:

> I don't think there's any question about the fact that what I've written about women and gynecology is also a fact about medicine for the aging. . . . Discrimination against the aged in medicine—it's just all over the place. You can make the case against medicine and you can make the same case against medical education, since students take geriatric medicine only as an elective. They learn nothing about older folks!

Yet these same graduates treat older patients as a part of their internship and residency, and eventually in private practice? "Yes," he answered, "It pays their office rent!"

Dr. Robert N. Butler, writing in a report for *Geriatrics* (National Institute on Aging) asserted, "The needs of older people have been much neglected in the training of health professionals, in the structuring and financing of medical services, and in the support of biomedical and behavorial research. Medical school curricula generally do not reflect the incidence and character of the multiple disorders of old age. Medicare is designed as if its beneficiaries were young."

We do read more often that some medical schools are becoming aware of the problem, though I am not quite certain that the results are what they expected them to be. The Medical College of Pennsylvania has instituted a program designed to help its young medical students become aware of the problems of the aging patients they may one day treat. With simulated handicaps such as blindness, failing hearing, crippling from arthritis, the students are required to accomplish simple tasks such as preparing dinner or taking a book off the library shelf. One would expect these young people to come out of the exercise thoroughly empathetic with the aging population. Too often, just the opposite happens. The *New York Times* reported this comment from one medical student, her ears plugged with cotton, her hands tightly bound in rubber gloves to limit mobility and dexterity, trying to use the telephone and get a correct number from the information operator: *"It sure makes you want to stay young!"* (Italics mine).

While such specialties as nuclear medicine, pediatric roentgenology, and neonatology take precedence in medical schools today, "the long-standing deficiencies in geriatric teaching represent the unconscious negative attitudes toward the elderly that permeate our society," Dr. Butler says. In the course of a medical education, the student will learn about a *quarter-million* separate pieces of information, very few of them relating to aging.

There are probably many subconscious factors that add to the inadequacy of our medical treatment as we grow older. The aging patient is no longer as aesthetically appealing as the younger one, and one result is that many examinations, as well as the communication of "caring," are performed less diligently—if at all. Overmedication and hasty, unnecessary surgical intervention follow these encounters all too often. At a dinner party one evening I heard a young gynecologist remark that he was "turned on" when he examined his younger female patients. Does that shock you? We have already admitted that some of our gods are really people.

Incidentally, there is an immediate knee-jerk reaction when someone mentions a male gynecologist who is less than adequate, too rough, or unsympathetic. "Go to a woman doctor," is the response. Sometimes it works, but remember that most of the women practicing medicine have been trained by *men*. The men run the medical schools and they run the profession. Don't be surprised if the female doctor reflects exactly the same predispositions and prejudices as her male colleagues.

In the field of surgery, the victims and beneficiaries are of all ages, but unfortunately, the threat increases as we get older. It has been estimated that only 20 percent of all operations performed today are essential—serious trauma or cancer surgery, for example, and other procedures required to save or extend a patient's life. The rest are questionable or unneeded. A study by medical researchers estimated that 25,000 of the 170,000 annual heart bypass operations did not significantly improve the patient's chance of survival!

Where finances are in direct relationship to the number of operations performed, the statistics rise in skyscraper leaps. Hospitals need to fill beds in order to survive inflationary costs. In addition, there are about 30 percent too many surgeons in a country already rich with medical practitioners, and all of them trying to make a living. Dr. Peter Bourne, who was President Carter's special assistant for health issues, put it more succinctly: "If one has to be really blunt about it, there's an economic incentive—the more surgery you do, the more money you get." Thus, a patient who gets a second medical opinion, may find that one recommends conservative non-invasive treatment whereas the original surgeon might have recommended "immediate surgery."

The expanding health-insurance plans had been making surgery easily available and affordable for the patient covered by a union contract or corporate plan. But, when the number of elective operations performed in the United States began to soar, corporations and insurance carriers began to demand second opinions, and some new union contracts—bitterly fought— have begun to ask for contributions to insurance payments by the employees. During the seventies, the number of operations rose 23 percent while the population increased by only 11 percent. Caesarean sections almost doubled, cataract extractions increased by over 40 percent, and prostatectomies rose by about the same figure. Not to our credit, the United States now has the highest hysterectomy rate in the world, more than twice that of Great Britain, four times the rate of Sweden! And, along with all this, the death rate from surgery has also soared.

Within the last year, a combination of "strange bedfellows" has arisen. Many of us have been demanding for years that the government must do something about the escalation of health care costs, especially for the people who do not have any coverage at all—somewhere near forty million. The corporations have also begun to take note, aided and abetted by the American Medical Association, which used to cry "Socialized Medicine" at any hint of reform. Watching health-insurance costs explode, the major corporations have not only begun to demand second opinions and to ask the employees to share the responsibility, as I've noted, but they also have joined the demanding public in asking that "the government do something about the escalating health care costs!" I never thought I'd see the day when I'd be a firm and vocal ally of Lee Iacocca or General Motors!

But the doctors, of course, have an answer to all of this. Dr. Mendelsohn wrote, "When doctors are charged with overmedicating their patients, the typical response is 'the patient wanted it.' This 'blame the victim' strategy is one that doctors employ to cover most of their sins, whether the transgression lies in pushing drugs or performing hysterectomies and Caesarean sections that their patients shouldn't have and don't need."

Somehow I cannot accept the premise that "we ask for it." The surgeons state that we put the pressure on them to perform surgery, that they are really doing it for us. A British surgeon, interviewed by a newspaper reporter, recounted the classic medical joke about the compliant patient. The doctor says, "Mrs. Smith, we're scheduling a decapitation next Wednesday," and Mrs. Smith answers, "Fine."

The only defense I can accept on the part of doctors practicing today is the soaring malpractice insurance premiums due to a plague of insurance cases leveled against the profession, with the concomitant multimillion dollar awards. As a result, many doctors have begun to practice "defensive" medicine, ordering many tests and writing many prescriptions with the thought that ignoring any avenue of diagnosis or medication might well result in a lawsuit. I accept that and I acknowledge the problem. All I ask is that in return, the medical profession try to understand how *we* feel during that visit to the doctor.

Frightened, vulnerable, alone, trusting, looking for an answer from someone we believe is an idol (and who believes it half the time himself or herself), potentially ill or suffering from what we've just been told is possibly a fatal illness if we don't do something about it right away—that instant!—what does the surgeon expect us to say: how does he expect us to react?

Someone very close to me visited her doctor, was examined, tests were taken and finally when she sat across from the doctor at his desk, *he turned to his recording machine,* swung his back to the patient and said into the microphone, "The patient has breast cancer and must undergo a mastectomy immediately!" The patient watched in disbelief and in horror. Two years later she was dead.

One of the books that came to my attention recently finally puts on the record all the stories that you and I tell one another when we discuss our doctors and the state of medicine (such as it is) in this country. It's called *Medicine on Trial: The Appalling Story of Ineptitude, Malfeasance, Neglect and Arrogance,* by Charles Inlander, president of the People's Medical Society, Lowel Levin, professor at the Yale University School of Medicine and Ed Weiner, senior editor of the People's Medical Society (Prentice-Hall). It's available from the People's Medical Society (address on page 130). What makes it so horrifying is that the material in the book is taken directly from the medical records, medical journals, and the documents that have already been published by the medical profession! If you think that I have been exaggerating, I suggest you read the book.

What, then, can *we* do? There are things we must *learn* to do. Dr. Mendelsohn advised, "Don't reinforce your doctor's feelings of omnipotence by allowing or encouraging him to patronize or intimidate you. Be on your guard, and make him explain and defend every diagnosis he makes, every drug he prescribes, every operation he recommends. Don't be in awe of him. Compel him to accept you as an equal, because you deserve his respect at least as much as he merits yours!"

And if surgery is recommended? Don't be afraid to get a second opinion. If necessary, Dr. Mendelsohn urges that you get on a plane and fly to some other city, where the doctor has no connection with your own surgeon. Tell him, by the way, that, whatever his diagnosis, *he* will not be retained to perform the operation. If you're still in doubt, get a *third opinion,* and don't be rushed into anything.

A few days ago I found an epitaph written by Matthew Prior at the beginning of the eighteenth century. As the surgery boom increases, it might well be noted today: "Cured yesterday of my disease, I died last night of my physician."

Hospitals Can Be Hazardous to Your Health

A few years ago Lois Gould wrote a novel called *Such Good Friends,* in which the husband of the heroine goes into the hospital for the removal of a wart, a simple operation. While undergoing surgery he dies of "complications." There is, of course, a word to describe this contingency that seems to be *increasing* rather than diminishing over these last few decades. It is a marvelously fluid word, one that rolls easily off the tongue and makes us sound well-read and knowledgeable. It is *iatrogenesis,* and it is such a superb word that I wish it did not describe so awful a situation—the risks of illness and medical complications that occur during a medical procedure initiated by the doctor, and having nothing to do with the *original* complaint or illness. The situation described by Lois Gould would be just such an iatrogenic event. And the hospital, always the leader in "medibabble," would term an iatrotgenic infection as *nosocomial* (hospital-related), another candidate for the chapter on future-talk. In other words, you go into the hospital to have your appendix removed and you acquire AIDS through the use of a dirty hypodermic needle. Welcome to the club!

Dr. Mendelsohn commented, "Hospitals *look* awesomely antiseptic. They are actually so germ-laden that 5 percent of all hospital patients contract infections that they didn't have when they arrived." The National Foundation for Infectious Diseases estimates that each year there are *two million* cases of nosocomial infections and between twenty thousand and sixty thousand deaths, one-third of them preventable!

In one hospital, a study showed that 36 out of 2,500 patients admitted for surgery suffered mild to severe complications because of mistakes by physicians! And of those, 36, 20 died, with 11 of the deaths directly linked to doctor error. Of the 16 who survived, 5 had serious physical impairment that could have been avoided. A story in the *Wall Street Journal* concluded that "most of the complications were due to poor judgment by the surgeon. Such problems included reaching the wrong diagnosis, delaying needed surgery, performing unnecessary or overextensive surgical procedures, or ignoring trouble signs because of overconfidence or misplaced optimism."

In the hospital itself, the guilt lies with almost every procedure, in almost every department, and the almost 100,000 nosocomial deaths in the United States each year only makes it evident that hospitals are not, indeed, the sterile institutions they would like us to believe. The rates are highest in teaching hospitals, and treatment-related infection is prevalent in almost every category of admissions from cancer to pneumonia to hemodialysis. Investigators have found that hand washing is not always done after a procedure, that catheters are ready pathways for bacteria, inadequate refrigeration threatens every patient with salmonella or worse, equipment is not cleaned properly, and even contaminated water in the hospital towers has caused outbreaks of Legionnaires' disease! As the authors of *Medicine on Trial* have so nicely put it, there are bugs in the system!

For those of us in our middle years and those who are about to be numbered among the elder segment of our population, the hazards of hospitalization should not be underestimated. Given the combination of an increasing number of chronic ailments and the penchant of doctors and surgeons to recommend some sort of drastic remedy, from drugs to major surgery, the risks of a hospital stay, no matter what its duration, are not trivial.

There is one more book that I'd like to recommend, and I suggest that you read it, then put it on your shelf in case you ever have to go to the hospital. Also available from the People's Medical Society (address on page 130), it's called *Take This Book to the Hospital with You: A Consumer Guide to Surviving Your Hospital Stay* (Inlander/Weiner Rodale Press), and it's an excellent guide about your rights, your demands, what to expect, how to protect yourself against "the medical mine field that stretches from the admissions desk to the cashier." There is information about which rights you sign away when you fill out the hospital consent form, who can get things done for you, and how to find out if the hospital has a consumer advocate, something that many institutions are now providing to the patient since we have begun to fight for our rights.

Now that we've finished with the hospitals for the moment, I'd like you to meet a business partner of the medical profession—the pharmaceutical concerns.

Our Aging Junkies

Voltaire wrote, "Physicians have been pouring drugs about which they know little for diseases about which they know less into beings about whom they know nothing." Since Americans over the age of fifty take about twenty-five percent of all drugs prescribed by doctors (and many that are not), this is still another area that concerns us, especially since chronic illness is an occasional companion of a longer life span.

We have reached a point where both we and our doctors expect that there is "a pill for every ill." If we happen to suffer from more than one illness, real or hypochondriacal, we begin to mix our pills—sometimes prescribed by more than one doctor, each unaware of the other's prescription!

"What is the response going to be when you take two drugs that conflict—or two drugs in combination with a nutritional item. . . ? Is it compatible with orange juice, for example, or liquor?" I was visiting St. Barnabas Hospital in the Bronx, where I had produced two films some years ago, one of them on chronic disease and aging. Janet Beard, who heads the Braker Home, sat at lunch with me and Dr. Manny Riklan. "I'm not too sure that the doctors know the response. I'm not too sure they take the time to read the literature—they get it from one side only, from the pharmaceutical side, and not from the pharmacological side."

For the doctor, there is a constant stream of new drugs that enter the market as panaceas for high blood pressure, diabetes, glaucoma, arthritis, heart attacks, cancer, digestive disturbances, and all the other diseases that can strike us as we age. At one time a stroke could dispatch us with relative speed. Today there are drugs that can keep us active and alive for twenty years or more.

Much of the doctor's knowledge comes from the salespeople who work for the pharmaceutical companies, and very few doctors have the time to read the literature that accompanies the samples flowing into every physician's office every day of the year. A veritable cornucopia of wonder drugs! Or are they?

We *expect* the doctor to give us a prescription when we leave his or her office. The doctor, in fact, is taught in medical school to give us something to take with us. A little token in Latin makes it all worthwhile. Too often the prescription is for a drug about which he knows little, though he prescribes it with great confidence, and he give us absolutely *no* information about what *the side effects* may be.

I mentioned earlier that my wife had been told by a doctor to give her ailing and aging mother Thorazine and he, in his wisdom answered her question about side effects with, "It's better you shouldn't know." She went immediately to the pharmacist and looked in his reference book. Much to her horror, she found that the side effects were potentially worse than the condition for which they were prescribed! Not only that: since most drugs today are tested on young and middle-aged people, the dosage for an elderly, frail, sickly woman of eighty-five pounds seemed terribly high. She cut the dosage herself and I quite forgot about Thorazine until I found an incredible story in Dr. Mendelsohn's book, a classic example of "the chicken or the egg." Thorazine is prescribed for psychic disorders: agitation, excessive anxiety, and tension. However, some of its side effects are symptoms resembling those of Parkinson's disease. When a side effect appears, the doctors then prescribe Artane, which has, in turn, its own side effects:

Dizziness, nausea, psychotic manifestations, delusions, hallucinations, mental confusion, agitation, and disturbed behavior.

Naturally, when *these* side effects are reported to the family physician, he immediately recommends another drug to counteract them: *Thorazine!*

Again we are vulnerable, for even the doctor knows too little about drug incompatabilities and side effects, and the pharmaceutical companies are in a profit-motive industry. The more they sell, the more they make. Of course, the drugs have all been tested and approved by the Food and Drug Administration. And, of course, the drug companies spend millions of dollars on research and on the advertising and promotion that gets their product into the hands of the physicians too busy to study its effects. Thalidomide was tested and researched. DES (diethylstilbestrol) has surfaced as the villain in vaginal cancer in the daughters of women in our generation who were given the drug during pregnancy. Bendectin, a supposedly well-researched and tested drug for morning sickness is now blamed for many of the same birth defects that were caused by thalidomide. And don't worry. If we do manage to stop the use of a drug or product, such as the Dalkon Shield, we soon find that it's no longer in use here—but it's being dumped overseas into Third World countries!

As we age, the horror stories multiply. Cases of drug misuse and misinformation are so common in our aging population that they seem to be the rule rather than the exception. There are stories of senior citizens sampling one another's pills. Drug toxicity emergencies rise as the population ages. Consumers aged fifty and over are the biggest market for over-the-counter drugs. We buy 60 percent of all arthritic and rheumatic pain relievers, 45 percent of all laxatives, and 25 percent of all nonprescription drugs, a market of $1.5 billion! Yet there are many over-the-counter drugs that have dramatic and sometimes damaging side effects when taken either alone or in combination with other prescription drugs.

For example, in the book *Nonprescription Drugs* by the editors of *Consumer Guide* (Beekman House), even a quick perusal is enough to make us sit up and take notice. I stood in the aisle of my local bookshop and opened the book to Chlor-Trimeton, a decongestant and cold allergy sold over-the-counter and manufactured by the Schering Corporation. In addition to the warnings and contraindications for persons with peptic ulcers, glaucoma, heart and kidney disease, and other ailments, the potential side effects include: increased blood pressure, nervousness, anxiety, tension, insomnia, tremor, dizziness, headache, sweating, nausea, vomiting, loss of appetite, palpitations, chest pain, difficult or painful urination, blurred vision, confusion, constipation, and rash. All these—and the drug is in the *non*prescription category! It makes me wonder just what medical time bombs are ticking away in the medications that are "just what the doctor ordered."

"Another thing about aging people," Janet Beard says, "if you look in their medicine cabinets, they have outdated drugs, some from one doctor and some from another. Doctor A doesn't know what Doctor B gave them. We call them, 'medical shoppers' and what we try to say to them is that you need *one* person to coordinate your health."

Each of the drugs in your medicine cabinet may be safe and each may be effective for the particular condition for which it was prescribed, but the "polypharmacy" that lies there can be dangerous if taken at the same time and if you are not completely familiar with potential side effects. In addition, many of the tranquilizers that are prescribed so readily today may well be habit-forming, and when you finally decide that you don't need the Miltown or Valium, the effects of withdrawal will make it almost impossible to give them up. Before you quickly condemn heroin and marijuana and crack, it might be wise to look more carefully at those rows of neat bottles of "establishment" drugs that line your medicine cabinet.

What, then, can we do? The answer is at once simple and complex. We must learn to protect ourselves from the quick and easy prescribing of drugs by our doctors (aided and abetted by the sales pitches of the pharmaceutical concerns) by acquiring as much knowledge as we can about what is being peddled to us. Don't expect your doctor to cooperate easily. If he is like most medical practitioners, even broaching a simple question is tantamount to heresy. Be firm and insist that she (or he) respond to your questions—if he (or she) won't, find another doctor.

- Invest in the book *The Essential Guide to Prescription Drugs* (James Long, MD, Harper & Row—revised from time to time). The book gives brand names both in the US and in Canada, the generic availability, how the drug works, when it should and should not be taken, how it should be taken (before or after eating, with milk, other fluids, etc.), and the possible side effects, allergic reactions, etc. Put the book on your shelf, and when you have gone through the rest of this list, take it down and *check your doctor.* Has the doctor omitted anything? Are the instructions given to you absolutely correct? Remember, it's *your* body and *your* health. And, frequently, it's also *your* money.

- Ask your physician what the side effects of the prescribed drug might be. Are there any warnings of reactions or interactions that you should know about?

- Discuss with the doctor any other medications you are taking and for what condition. Include over-the-counter medications, laxatives, and vitamins.

- Try to write down what the doctor tells you about what he/she prescribes. Most of us are so tense during a medical visit that we tend to forget the instructions, or we may think they'll be perfectly clear on the medicine bottle. Is the pill taken on an empty stomach, after breakfast, before bedtime? Should you avoid driving after taking the prescribed dose?

- This is most important: Is the doctor, in fact, giving you the smallest possible dose to attack the problem? I have never been able to understand why a one-hundred-pound female may be given exactly the same dosage as a two-hundred-pound male.

- If you should develop side effects, report them to the doctor at once. And if your physician then tries to prescribe still another drug to eliminate the side effects, you had better question him even more rigorously!

- Above all, as I suggested right at the beginning, check it all out when you get home by using the guide to prescription drugs. *And, don't feel guilty about it!*

There is one more point, and it has to do with the economics of the drug world. The pharmaceutical companies would like you to use only their brand-name medications and they do what they can to encourage the doctors to prescribe Miltown, for example, rather than the generic meprobamate. Both are the same drug but brand-name drugs are expensive and, in many cases, a waste of your money. Certainly there may be a time when a particular drug is recommended because of patient sensitivity or the fine-tuning of a specific brand (or the nonavailability of the generic equivalent). But one survey in New York found that the vast majority of brand-name prescriptions were written for the commonest of painkillers, tranquilizers, antihistamines, diet drugs, and antibiotics. Each year patients in New York City alone were paying over $10 million too much for the privilege of using a brand name.

Ideally, I wish we could all follow Sir William Osler's advice that a doctor's first duty is "to educate the masses not to take medicine." Failing that, just amend the statement made by our ex-family physician, "It's better you *should* know!"

How to Shop for a Doctor

With it all, we need our physicians, even our surgeons. Not even the angriest of modern medicine's critics would suggest that we return to the practices of the past century, at least not in a technological sense. (There is no doubt that we would like to reinstitute the house call and some empathy.) But so much energy has been devoted to the treatment of sickness rather than the maintenance of good health, the expansion of a complex and expensive hospital system rather than the advancement of nutrition and disease prevention, a dependence upon our doctors rather than taking responsibility for ourselves, that both we and our physicians have become trapped in a spiral of impersonal and inflationary medical care.

In instances of acute illness, when we *must* see a physician, we are frequently left with an inadequate choice. As people who are in midlife and older, it is inconceivable that we should be without medical help when we need it. Yet many of us feel anger, hostility, and fear toward a profession we were taught to admire and to accept without question.

We shop for our automobiles with care and with exquisite attention to minute details of image, performance, appearance, and durability. Our refrigerators are purchased on the basis of thorough investigation by Consumer's Union and the references of neighbors and friends. If the accountant should make a serious error in our income tax returns, we would strongly consider changing accountants. And if salespeople treated us with the same lack of human concern shown by some of our doctors, we would certainly begin shopping around. Why, then, do we accept from the medical profession—when our health and our lives are at stake—what we would not tolerate from anyone else? Let us first of all take a good, hard, realistic view of our physicians, taking note of the saying that my wife, Sheryl, likes to quote: "Remember, 50 percent of all doctors graduated in the lower half of their class!" Then let us shop for our doctors with the same care and attention to detail that we give to purchasing our new automobiles.

I Want a Doctor Who Is Willing to be Interviewed before I Commit My Health to Him or to Her.

This is an idea that is absolute and total anathema to almost every doctor! And yet, it is all so logical. When we found that our doctor, Bob Levin, was retiring, we set to work over a period of months, calling general practitioners and internists who had been recommended and telling the receptionist—or nurse—that we would very much like to "interview" the doctor before submitting to an expensive examination and the commitment to him or to her. The responses were incredible and would probably be funny if they weren't so awfully serious. One would think that we had asked the doctor to provide us with a free supply of cocaine sight unseen.

- "That's not the way we work," said one voice. "First you have to take a physical exam (six hundred dollars for the two), and then the doctor will see you. And by the way, we don't have an open appointment for six months."

- "*Interview* the doctor?" A long pause. "Oh, I don't think he'd like that." We hung up.

- "We can't do it. The doctor is never interviewed first." This response came from the nurse who worked for a doctor who was head of Doctor-Patient Relationships at a major medical school!

We finally found two doctors who agreed to the "interview" and only one seemed at ease and understood what it was we were trying to do. Currently, he is our doctor of record, but he is still on trial. We spent over an hour with him, asked at least a hundred questions, and we liked him a lot. We shall see. (He did *not* charge for the first visit.)

I Want a Doctor Who Can Separate My Chronological Age from My Physical Condition.

I am no more prone to aches and pains than I was ten years or twenty years ago; I am no crazier, nor am I more senile, and neither are most of my peers. As a matter of fact, I probably was more crazy at seventeen than I am now.

I Want a Doctor Who Is Open to New Ideas.

Medicine is too quick to turn obdurate at the first suggestion of an idea that goes against its teaching or threatens its status. It took poor Dr. Ignaz Semmelweis a torturously long time to convince his colleagues that postpartum infection was caused by their not washing their hands before a delivery. The posture of medicine has not changed very much since then (especially when we read that nosocomial infections are still caused by nurses and doctors who don't wash their hands properly). I want my family physician to accept the holistic concept of medicine: that I am a whole person who is suffering from a disease. I resent anyone's referring to me in a hospital as "the gallbladder" or "the hernia" as so many physicians seem to do. If I discuss chiropractic with my doctor, I would like the courtesy of a hearing and a discussion of a drug-free, surgery-free alternative, rather than being dismissed with a sigh of resignation or the vituperative evaluation of any chiropractor as "Quack!"

I want the same response and openness of acceptance if I ask about acupuncture, biofeedback, the Feldenkrais method or the Jacobson technique, rolfing, shiatsu, yoga, Gestalt, or homeopathy.

If there is a disfiguring or life-saving operation involved, then I certainly want my doctor to be open to new therapies, new techniques, new approaches. Certainly, if I were a woman of my age, I would want to know much more about the alternatives in treatment open to me if I were to find a small lump in my breast one morning. For years many surgeons have accepted the Halsted radical mastectomy as the only solution to breast cancer, although newer and more desirable techniques and treatment combinations have evolved. I was present in a surgeon's office when he recommended immediate hospitalization and surgery to take care of a lump in the breast. When asked for the alternatives, or what would happen if nothing were done, he turned condescendingly, and asked almost with hostility, "Am I hearing you correctly?" The patient walked out, never to return. The surgery he was recommending, incidentally, turned out to be unnecessary.

There are times when it is not only the doctor who has a closed mind to new ideas, but the entire medical profession. Frankly, I worry about it. When I produced my Academy Award nomination film *To Live Again* (1963), I had the honor and the pleasure of working with the brilliant neurosurgeon, the late Dr. Irving Cooper of St. Barnabas Hospital in the Bronx, New York. A young man at the time, he had recently developed a remarkable operation that involved working deep within the brain for relief of the symptoms of Parkinsonism. The technique, cryosurgery, required the insertion of a probe into the thalamus and the lowering of the temperature in that area to below freezing to halt the incapacitating tremors or the rigidity of dystonia in patients who had appeared to be totally destroyed as human beings by the disease.

I watched him perform operation after operation, always in awe of the results—the tremors stopping as the patient lay awake on the table, fingers able to move, hands able to function. I fully expected the medical profession to rise in one loud cheer of acclaim, but it did not happen! Dr. Cooper, unfortunately, was "too young." Others who had attempted similar operations had failed, either through paralyzing their patients or by killing them altogether. Though he had operated successfully on over six thousand patients, there are some doctors who, as late as the early eighties, still believed that it was a fraud, that he had used hypnosis, and possibly that he was a witch doctor, I imagine. Before he died, he published a book, *The Vital Probe* (New York: Norton), a remarkable and sensitive history of his medical life. I recommend it to anyone who thinks that I am exaggerating when I condemn the world of medicine for being rigid, unyielding, and closed to new ideas.

I Want My Questions Answered.

I don't want to be passed off with, "Am I hearing you correctly?" or "It's better you shouldn't know." I don't want to be treated with a lack of respect and I don't want to be patronized. I demand integrity and I demand accountability in the answers my doctor gives. And I want *time* to discuss my questions and get the answers. I realize that "time is money," but my health is more important to me—and it should be to my physician.

I Want a Doctor Who Is Conservative in His Treatment.

There is generally time to discuss, time to consider, time to decide if a major procedure is indicated, especially in the elective area of surgery. I want my doctor to be stingy with recommendations of surgery, drugs, or extensive testing. In a recent survey, nearly half of the registered nurses across the country believed that between 30 and 50 percent of all operations and up to 50 percent of all hospital stays were unnecessary. I resent any diagnosis that might make me part of that statistic. We have a marvelous physician here at Fire Island in the summer, named Dr. Bob Furie, who is more to my liking. The doctor suggested to a friend of mine, who had been feeling unwell for a week or so, that he would be watching him, and in the meantime would treat him with "intensive neglect." The treatment worked, even though it is probably not taught in medical school.

I Want a Doctor Who Values a Second Opinion.

It is not a sign that I lack confidence in my own family physician that I sometimes want the opinion of another doctor in a case more serious than the Asian flu. I would, in fact, appreciate his or her suggestion that I see another doctor to confirm or deny the diagnosis. As I advised earlier, if you do go for a second opinion, make sure you tell the surgeon or physician that *he* or *she* will not be the one who will treat you.

During a particularly difficult time in my own family's medical history, I read a remarkable book by Rose Kushner, *Why Me?* (Harcourt, Brace, Jovanovich) an account of her own experience with breast cancer. Over a period of several weeks I spoke with her by telephone at her home in Maryland. Her support helped tremendously through that trying period. Along with a growing number of people in the medical profession, she strongly advocates that a woman undergo a two-stage approach to the breast biopsy, and that she never go into an operating room not knowing whether she will come out with only one breast intact.

It is just as important, she insists, that the patient obtain a second opinion, realizing that there is *time* to do it; she should not, must not, be rushed by the surgeon into a disfiguring and emotionally devastating operation. Her analogy, as strong and direct as she is, was delivered in a speech at the Women's Health Fair in Miami: "If you had a $50,000 Rolls Royce and it developed a knock, would you drive it into the nearest service station? Would you accept the corner mechanic's estimate of what was wrong—especially if he said it would cost $10,000 and he couldn't even guarantee it for six months? Of course not. You'd get another mechanic. And that's certainly what you should do for your body."

I Want a Doctor Who Chooses Home over Hospital When He Can.

If I am ill, I want to be surrounded by loved ones, and pampered a bit and have homemade chicken soup when I need it. In most cases, I am better off at home, while modern medicine chooses the hospital as the first and last resort. As a matter of fact, too many doctors choose the hospital as the final stop in a terminal illness when the patient would be much better off in his or her own home. It is an ongoing conflict between the philosophy of humanity and the pragmatics of medicine. The medical profession fights violently against a baby's being born at home and it is just as rigid in recommending that we also die in the isolation of a hospital room. It is changing slowly, but only through the pressures of patients and families.

Above All, I Want a Doctor Who Believes in Prevention.

I want a doctor who likes me but doesn't really want to see me, because he and I both believe that a great part of the preventive role in medicine is *my* responsibility. Should I genuinely need him, I want him to be available to me, for I will only call when the necessity is real.

Doctors are becoming more aware and awareness may well be the first step on the road to change in attitudes. A research economist, speaking at a meeting of the American Society of Internal Medicine, commented that many patients are, indeed, questioning who is responsible for their state of health, and they are discovering that the duty is theirs rather than their physician's. He went on to say that increased attention to diet and exercise by patients would affect the livelihood of doctors, as fewer and fewer people would seek medical care. Somehow they will survive our independence! *Pediatric News* carried an item in which a psychologist recommended that doctors give their patients a questionnaire at least once a year. "A patient questionnaire is an excellent practice management tool. It is also a superb patient relations tool; the request for their input sends out to patients a strong message: 'We care.'"

I certainly hope they do.

An Apple a Day: Prevention—Not Intervention

During World War I my father was wounded three times, once quite seriously when gangrene began to infect his injured leg. One morning, as he lay in a field hospital, a surgeon approached his bedside, handed him a piece of paper, and asked him to sign.

"What for?" my father asked. He was only nineteen at the time.

"We have to amputate your leg to save your life," the doctor answered perfunctorily.

My father pushed the paper aside, turned away and said, "Not me. I was born with two legs and I'm going to die with two legs."

The gangrene disappeared and my father survived the war intact. For *sixty years* afterward he never visited a physician. "I don't like doctors, I don't trust doctors," he would say every time I tried to convince him that a current illness might well be looked at. And he was always right.

Just a few years ago my father hurt his wrist while at work and, after a few days of pain, I convinced him that it might well be a slight break, which it proved to be. Reluctantly he visited my family doctor with me, and as he took the medical history, the doctor asked, "When was the last time you visited a physician?" My father answered, "Nineteen-eighteen." The doctor looked up and smiled. "You're none the worse for it!"

The responsibility and many of the decisions that relate to our health and well-being are actually up to us. We are finding that commonsense approaches to health are far more effective than technology and sophisticated medical techniques. The American medical profession is self-laudatory in its public relations; yet an infant is safer being born in Denmark, Japan, Belgium, the Netherlands, Switzerland, Finland, or even Singapore than here in the United States. Fourteen other countries have better life-expectancy statistics than the United States, and in spite of the self-acclaim of modern medicine, today's forty-five-year old male can look forward to living only three to four years longer than his counterpart in 1900! And that was before the age of miracle drugs and the marvels of twentieth-century surgery! (By way of explanation, it is in the area of *childhood* disease that medicine has been most successful, thus allowing *more of us* to live longer.) Doctors cannot give us our health habits. Weight control, regular exercise, good nutrition, not smoking, avoiding excessive intake of alcohol are all part of *our* responsibility to ourselves, not the obligation of our doctors. In the recent past, the AMA suggested that we eliminate the routine annual physical examination. This was taken a step further by Dr. Mendelsohn when he wrote, "The door to the doctor's office ought to bear a surgeon-general's warning that routine physical examinations are dangerous to your health. Many studies over the last decade or so have established that the annual physical examination is a waste of money and a waste of time."

Research groups around the world are beginning to discover that more and more of our diseases of aging either are caused by or can be cured by diet and nutrition. Osteoporosis, or brittleness of the bone, for example, is an important disease among older women and is generally associated with almost 200,000 hip fractures a year. New Zealand researchers have found that a low-calcium and high-salt diet may well lead to an increased risk of developing the disease, while the National Institute on Aging issued a report indicating that a balanced diet with adequate levels of calcium and vitamins, sufficient exercise, and avoiding cigarette smoking and heavy drinking, might help in *preventing* the onset of osteoporosis.

Small segments of the medical profession are also beginning to move into the area of *wellness* rather than sickness. The Gerontology Research Center of the National Institute on Aging began to investigate such areas as adult nutrition, geriatric medicine, and the pharmacology of aging as far back as twenty years ago. They were also in the forefront of the attempt to promote mandatory courses in geriatric medicine in the medical schools, where it is now passed off, for the most part, as an elective subject.

Occasionally we also hear of an innovative and enlightened program that throws off the straitjacket of previous medical treatment and opens potentially new frontiers of preventive medicine. Mt. Sinai Hospital in New York began a program many years ago, devoted to improving the *quality* of life of the aging. Following that, the establishment of a geriatric chair in medicine at Mt. Sinai by Dr. Robert Butler, has begun to move the hospital into the forefront of health care for the aging.

St. Barnabas Hospital in the Bronx instituted satellite health centers, in a outreach program brought right into the community itself. "The hospitals and the medical community have a role in teaching about smoking, about losing weight, about high blood pressure and how to check your own," Dr. Manny Riklan told me; "a health education program *before* you get sick."

The centers serve the community and in each of them a health educator teaches about hypertension, what foods to eat, what foods to avoid, exercise, and the treatment of diabetes and arthritis. "The programs are run just like a college," Dr. Riklan explained, "with the 'students' taking a test and actually getting a diploma when they graduate. The doctors are some of our younger people who must become familiar with the problems of aging as well as some who are semiretired. One of our doctors is seventy-three." It is another beginning.

I have a very dear friend who is an inveterate and very typical heavy smoker. It has created a series of problems for her as it does for most smokers, and she suffers from emphysema and all its symptoms, ranging from loss of breath to terrifying coughing fits. And still she smokes, though she has tried to give it up time and time again. Like so many friends I have tried to persuade her to do so, sometimes with a smile, sometimes with anger, and sometimes by slipping the latest pronouncement from that most marvelous Surgeon-General C. Everett Koop (and I was sad when he retired!). With all her charm, my friend looks back at me and agrees, and then she says, "If only my *doctor* would scare me and tell me to give it up, I would!"

For my dear old friend, about whom I worry too much, and for all of us at this point in our lives, it is time. It is time that we stopped looking to our doctors and time that we faced up to the facts of life—and the facts of death. It is time that we stopped thinking that an unending stream of money can create new technologies that will keep us healthier, if poorer. Whether you like it or not, only *we* can make a dramatic impact in the *maintenance* of our good health. Like it or not! It is about time!

14 "Drink Your Milk! It's Good for You!": Some Thoughts About Nutrition and Exercise

> Though I look old, yet I am strong and lusty.
>
> —William Shakespeare
> *As You Like It*

I have a confession to make. I am a supermarket voyeur. Along with you, I push my basket down the endless aisles, awed at the abundance and the variety, seldom able to find a product my first time through. And as I shop I look into the baskets of those who pass, making a mental note of the products they buy and what they're planning to have for dinner that evening. Through it all, I generally come to one inflexible conclusion: *I would not want to be invited to most of those homes to dine!*

Frozen TV dinners, microwave specials, packaged puffed, sugar-coated cereals, tissue-textured white bread, frozen lasagna, instant coffee, nondairy chemical creamer, potato chips, Fritos, corn chips, soda pop, processed meats, ten-pound bags of sugar, plus plenty of animal fat in the form of chopped beef, steak, and bacon: the baskets overflow with colorful boxes, most of them advertised on television and in our consumer magazines, and many of them offering discount coupons to the unwary shopper. The prices are high, of course—even with the discounts—for they include the processing, the advertising campaigns, and chemical additives and preservatives.

For a country as rich as ours, as ingeniously inventive when we are forced to be, it is amazing how few people understand that we are essentially a nation of overweight and malnourished individuals, though we consume more food per capita than anyone else in the world. The blame can be apportioned—part of it—to ignorance, part to laziness, part to stubbornness, and a great part to a dependence on "experts" who know less about nutrition than we do. The unfortunate part, however, is that we are allowing our children to follow the same bad habits and to indulge in a vast cornucopia of non-nutrition.

My mother was, perhaps, typical of a generation of immigrants who had struggled very hard and were determined that their children would never go hungry in a land of plenty. The end result of their hard work, their sacrifice, and their dedication would show up in progeny who were obviously very well fed. I was so skinny as a child that it was painful for me to wear a bathing suit. An early photo, taken at a lakeside resort when I was thirteen, clearly shows the full number of ribs on a gangling frame, even though the picture has faded after all these years.

For my mother this was a torment, and along with the constant reminders to "Eat!" or "Have a little more," my nemesis was an obese friend named Harold. To coax me onward toward her goals for me, my mother constantly commented, "Look at how nice and healthy Harold looks!" while placing before me custards covered with heavy cream, fat-encrusted steaks and lamb chops, eggs and bacon, chocolate cake, and "rewards" of sugar-coated jelly beans. Of course, she meant well and I managed to survive—as we all did—overcooked vegetables with the vitamins drained out along with the water; well-done steak; and a constant diet of cholesterol, saturated fat, and sugar. To top it off, my mother was a terrible cook, and I was one soldier in World War II who did *not* want to come home to "Mom's apple pie"!

Modern technlology has taken over where mother left off. We learned to process foods to make it easier to prepare meals for a busy family. We invented the now-beloved microwave, while television came along and prospered, helping to push the new millenium—instant cereals, enriched food, chemically preserved, sugar-rich junk food snacks—to make us what Dr. Gae Gaer Luce (*Your Second Life,* Boston: Delacorte/Seymour Lawrence) called "the world's proving grounds for cardiac disease," adding that "we are about to become the diabetes capital of the world." For there is evidence that, along with our convenience, we are paying a terrible price. *Our diet may be related to six of the ten leading causes of death in this country.*

This is another area where the media and the corporations of the country well deserve to be on our hit list. The Senate Committee on Nutrition and Human Needs issued a report some fifteen years ago, signed by then-Senators George McGovern and Charles Percy, that said in part:

Television advertising of edible products, often containing little or no information on nutritional content, shapes early food selection. And most of what is advertised is food with no nutritional value.

The incredible thing is that this has not only *not* changed, but the hype and the misinformation has gotten worse. Now that the advertisers have gotten hold of the word *natural* and now that they know that "less salt" means nothing at all, they have continued to run rampant over our TV screens—and we have continued to buy.

As far back as 1972, the Ninth International Congress of Nutrition reported that "50 percent of the money spent on television food advertising may be negatively related to health . . . items that may be generally characterized as high in fat, cholesterol, sugar, salt, or alcohol." Just take a look at the Saturday morning children's shows—and you'll see what they mean. (Except for beer, which comes later in the day!)

One would think that the medical profession would be of help to us here. But that, too, is not the case. When was the last time that your doctor spoke to you about nutrition? When was the last time he or she sat down with you and discussed the alternatives relating to good eating and good health? Probably never, because most doctors know *nothing* about nutrition. It is not taught in the medical colleges because it is basically a preventive science and is not normally directed toward the cure of a particular disease. So when your family physician gives you a loving pat on the shoulder and says, as you leave the office, "I'd like to see you take off five pounds," you have received a full dose of nonadvice because he can't really tell you how to accomplish the feat.

The dieticians and the so-called nutritionists who work in the hospitals are not much better. Have you ever looked carefully at hospital food from the point of view of nourishment? If hospitals were so marvelous in their dietary practices, why would so much sugar-loaded gelatin dessert be served to patients? Dr. Robert Mendelsohn reported on one large Boston hospital that tested surgical patients for protein and calorie malnutrition. Half of them were not getting sufficient amounts of either one "and 25 percent were sufficiently malnourished to lengthen their hospital stay. Other studies have discovered malnutrition in from one-quarter to one-half of the patients in hospitals. *It is a common cause of death among elderly patients.*" (Italics mine).

Sometimes there is black humor attached to the stories that we read, and we laugh with a little knot in our stomachs at our helplessness and vulnerability. The *Washington Post* once sent a reporter to the cafeterias of the government agencies most concerned with health, nutritional protection, and the dissemination of health information: the Food and Drug Administration, the Department of Agriculture, and the Department of Health and Human Services. She found that they specialized in greasy fried meats and potatoes, with little attention to fresh fruits, vegetables, and low-calorie foods. They're called "Uncle Sam's fast food emporia." Indeed, even *we* don't have to be patients in a hospital to prove all of this. Just leave your friend or relative and go downstairs to the hospital coffee shop and look at their menu. Two days of eating there, and you well might end up on the patient floor—as a patient!

When the Senate committee reported, it said, "Since the beginning of the century, the composition of the average American diet has changed radically. Complex carbohydrates—fruits, vegetables, and grains—which were the mainstay of the diet now play a minor role. At the same time, fat and sugar consumption have risen to the point where these two dietary elements alone now comprise at least 60 percent of the total caloric intake."

Add to all this the stresses of modern society; the prevalence of smoking and alcohol; the spreading clouds of pollution, even in formerly smog-free cities like Denver and Salt Lake City; the injection of hormones and preservatives, and the ripening of vegetables and fruits by injecting gases—or, in the case of apples, making them redder with the chemical Alar, until the public began to boycott the fruit in protest—and we begin to see then why all of our nutritional bad habits can have a negative effect on our life expectancy and our resistance to disease. It becomes even more important to us as we grow older. And—rich as our nation is—this is one area where money doesn't seem to save us. In fact, it is our *affluence* that may be making nutritional matters worse.

On a film trip to Vancouver, Canada, searching for a place to have a quiet dinner with my crew after a hard day's work, we were sent to the "best" restaurant in the city, a place called the Mansion, an elegant and stately house in a quiet section of the city. I scanned the menu for a simple, wholesome selection, something honest, nutritionally acceptable, and unadorned. My search was, of course, in vain. The more expensive the restaurant, the more complex the dishes are apt to be. I found a classic and read it aloud for my companions to hear:

Beef, Veal, and Pork topped with Crabmeat . . . Foie Gras and Artichoke Bottoms, Sauce Bernaise.

My mother would have urged, "Eat, it's good for you. Maybe you'll look like your friend Harold!" But if she were alive today she might very well have laughed with the rest of us. It is never too late to change and in only the past few years the change has been surprisingly evident almost everywhere we look.

To be sure, it has taken time. The results of drinking hemlock are almost immediate, but the destruction caused by bad diet, smoking, obesity, and lack of exercise may not make itself felt until well into our middle or later years, in the form of chronic disease or premature death. Still, it is amazing to hear that *two-thirds* of the households interviewed by the US Department of Agriculture's Economics and Statistics Service reported that they were making dietary changes for reasons of health and proper nutrition! Up to 20 percent had actually reduced their consumption of bacon, sausage, hot dogs, luncheon meats, eggs, beef, and pork, while increasing their intake of poultry, fish, fruits, and vegetables.

This awareness has even extended into the area of insurance. A growing number of companies have begun to offer reduced premiums for their policy-holders who do not smoke or drink, who keep their weight down, and who exercise regularly, with an awareness that our bad habits are killing many of us before our time, and are crippling millions of others unnecessarily:

- Obesity is one of the biggest health problems in our society. Dr. Ken Walker was quoted in the *Canadian Medical Association Journal* as saying that the extra pounds equal diabetes and atherosclerosis and, if the extra pounds were wiped out, "you could fire half the nation's doctors and close half the hospitals."

- As little as a ten- to thirty-percent weight reduction can lower the blood pressure significantly, the *New England Journal of Medicine* has reported.

- Researchers are beginning to discover that lack of correct nutrition may be one of the causes of senility in the aged. And, as we grow older, what we eat may affect our vulnerability to osteoporosis, periodontal disease, anemia, and even starvation.

- Coronary disease and strokes can be directly associated with our diets of high fat and high cholesterol as well as the severe effects of smoking, from emphysema to lung cancer, the constant denials of the cigarette industry notwithstanding.

When my father reached the age of seventy-two, he had been smoking for somewhere around sixty years or so. He began about the age of eleven or twelve, and on his seventy-second birthday, he gave up his beloved cigarettes, all two packs a day. The only reason he would give me when I asked him why was, "I just thought I'd feel better." I often think of his answer, and his remarkable willpower after so many years of inhaling carcinogens, especially when one of my friends tells me that he or she "would like to quit" but "can't seem to do it."

When my father was eighty-six, he was still smokeless. An unfortunate auto accident, in which he was the passenger, sent him to the hospital for a period of six weeks in the intensive care unit before he finally succumbed and died. Unfortunately the years of smoking had affected his lungs sufficiently so that they just could not function properly when he really needed them. He was a tough old guy, though.

There is no doubt that too many of us smoke too much, drink too much, eat too much. As we age, we should be cutting down our intake of food, yet many of us increase the amount we eat. Dr. Eleanor D. Schlenker brings the subject right back to the area of *our responsibility:* "Many factors determine the health and life span of older people. The individual has little, if any, control of some of these (for example, pollution in the air). But nutrition is one factor which, for most individuals, is subject to a certain amount of choice. Proper nutrition throughout life has been suggested as one of the best means of minimizing degenerative changes as well as increasing life span."

What is proper nutrition? We are just beginning to learn what our grandparents may have instinctively known so many years ago. We are going back to the basics and, as with our physicians, we are beginning to read the labels and to question.

We still can't understand *everything* they tell us and the technical names can be awesome and frightening. But the basic information must be there and, if you are on a restricted diet or you feel as I do that sugar and salt are dangerous to your well-being, at least you have some indication of the amount of the ingredient, though the FDA would like to see the law changed to list the *percentages* used.

Keep in mind, too, that the two most common additives to processed foods—sugar and salt—can also masquerade under other names: *sugar* as corn syrup, dextrose, sucrose, maltose, lactose, fructose, glucose, or invert sugar; *salt* as sodium, sodium chloride, or sodium diacetate.

Naturally, the manufacturers will come up with various methods of muddying the waters and major consumer groups would like to see the law made more precise for such terms as *low cholesterol* or *dietetic*. The term *salt-free* may indicate no sodium chloride, but other types of salt may be present.

One of the most misused terms is the label, *Natural*, for it means one thing to some of us and something entirely different to every manufacturer who has discovered that it is the magic word of marketing. It means—to put it bluntly—nothing! Look at the labels on most commercial "natural" products and you will probably see that two of the leading ingredients are salt and sugar. They are, after all, natural, are they not? And, the most recent discovery by supermarkets and suppliers around the country is the word, *organic*. Realizing that the consumer has become more and more aware and even more frightened of the use of chemical fertilizers and insect repellants, the demand for organically grown produce has mushroomed. The problem, as always, is how do you know that you are really getting an organic product just because the label above the fruit or vegetable says so? Do I mean to say that food suppliers would cheat? Don't be ridiculous!

There is one other factor that has become evident to me in my years of writing cookbooks and my publishing days with Rodale Press. If the real, honest-to-goodness natural product like grains, is economical, easy to prepare and tasty; if I use fresh herbs and spices in my cooking instead of shakers full of salt; if I even bake my own bread, which so many of us now do . . . then *why* would I buy the processed products that now proliferate and promise me that they are healthy for me? The reason is quite simple. Aided by the food industry, natural food products and ingredients that are actually good for you and taste just wonderful have been labeled "health food" and saddled with the subliminal message that they taste just lousy. Witness some of the advertising that has come out in the past few years:

- Oroweat Bran'nola, Honest Bread (!) It tastes so good, you'll forget it's good for you.

- If Prince Superoni didn't taste so good, you might think it was a health food.

- Thomas' Protein Bread. How can anything so nutritious taste so delicious?

For someone like me, as well as other business people all over the country who travel a great deal, another source of nutritional frustration comes in the hotels, motels, and restaurants at which we are obliged to eat. Run by large corporations in many cases, guided by magazines and marketing techniques that emphasize "portion control," specializing in food shipped frozen and microwaved at the last instant, these places offer breakfast, lunch, and dinner that are superb studies in chemistry but are not a balanced diet. And, I have not even mentioned *the airlines*. Words are best left unsaid.

I am a latecomer to the world of good nutrition. Though I am no missionary about it, I do believe that these past twenty years have seen a tremendous improvement in my health and well-being, and my weight has been easier to keep in check. Thus the food that I encounter on my constant travels can be disappointing, to say the least, as well as a perpetual source of resentment toward the lodging chains and restaurants whose offerings have so lowered the standards of our diets. As a result, I generally take my own picnic meals aboard airplanes, buy fresh fruit and eat it for breakfast in my room, and let the eating establishments know that I am displeased when they serve an array of artificial swill that they would pass off as "gourmet cooking." Of course, I am also, occasionally, not pleasant to be with.

But with all my complaining, I begin to see a small shaft of light shining through. A pamphlet issued back in 1972 by the US Department of Agriculture (and revised in 1974), *Food Guide for Older Folks*, stated that "nutritionists [!] have developed simple food guides to help people make good choices whether they eat at home or eat out." The recipes included frozen dinners, canned and frozen main dishes, processed cheeses, canned corned-beef hash, ground meats, dried beef, frankfurters, canned macaroni, bacon, salt pork, beef drippings, and as much as half a teaspoon of salt per recipe!

The pamphlet was eventually withdrawn and a new one was issued a short time later. (*Nutrition and Health*, Superintendent of Documents, US Government Printing Office, Washington, DC 20402.) The change in approach in just a few short years is nothing short of astounding and the new pamplet lists the seven basic guidelines right on the cover. Gone are the salt pork and the beef drippings. In their place are whole grains, fresh fruits and vegetables— and the avoidance of salt, sugar, cholesterol, and too much alcohol! The seven points contain some very good advice.

Eat a Variety of Foods

As we get older, we may (and should) cut down on the amount of food we eat. Thus the variety, rather than the amount, of food can give us a well-rounded diet of vitamins, minerals, amino acids (from proteins), essential fatty acids (from vegetable oils), and energy in the form of sufficient calories.

- Fresh fruits and vegetables are an excellent source of vitamins, especially C and A.

- Whole grain products provide B vitamins, iron, and energy as well as fiber. Indeed, whole grains are truly the best way to get natural fiber, ignoring the claims of the manufacturers of processed food. The moment we process anything, we destroy a good part of its food value.

- It is no longer believed that "milk is only for babies." Milk and its by-products are excellent sources of high-quality protein, calcium, and vitamins, no matter what our age.

Many of us believe the biggest waste in the food chain is the rich, fatty meats that we love for their protein. There are more efficient ways to get whole protein, though I doubt that this advice will ever be listened to in a "steak-crazy" nation. A combination of grains and legumes can make a full protein meal, the equivalent of a large portion of steak, and without the saturated fats. The same protein content can be found in a teaspoon of sunflower seeds! The beef industry, finally seeing the handwriting (or graffiti) on the consumer wall, has begun to mount a campaign to bring the consumption of beef up again, for there has been a very decided move to chicken and fish by America's shoppers: Low-fat beef is the newest pitch, but animal fat is animal fat—and it's the kind you don't want.

Also be aware of the fact that the processed foods you buy are changed by the very treatment used in bringing them to your supermarket shelf—generally a diminution of food value, as I mentioned earlier. The RDAs (Recommended Daily Allowances) are also meaningless, for they vary for children, teenagers and older adults. We are not homogeneous, shot-from-the-same-cannon, like our processed cereals. Some of us have special needs because of illness, the size of our frame, or just plain preference in foods.

Not too long ago, a dear friend of mine specifically wrote a cookbook directed toward that group of us who *do* have special dietary demands. It's called *Eating Well When You Just Can't Eat the Way You Used To* by Jane Wilson (Workman Publishing) and I recommend that you take a look at it if you do fall into that category. It also covers the problem of preparing a meal for only one person while still considering nutrition and health.

Maintain Ideal Weight

The heavier you are, the greater your chances of developing the chronic disorders that plague our age group. The country is rife with high blood pressure, diabetes, and strokes, much of it the result of excess weight and bad diet. The change that has come about, however, since we were kids is that body weight is no longer based on a rigid height-weight ratio. At last they have taken into consideration the fact that my metabolism may keep me thinner than yours keeps you, and that my frame size and bone structure are different from those of my peers. In fact, some of us can eat large amounts of food and not seem to gain weight, while others merely take a snack once in a while and yet put on too many pounds too quickly.

Suggested Body Weights		
Height	**Men**	**Women**
(Feet-inches)	(Pounds)	(Pounds)
4'10"		92-119
4'11"		94-122
5'0"		96-125
5'1"		99-128
5'2"	112-141	102-131
5'3"	115-144	105-134
5'4"	118-148	108-138
5'5"	121-152	111-142
5'6"	124-156	114-146
5'7"	128-161	118-150
5'8"	132-166	122-154
5'9"	136-170	126-158
5'10"	140-174	130-163
5'11"	144-179	134-168
6'0"	148-184	138-173
6'1"	152-189	
6'2"	156-194	
6'3"	160-199	
6'4"	164-204	

SOURCE: HEW Conference on Obesity

Somehow, the old nursery rhyme keeps coming back to me as I write this: "Jack Sprat could eat no fat, and his wife could eat no lean." (On the other hand Jean Jacques Rousseau said, "Let them eat cake!" No, it was *not* Marie Antoinette who said it first.)

Don't try to lose weight too rapidly and don't indulge in the crash diets that are the fad these days. Try to lose weight gradually—a pound or two a week. And don't go off too far in the other direction. Severe weight loss can be the cause of everything from hair loss to skin changes, intolerance to colds, constipation, and even mental disturbances.

Avoid Too Much Fat, Saturated Fat, and Cholesterol

Eating foods that contain large amounts of saturated fat and cholesterol tends to elevate the blood cholesterol level in most adults. Though there is still some controversy, evidence seems to point to a high cholesterol level as the prime villain in early heart attacks, especially if you suffer from high blood pressure and you smoke.

- Select lean meat, fish, poultry, and dried beans and peas as your sources of protein.

- Moderate your use of eggs and cream, butter, hydrogenated margarines, shortenings, palm oil and coconut oil, and cut down your consumption of organ meats such as liver. With regard to coconut oil and palm oil, you'll notice (if your read the labels) that they are a common ingredient in such items as the nondairy creamers now so prevalent on airplanes and in restaurants. They are loaded with cholesterol and food processors are busily trying to find substitutes, again through consumer pressure.

- Trim the excess fat off meats.

- Broil, roast, bake, or steam rather than fry or deep-fry.

I do note again that the food industry seems to be listening. Not to be outdone by lean (mean) beef, the egg producers, hurt badly by the severe drop in consumption, have now begun to develop a low-cholesterol egg. Again, we shall see, and I would love to see them succeed, since eggs were once my favorite food. (Before my doctor told me my cholesterol count!)

Eat Foods wth Adequate Starch and Fiber

This is an area of much myth, like everything else that seems to affect us as we age. My wife and I were working on a book (*Sheryl and Mel London's*

Creative Cooking with Grains and Pasta, Rodale Press) that required testing a range of whole grains including barley, oats, rice, amaranth, bulgur, corn, and wheat. It went on for two years—for breakfast, lunch, dinner, and snacks we invariably had dishes made with grains. The first reaction to all of this from our friends was, "Boy, are you two going to get fat!" especially when they heard that the book had a vast array of pasta recipes. We not only did *not* get fat—we felt better and we actually *lost* weight during part of the testing process! Working on that book has changed our dietary lives and our eating habits, for we still consume large amounts of whole grains and complex carbohydrates. And our weight is still down, about seven years later.

The major sources of energy in our diet are carbohydrates and fats. If, as good nutrition suggests, we lower our intake of fat, then we should increase our caloric intake of carbohydrates. Carbohydrates also help us maintain our weight, since they have about half the calories of fat. However, the *simple* carbohydrates, such as sugar, give us a "quick fix" with calories but provide very little else in the way of nutrition. The *complex* carbohydrates—beans, peas, nuts, fruits, whole grains, and cereals—provide other essential nutrients in addition to the calories. I've read with interest that the sporting world has replaced the familiar pregame or prefight steak with pasta. And so have the long-distance runners. And so have our local joggers.

There is another element that makes the addition of complex carbohydrates important to our nutritional needs. Anthropologists and other scientists have been studying certain African tribes for years, wondering why their incidence of bowel cancer is so low. Their diets are heavy in whole grains, and whole grains add fiber, an element quite low in the average American diet. High fiber content also reduces the symptoms of constipation, diverticulosis, and other modern complaints of irregularity. Millet, a remarkable, high fiber grain that is consumed universally in Africa, is fed to our birds here in the United States!

Avoid Too Much Sugar

I must admit that my diet as a young person, now changed so radically, left me with dreams of jelly beans and Milky Ways (frozen). But I paid a price for all that nonstop munching of candies, chocolate, and rich desserts. My teeth have gone through enough reconstructions, excavations, and probing to make them eligible for an archaeological foundation grant. The average American consumes about *130 pounds of sugar a year* in coffee, jams, jellies, desserts, soft drinks, cakes, pies, breakfast cereals (read the labels on those!), catsup, and ice cream, and none of it is nutritionally necessary.

Cutting down for someone like me means an increase in the use of fruits, carrot sticks, nuts, or a piece of whole grain bread as snacks. For anyone in middle age and beyond, the junk foods are better left untouched. I do admit, however, to a little tinge of envy when I used to see a jar of jelly beans on the desk of the man in the White House. And I do also admit that I still keep a few frozen Milky Ways in the freezer—*for guests!*

Avoid Too Much Sodium

The next time you visit a middle-America restaurant, look around you at the diners. Undoubtedly, you will see the food arrive at the table, and *without even tasting* the dish, people will grab for the salt shaker and vigorously pour a snowstorm of it on the food. In addition, the chef back in the kitchen has also added his or her contribution in order to make the entrée taste "better."

This seems to be one of the most difficult areas in which to abide by the sane rules of nutrition and maintenance of health. We salt our food almost by rote, both in cooking and when it reaches the table. My wife and I thought that writing a book on grains would necessitate the use of salt, even though we normally do not use it in our house. We felt the same way when we did our book on fish (*The Fish Lovers' Cookbook*, Rodale Press). And both times we were wrong. The clever use of citrus, spices, and seasonings, the use of herbs, and the fact that it is quite possible to learn to enjoy food by tasting its natural flavor, can reduce the amount of salt intake enormously. Our learning experience then led to yet another book that eliminated the use of salt while still providing superb flavor, *The Herb and Spice Cookbook*, (Rodale Press).

One morning, Sheryl burst into my office bearing a gift of two large bowls of warm, freshly made popcorn—*without salt*. In my childhood that would have been sacrilege, for anyone in his right mind knew that popped corn must be flavored by a large supply of salt. It is just not true—and I suppose that I've come a long way. The snack tasted absolutely superb au naturel.

It has been proven time and again that populations with a low sodium intake have less trouble with hypertension and high blood pressure. Japan, for example, uses large amounts of sodium in seasonings such as soy and in pickled condiments and salt-dried fish, and the hypertension rate is astronomical. In America, most of our salt intake is hidden in processed foods—potato chips, pickled products, condiments like steak sauces, cheese, cured meats, and yes, commercial popcorn! This is an area where reading the labels can help you determine the salt content and assist you in the reduction of sodium in your diet.

Take Alcohol in Moderation

The seventh piece of advice given by the USDA and the Department of Health and Human Services is to keep your intake of alcohol moderate if you do drink. Alcoholic beverages are high in calories but very low in nutrition.

Other sources of information are available and an avid reader of any of today's magazines and other literature can quickly become at least a little familiar with the rules of nutrition and good health. They are really quite simple. The National Retired Teachers and the American Association of Retired Persons distribute a helpful booklet, A Guide for Food and Nutrition in Later Years. It covers supermarket tips, nutrients and their food sources, and special diets, and there is even a small section on how to make eating alone more palatable and enjoyable. (Write: Society for Nutrition Education, 2140 Shattuck Avenue, Suite 1110, Berkeley, CA 94704)

The National Council on the Aging publishes a pamphlet, Eating Well to Stay Well (600 Maryland Avenue, S.W., West Wing 100, Washington, DC 20024) designed to inform and encourage older adults to eat in a sensible and healthy way. It includes guidelines based upon government parameters, life-style suggestions to maintain health despite existing chronic conditions, and a list of resources.

Nutrition is still a new and evolving science. Many of the theories are not yet proven and new ones surface every day. It is one of the reasons that the subject of nutrition is so fascinating. The director of the Santa Barbara, California, branch of the American Institute of Family Relations claims that the food we eat is responsible for emotional problems in three out of every four marriages. She reported in an article ("I'm a Natural," March 1981) that one case is fairly typical. The woman was severely depressed and the man extremely irritable. She advised that the couple stop their consumption of sugar and refined flour and reduce their intake of coffee. "Their relationship turned completely around," she wrote. "Her depression lifted. He went from being testy to amiable. They were like honeymooners again."

And don't be surprised, given the new and growing interest in how we eat as well as what we eat, if that old children's nursery rhyme is eventually revised from "Jack Sprat could eat no fat," to "Jack Sprat should eat no fat." It would be very good advice, indeed!

The Agony and the Exercise

During the summer months it begins very early in the morning, usually as the sun makes itself felt here on the ocean's edge and my typewriter has yet to compose its first words, a cup of coffee steaming at my elbow. The rhythmic pounding on the boardwalks outside sends a ripple through the beams of the house, sometimes the drumming of two Adidas or Nike-clad feet and at other times a couple moving in cadence with their own silent clock. The joggers have begun and they do not stop their exercise no matter how hot it becomes, though the agony is more evident on their faces and in their sweaty bodies as the temperature and the humidity climb.

They are of all ages, shapes, and sizes, men and women and little children, as well as panting dogs tied to the runners by a leash, all being initiated into the cult of masochism. One runner passes, actually pushing a three-wheeled baby carriage as he jogs, with the child fast asleep and oblivious to what is going on. I walk outside and watch with awe the self-flagellation, the punishment, and the misery. But then I do not understand and I suppose I never will. I am not, by nature, a deliberate exerciser and no matter how often the runners explain to me that what I am seeing is actually rapture and ecstasy, the beatitude of exertion, I am among the uninitiated, the unbelievers, the infidels. Suffice it to say, there is exactly one mile from the village store past my house and back again, and so they will be here again tomorrow morning and all through the day, their breathing sounding, as Sheryl puts it, "like an obscene phone call."

I have teased and I have been teased through all these years of proclaiming that "exercise is destructive to the muscle tone," for I know that deep, deep down I believe quite the opposite and that, particularly at our age, exercise can do much to preserve our physical fitness and help the body resist disease; delay sluggish circulation; and maintain the strength of our muscles. It is just that I have been lucky and am the end product of a career that has entailed a tremendous amount of physical labor. In short, as Alex Comfort has written, "The best exercise is work." And I still do my share of hauling film equipment up mountains at fourteen thousand feet or a half mile down in a coal mine, constantly pacing while I direct my films, working a twelve- to fourteen-hour day on location, and having a "hyper" Type A personality that does not let fat sit very long on my frame. But I will not, by any stretch of the imagination, punish myself by jogging or by playing tennis. There are other alternatives for each of us.

We are, by nature, a sedentary society, unaccustomed to moving very far from our television sets, and it is no accident that the phrase "couch potato" has come into being recently. We are slaves to the automobile that becomes our seven-league boots to the supermarket, school, our social affairs, and the fast-food emporia. There we can sit again and indulge in still more saturated fats and junk-food cholesterol. To top it off, we probably have sat at a desk for thirty years or more.

One day as we hit middle age (whatever that is), we begin to see ourselves with too much bulge in all the wrong places and cellulite overflowing its boundaries, and we decide that it's time to exercise! Violently! Immediately! To make up for all that lost time. Or else we decide that it's not worth the effort and we just let nature take its course. The first choice is dangerous and can bring on cardiac failure. The second choice portends inevitable destruction of the muscle tone and chronic fatigue. As a matter of fact, the National Aeronautics and Space Administration (NASA), in its early studies for the space program, found that each three days of total inactivity corresponded to a loss of *one-fifth* of a person's maximum muscle strength!

A group of British doctors voted on the side of *vigorous* exercise when they studied almost eighteen-thousand middle-aged men and found that those who engaged in active and strenuous sports and other fitness exercises had only half the incidence of coronary heart disease as those who did not exercise at all. Those that got heart disease suffered less severe effects and fewer died. In a report in *Lancet,* the British medical journal, they concluded that "vigorous exercise is a natural defense of the body, with a protective effect on the aging heart against ischemia (lack of blood supply) and its consequences." If, when we reach middle age, we have been exercising strenuously for many years, there is a good chance that we are maintaining our dedication to racquetball or squash, tennis or jogging, or even two rounds of golf each Saturday afternoon. For those of us who have exercised spottily, if at all, there are a number of other ways to keep our bodies fit and limber at fifty or seventy or older.

On my very first trip to Hong Kong back in the early sixties, I looked out of my window one foggy morning and watched in awe as a vast number of people, most of them elderly, moved gracefully through a series of exercises. Each person seemed to move entirely on his or her own in a rhythmic, predetermined, graceful series of balance shifts, gentle thrusts, and wide arcs. It was my introduction to the remarkable ancient Chinese exercise t'ai chi ch'uan. I have watched it many times since then and have photographed it for travel films, and just recently I investigated it more thoroughly by attending a beginner's class at a local school. It is just one example of what many of us can do to stimulate circulation as we get older, to use grace and balance and rhythm, and to combine an art form with tradition in keeping ourselves more fit and active. There is no need to take up tennis at the age of fifty or sixty!

For some of us, exercise can be vigorous and active and competitive. For others of our group, it need not be the Jane Fonda aerobics tape, but it can well encompass dancing, movement, programs offered at the local "Y" in yoga or t'ai chi, or it can be just *walking* on our own. At a conference held at the National Institutes of Health in Bethesda, research participants from the United States, Canada, and Western Europe agreed that walking was the most efficient form of exercise and one that can be safely followed no matter what one's age.

And so, I gently withdraw my constant and long-standing maxim that exercise is destructive to the muscle tone. As we enter middle age, and certainly as we approach Otto von Bismarck's magic number of sixty-five, and then as we move into the later years, it is, indeed, more important to us that we stretch more, bend more, and sit less, no matter how we choose to accomplish it.

On this lovely morning, as the sun begins to creep up slowly, I shall take my coffee cup, walk outside my door, and *smile* at the joggers as they gasp their way past my house.

PART III

The Changing Face of Aging

We are not without our problems, our emotional letdowns, our deep and agonizing questioning of ourselves as we enter into and travel through middle age. Indeed, I admit that it gets even more difficult as we begin to anticipate and then analyze that mythical—soon to become real—milepost, the age of sixty-five. My grandmother used to say, "Who ever told you that life would be easy?" And thus my friend, Jonathan, just turning fifty, is going through those pangs of "Whither go I?" at this time in his life, unable to believe that the years have gone by so quickly and that over one hundred friends at his birthday party will help remind him that his children are grown (his "baby" daughter now an assistant district attorney!) and that he has survived quite well through this half century. He will also manage to weather the next decades with ease, once he overcomes the awe that seems to come with the idea of having lived fifty years.

There is no doubt that someone of twenty cannot know what it is like to be fifty or sixty. Think back to what you considered "old" when you were a child. One of my mother's contemporaries always struck me as the most mature woman I had ever known. I was then four. Later I found out that she was all of twenty-five when I had those thoughts. The police begin to look younger and younger to you now, don't they?

I state none of this in a negative way, for I am referring as much to the joys of aging and maturity as I am to the problems that are a part of this aging process. Jonathan's reaction is, perhaps, universal in the sense that all of us have felt the onset of middle age as a turning point throughout the generations. Sometimes it strikes as early as the age of twenty-five; for others it comes at forty. Society does little to relieve the shock, as we have seen.

But, in addition to the self-awareness that comes with merely reaching whatever age we consider to be the middle of our lives, there are also the dilemmas that we face merely because we are living in a *particular time*. In that way we are very special, for these are problems that have belonged to no one else. They are very specifically *ours*.

We are the first generations to find ourselves in a world where we are destined to live longer than any who have preceded us. And yet we seem to retire much sooner than our fathers and our grandfathers did. This longer projected period outside the work force brings with it the necessity for more orderly and detailed financial planning, but the ravages of inflation are threatening the secure patterns that we thought we have developed.

To make matters even more threatening, the Social Security system is under severe attack, though the optimists among us watch it with fingers crossed, knowing that we will somehow survive the problem as we have persisted through so many others in our lives. There may even be cold comfort in the fact that our grandparents, and those who came before them, did not even have a system of retirement benefits, either governmental or private.

But there is one area where this longer expected life span has brought with it a new, serious, and deeply emotional set of complications for those who are entering middle age. No other generation has had to face, to the same extent, the realities that have come for so many of us who have elderly parents who are still living.

There are three-generational families and not a few with four generations still alive, sometimes living in the same household. It is not unusual to find a still newer phenomenon—two generations of *retirees* in one family. And thus, just when we feel we have discovered our freedom, the children gone, we suddenly hear a cry from the other direction. The generation gap reverses and it is our parents who seem to need help, and they inevitably turn toward us, their middle-aged sons and daughters. We have been dubbed "The Sandwich Generation" and in this area *we* are the pioneers, for no one before us has—or could have—written the rulebook by which we can find our way. It is a new responsibility in a life that has held so many changes.

15 ✸ Well, We Can Always Put Them on the Ice Floes

Cast me not off in time of old age; forsake me not when my strength faileth.

—Psalms 71:9

The books and the advice came too late to be of any help to us. We were in the beginnings of an awareness of the problem and an occasional newspaper article told us that we were not alone. Even now, almost fifteen years later, I am not quite certain how we might have approached things differently. I have learned, however, that my solution to the situation was quite wrong; that my wife, Sheryl, in her stubbornness, was far ahead of her time.

Almost ten years after the problem had surfaced, I watched Dr. Stephen Z. Cohen, author of the book *The Other Generation Gap* (paperback, Warner Books) on the tape of a television program and I nodded in mute agreement as he told the interviewer:

> People have always had parents who have grown old and have needed assistance, but what's special in our country today is that so many more people are living to an advanced old age. We now have approximately 23 million people in the country who are over age sixty-five, and the prospect is that many more will achieve seventy, eighty, ninety years of age. Living that long poses many problems for the older person and for the children. There's the prospect of living with a variety of chronic illnesses and that means that people are going to turn to their children most frequently. Unfortunately, there has been very little discussion of these problems in the country.

My mother-in-law Kitty's slow and agonizing decline took place over a period of five years, beginning when she was eighty. For the first three of those years

171

the chronic diseases seemed to vie with one another to make themselves known. Added to the rapidly diminishing eyesight caused by glaucoma, the symptoms of Alzheimer's disease (senility) had begun to make themselves felt, from being unable to choose her own clothing—wearing a sweater as a hat—to the mismatched pieces of silverware placed on the table before her dinner—two knives on one side of the plate, a fork, a knife, and a tablespoon on the other. Her conversations were vivid remembrances of minute details that occurred in 1934, but she could barely recall what she had had for lunch two hours before. That most remarkable computer, the brain, had begun to accept nothing new while continuing to function exquisitely in the past.

To this day, I am not quite certain that the symptoms of senility and of the Parkinson's disease that later struck her were not the result of the side effects of Thorazine and the other drugs that had been so liberally prescribed for her. Whatever the cause, the symptoms were there and the degeneration continued. The generations were reversing, and on that tape so many years later, Dr. Cohen described it all quite accurately, and I'm quite certain that some of my readers have already gotten a chill of recognition:

> There is an expectation, a long-standing tradition in our culture, that somehow we are required to take care of elderly parents. It dates back to the commandment, "Honor thy father and thy mother." Yet, for many people, the fulfillment of that prescription is very difficult. And, for many middle-aged people, the caring for an older person over a long period of time poses terrible problems. For some, the relationship that existed over a period of time becomes strained and painful for both parties.

Dr. Cohen might well have added, "and painful or destructive to the marriages of middle-aged children." There are new decisions to be made, the normal expectancy that it might all disappear in time, knowing full well that it will not. There are the differences of opinion, the guilts and the anxieties of commitment, the pressures, and the anticipations of the months, the years to come.

Kitty was of her generation, just as we are of ours and our children reflect the particular values, virtues, and imperfections of theirs. Outwardly frail, with a cameolike beauty that remained with her until the day she died, her luminescence gave a sense of delicacy and helplessness that covered a great reservoir of strength and determination. Her credo, as expressed to us when we were first married and we told her that we had decided not to have children, was, "Who will take care of you when you're old?"

By the end of the third year, when she was eighty-two, the occasional observation of Kitty's daily life, the telephone calls several times a day to see that she did not turn on the gas stove and leave it unattended, had become a constant routine of supervision. She still lived in her apartment only a block away, but now the trips that Sheryl made became more frequent, the daily exercise walks to the park more frustrating and time-consuming. The diseases continued their inexorable march and the drug therapy only added to the toll, making Kitty still more dependent, still more disoriented, and more in need of constant attention.

To make matters still worse, Sheryl's older sister, then in Florida and retired, was unable to share the burden. She had contracted cancer and was to undergo a mastectomy. The responsibility fell with all its weight on one person, Sheryl. Since that time, I have learned that this is quite common. One child bears the cross and it is most often a daughter. This has not changed one iota since that time, twenty years back; *92 percent are women!*

After that third year, my reaction was simple, American, knee-jerk response—possibly an answer that many readers will have thought of as this chapter unfolds. It is the first, almost immediate answer in our country to the problems of aging and chronic disease: "Put her in a nursing home!"

Sheryl adamantly refused. "I wouldn't put my dog in a kennel," she retorted each time I brought the subject up. "I certainly am not going to put my mother in a nursing home." There had to be a way, she firmly maintained, to handle the problem without taking Kitty from familiar surroundings and isolating her, to let her retain her dignity, and to give her the kind of care and consideration that is so sorely lacking in America's geriatric wards.

I had worked in nursing homes and in the chronic disease wards as a filmmaker and I had seen the emotionless, empty, deadly stares of the patients who sat interminably doing nothing. I had seen the halfhearted attempts at "arts and crafts" and the shocking conditions that existed even in the "best" of homes. I had come back from my film trips emotionally exhausted and unable to get the images from my mind, all of them indelibly implanted as they had been on the film we'd shot. Indeed, it was not until just this past year that I finally saw one group who actually achieved what we had looked for all those years—the Little Sisters of the Poor and their care of the aged poor. But even at that time, faced with the rapid deterioration, the physical and mental retrogression of Kitty, my own mother-in-law—and knowing what I did then about the conditions of the nursing homes that I had inspected—I immediately thought of quarantine, the surgical removal of the patient from active society.

It was a time when black humor became rampant as the difficulties mounted. I recalled the wonderful book about the Eskimos that I had read while still a teenager. The elders of the community—no longer able to function in an environment that was now hostile and threatening, no longer able to chew and soften walrus hides with teeth that were worn to the gums— were put on the ice floes to drift outward into the Arctic Sea, their fate accepted by them and by the younger members of the community, who would one day also ride the ice floes to their destiny. I remember, too, reading of the anxious daughter of one of the elders who shouted to her father, "Jump into the water, father, and put your head under. It will be easier that way!" Indeed, there was a wonderful black humor postscript to this story, for I received a letter soon after publication of the first edition of this book, and was told by an irate reader that she found me quite depressing, "particularly for the story about the Eskimos!"

Over the next two years, Kitty's condition deteriorated even more rapidly, and I learned much about caring and responsibility and devotion as I watched Sheryl handle it. The resolve that the mother had shown so often in her lifetime was obviously passed on to her younger daughter through the family genes, for Sheryl was quite determined to see it through and to find help somehow. It was not, by any means, easy. The drug intake and the rapid physical deterioration continued, finally making Kitty bedridden and incontinent. She was blind. She took very little food. The mother had become an infant, helpless and swathed in diapers, yet her daughter did not yield even an inch.

She actually found help. She determinedly pursued her original intent that her mother would not be left to die in a strange and foreign place. She probed the community social services, explored by telephone bureaucratic mazes of nonanswers, noninformation, misinformation, and double talk. Some of her most important leads came from a remarkable ophthamologist, Dr. Ralph Salatino, who suggested organizations that were specifically designed to help the legally blind. From them, other bits of information surfaced. Sheryl discovered that there *are* people and organizations that not only listen, but can move mountains if they choose. There are an increasing number of community resources that can and do assist middle-aged children in caring for their older parents, and in the time since the first edition of Second Spring was published, still more organizations have expanded their work in this area, especially in the support groups for Alzheimer's disease. (More of which I shall discuss later in this chapter, along with some names and addresses to turn for help.)

Since Kitty was legally blind, she was entitled to additional Medicaid money with which to survive. There were medical and social programs at that time that would help in the purchase of the horribly expensive drugs, the food supplements, and even the medical paraphernalia that began to fill her room. The costs of all this care are no small matter if the children are forced to pay for the help. With medical costs soaring, any family might be financially destitute within months. Ironically, over a period of eight years, an aging president cut back program after program designed to help the aged and the indigent (and the children), with some slack being taken up by the private sector, the states and the more progressive cities, while others barely exist. Were it not for the programs that Sheryl uncovered, we would have been economically devastated, stripped of our savings. I have nightmares when I think of the administration in Washington that so callously cut back on these programs, unable to understand that they may well have represented salvation for the *middle class* as well as the poor of our country.

But the final and most critical help came from the homemaker program of our city. It provided a remarkable woman named Ivy Thomas, who cared for her bedridden patient for over a year, and she was with her until the moment she died at four o'clock on a fall afternoon.

It has been fifteen years since that terrible time, and Sheryl had not changed her mind. She would do it again. My solution would not have worked, for this way Sheryl is at peace with herself, without guilt, knowing that she did the best she possibly could. The situation, of course, was an extreme one, and I recount it here as only one example of what can happen as our parents age. Luckily, it is not the typical case, but it made me search deeply for the reasons behind my reactions.

Like many of my peers, I am the victim of still another set of myths about the aged, another series of social lies that distort our thinking when the problems of elderly parents become a personal burden of conscience. It is no small comfort to me to learn that I am not alone, that seventy-five percent of all nursing students polled in a recent study thought that almost all people over sixty-five were residing in nursing homes, just as my friend thought when we discussed the film *Cocoon.* When young psychologists were asked about it, thirty-five percent thought exactly the same thing. In fact, the actual statistic is astoundingly low—only *four to five percent* of the elderly are institutionalized! Even then it is usually a last resort—these are older people without families, immigrants who came to this country alone and who never married, widows and widowers without other means of family support.

Again, a large part of the blame for this perpetuated myth is our dear old friend, television. Although an occasional documentary (unwatched for the most part) does tell the truth about our problems with aging parents, a more typical representation was that of a drama in which Molly Picon starred some years back and which I had the misfortune to watch. It was called *Grandma Didn't Wave Back,* and the plot revolved around the reactions of an eleven-year-old girl to the fact that Grandma was getting senile. Grandma's children, the girl's parents, thus decide that Grandma has to be "put away." Deep in my files I have the notes that I share with you, along with my previous review of *Middle Age Crazy:*

- Even though it is stated that not *all* people become senile, it is implied that it is exactly what does happen. Grandma says, "When you grow old, the change is forever. We dance to the music of our own time." The reaction of Debbie, the little girl, is classic gerontophobia: "I don't want to get old!"

- The family is well able to care for Grandma, if they had the slightest urge to do so. However, the first talk is of "putting her away," to which Debbie compares it with her dog, who was "put away."

- The nursing home to which Grandma is finally sent is Hollywood's version—in spite of all the statistics and reality to the contrary. Grandma has a lovely single room overlooking the sea, obviously on multimillion-dollar real estate, with a view of sea gulls.

- Grandma tells Debbie that she "wants it this way."

- Considering the plush accommodations of the home, a little help—which the family could well afford—might have solved the problem without the nursing home.

- The show was a cop-out.

In spite of what we think, and in spite of what shows like the above seem to indicate, it turns out that our middle-aged brothers and sisters do *not* heartlessly dump their parents, abandoning them to an impersonal end. In fact almost *eighty percent* of the people over sixty-five in our country are living with someone else, not necessarily their children, and usually right in the communities in which they have *always* lived! And the people who do retire to age-segregated communities do so voluntarily. And, with the development of age-integrated planned communities such as Palm Coast, many of our middle-aged and elderly actually make the move to begin a second career, and to continue their lives surrounded by children and young adults. Over all, older Americans are not so likely to live with their children or to receive financial help from them as they once were. Even here, the world of aging is undergoing tremendous changes.

In a report published by the Department of Health and Human Services, Professor Alvin Schorr of Case Western Reserve University concluded that only one-sixth of elderly parents live with their children, compared with one-third in 1952. In addition, five to ten percent received financial assistance from their children in 1961, while only two to three percent do so now. There have been studies, in fact, that show that more cash assistance flows *downward* from older parents to their middle-aged children and grandchildren than in the opposite direction! This has become especially true as housing costs have skyrocketed, and many first mortgages and cooperative apartment purchases are funded by the *parents* rather than by the children.

Still, there is no doubt that this new resettling of the generations is creating problems. As Dr. Cohen said, "Where the relationships have been close and the children and parents have been together for a long time, those children respond naturally to the needs of the parents. But where there has been a considerable amount of emotional distance or where the children live a thousand miles away, this is a major problem."

The demands of the aging parent may be minimal—merely a request that we be more available or supportive—or they may be as extreme as Kitty's and the tyranny of helplessness. But it is all so unexpected and it is not easy, certainly. There is guilt on both sides of the generation gap. And there is no small amount of anger and resentment on the part of the children, who thought they could finally see the light in their own careers, their own dreams of relaxation and recreation, only to find themselves confronted by the new demands of their parents.

There is an interesting sidelight to all of this. Many feel that, except for the small percentage of very real physical or chronic problems, it is quite possible that, in many instances and within the normal cycle of the aging process, it is *we, the children, who help create the situation in which the parents become dependent upon us.*

The physical changes of aging are almost predictable. There are changes in hearing—it took my father almost ten years to admit that a hearing aid might help. And Sheryl, quite recently, has told me that "you play the radio too loudly." Our eyesight certainly does not improve with age—how many of us will read this book while wearing glasses? Or, if you cannot admit that you really *need* glasses now, how far from your eyes are you holding the page? When the arm length is outstripped by the blurring of the words, you will finally admit that something must be done!

There is a slowing down of many life processes as we age—we don't move quite so quickly, we breathe more rapidly with minor physical exertion, we become more deliberate in our movements. The children watch all of this anxiously and are all too ready to rush in, to intervene in what should be considered a normal process.

The slight case of forgetfulness, passed over when it occurs in youngsters, becomes cause for worry about creeping senility in our parents (or ourselves). We are so quick to use the word. I do it myself. Senility. More accurately, senile dementia or *Alzheimer's* disease, named for the doctor who isolated it. It is part of another damaging myth that creates unnecessary anxiety and anguish. "I believe more people fear senility, fear growing old and losing their minds and being put away than fear cancer," said Dr. Robert Butler, who is currently Brookdale Professor of Geriatrics and Adult Development at Mt. Sinai Medical Center. It is just this fear that creates our own foreboding as we see our aging parents become more forgetful, and we too rapidly step in to "help." Likewise, our doctors are too quick to diagnose a condition that might well be caused by a vast array of other factors.

Only a minority of the very old show signs of forgetfulness and confusion, often the harmless and normal effects of the body's slowing down. For others, it can be caused by the stress of retirement; loss of income; bereavement; depression; diseases of the heart, thyroid, or lungs; liver infections; nutritional deficiency; or the cocktail mix of drugs given too freely to control the aging mind and body.

Even discounting illness and imagined disorders, we are too quick to interfere with the agenda and the independence of our parents' lives, just as our children try to do with us. Think of our response when one of our parents, perhaps widowed for ten or more years, decides to remarry at the age of seventy-five or eighty! A thousand reactions and emotional depths are suddenly thrust upon us, the middle-aged children. I have observed resentment and jealousy, feelings of loss, anger at financial arrangements, and discomfort at the reemergence of romantic and sexual activity. I have even heard this phenomenon described by one woman as a "traumatic nightmare!"

Yet it is just this kind of *independence* that the aging parent so desperately needs. It is the continued functioning of parents on their own that helps maintain their strengths and their abilities, making them less dependent upon their children. "Most people can be helped with occasional intervention in their lives," Dr. Cohen says, "Gerontologists are coming to see that "the independence of the parent, the continued functioning as much as possible on his or her own, is far better than putting them in a nursing home or moving them into the children's home. With occasional help, they may be able to continue functioning independently for a longer period of time."

Most of our parents need only occasional help. And, if there is no single solution for every family problem, there *is* one universal word to keep in mind—*independence*. We are, the author included, too quick to want to infantilize our parents the moment they show signs of aging or of needing a small amount of help in keeping their self-sufficiency and their dignity. At the same time that *we* resent being judged by our chronological ages, we begin to do the very same thing to them, knowing full well that there are people in their eighties and even their nineties who are active and mentally alert; who remain in the community as participating citizens until their deaths.

It is a good idea to step back and analyze what can be done and what *should* be done before rushing in and making a decision that requires them to move in with us or isolating them in a nursing facility. There are aging men and women who need only an occasional bit of help from a friend, a neighbor, or from us, and with that help they can remain active right where they live. Being in touch with *life* is a more effective solution than the isolation we sometimes decree for them. It is interesting to note, also, that more than five million people over the age of sixty-five—over 20 percent of that segment of the population—have no children, and yet most of that group are *not* institutionalized.

Senator Bill Bradley once commented, "Individuals placed in institutions suffer a variety of costs. They are uprooted from their homes; they are severed from normal contact with their family, friends, and community. They experience a serious loss of personal dignity and independence." The statistics vary. The Senate has found that between 10 and 20 percent of the 1.5 million Americans in nursing homes could live in their own homes if they had adequate help. The Gray Panthers consider the entire situation a scandal and claim that 40 *percent* of the people in nursing facilities are capable of being on their own, given some help from the community.

Some Suggestions: Where to Begin

What then, can be done? If your family situation is one in which your parents are still living but the need for help seems to be growing, it might be wise to investigate the assistance available right in your community before making any drastic decisions or feeling that the world is coming to an end. Having gone through much of it myself, I know the feelings of panic mixed with unease as one turns toward a vast maze of hoped-for solutions. It is quite possible that your parents will never have to live in your home. It is even more probable that you will never have to make the decision even to look at a nursing facility. It will take time. There will be frustrations and, frequently, you will feel that the search will never come to fruition. But, it can be done, and more and more avenues of help seem to be available for information.

A good place to begin is either the local bookstore or the public library, since some of the recommendations may well be out of print by now. I wish that many of them had been written before the years of our own family hardships, especially those that give listings of places to which someone can turn for help or advice. I particularly liked Dr. Cohen's excellent book *The Other Generation Gap* because he believes that a great part of the solution is in *understanding* the process of aging, as well as assessing our own emotional reactions to the new family problems of our generation. Most important of all, Dr. Cohen believes that there is much that we can do to prolong the independence of our parents, utilizing both our own efforts and the help given by community organizations such as Meals-on-Wheels and the visiting nurse services.

Beginning about 1975, many other books have been written on the very same subject, and from each of them there is something to be learned before you begin the long process of discussion with your family, the endless and frustrating telephone calls, and the probing that will eventually help you to find your own solution.

When Your Parents Grow Old, by Jane Otten and Florence D. Shelley (Funk & Wagnalls) is valuable as a basic resource book. In the beginning realization that a severe parental problem is arising, we need new ideas. The names of organizations have a tendency to blur into a meaningless alphabet, and what holds for one state or community may not be available in another. The book contains an appendix on "Where to Write" including Federal Government Programs, Consumer Information, Crime Prevention, Health, Housing (both city and rural), Legal and Financial Management, Nursing Home Information, and Volunteer Programs. A second appendix lists organizations to which you might turn for information and help, including National Organizations for Older People, National Health Organizations, Home Care, and Government Agencies on Aging for each state in the country.

A more recent book, *Older is Better* by Elizabeth Vierck (Acropolis Books

Ltd.) is one I would recommend for only one reason. The list
go for help are the subject of most of the book (the rest of w)
by as rather slight). State by state the author gives names and ⌐
almost every type of agency available with addresses and telephone nu⌐
bers—ranging from government agencies on aging to regional and local
commissions that deal with Human Services.

You and Your Aging Parent by Barbara Silverstone and Helen Kandel Hyman
(Pantheon Books) covers much the same psychological and emotional ground
as the others, including guilt, disruption, and facing up to the reality of the
situation. It explores what the authors call "the endless possibilities" that are
available to those aged sixty-five and over. For our parents, as well as for us,
they point out that by knowing the alternatives, there may be less to dread
these years. One appendix lists the state offices on aging plus informational
and referral services across the country. A second section gives addresses
under Homemaker-Home Health Aid Services, Family Service Agencies in
the United States and Canada, Volunteer Service Organizations, and Opportunities for Paid Employment.

There are others, certainly, and a quick look at the bookshelves will bear
out my comment that the subject is becoming more important to the middle-
aged child. Old People Are a Burden—but Not My Parents by Marcella Blakur-
Weiner is another. And, if your parents have begun to develop the chronic
diseases that often accompany the aging process, a book by Lawrence Galton
(Don't Give Up on an Aging Parent, New York: Crown) may give you a better
understanding of just what medical science has learned about everything from
arthritis to memory loss. Galton calls them the "so-called illnesses of the
aged" and is a great believer (along with me) that doctors practice what he
calls "condescension medicine"—what can you expect when the patient is
getting older?

There is yet another updated book that may well give you some ideas on
where to turn for advice. Handbook of Human Services for Older Persons by
Monica Blychowski Holmes and Douglas Holmes (Human Sciences Press,
233 Spring Street, New York, NY 10013) provides an overview of information
and referral services; multipurpose senior centers, homemaker and home
health agencies; legal, residential repair, employment, and day care services
as well as nursing home advocacy. It is more technical than the others and
each chapter has been written by a different author involved with social
welfare and community work, but it is listed here as still another resource that
may be of help to you.

In addition, today's magazines and even the television documentary programs have begun to concern themselves with the problems of middle-aged children with elderly parents. My files are crowded with new ideas, new approaches, new thinking—all designed to keep the elderly independent and active instead of being incarcerated in institutions. Even the corporations, believe it or not—at least, the more forward-looking ones—have begun to take notice. The most recent union contract negotiated with AT&T takes into account for the first time that employees who have family problems requiring that they be absent from work not be penalized. One of the agreements negotiated in 1989 is to allow unpaid leave of up to one year to care for ailing relatives, a similar arrangement for parental leave. During that time, the employee continues to receive certain benefits and is guaranteed his or her job upon return to the company. IBM, Travelers, and thirty-three other companies have set up hot lines over which employees can call for help and advice. The Gray Panthers have encouraged and pioneered intergenerational living, where young and old share living quarters. As a matter of fact, Maggie Kuhn shares just such a house in Philadelphia with younger people, most of them about the age of thirty. The occupants learn from one another and give mutual help in a group setting. The idea is spreading.

In California a small organization called Housing Alternatives for Seniors provides a "matchmaking" service for people like our parents who should no longer live alone, or who don't want to live by themselves after widowhood. Actually, the founders prefer to call it a service that finds "roommates," compatible partners for strong, elderly people who want companionship and who want to retain their independent life-styles.

In New York, a pilot program began recently that takes into consideration yet another problem. What happens if the middle-aged child is separated from the parent by a distance and thus cannot be available to give day-by-day assistance? It's run by the nonprofit social-care agency Selfhelp and it's called *Elderlink*. It fills a very needed gap for middle-class people, since there are still some publicly financed programs for the indigent, but absolutely none that we can turn to for aid and assistance. The costs are minimal and the group is available by telephone to the distant son or daughter, and their program includes visits by a geriatric social worker, evaluation of the problem, weekly check-in phone calls and a monthly consultation with the children. Although it's basically a New York service, a phone call (with no charge for the initial consultation) might give you some leads as to just where to turn. (1-800-435-7666—the last seven digits spelling HELP MOM.) It is possible that other programs across the country are also being developed to pursue this particular problem.

When it comes to the dread Alzheimer's disease, a great many things have taken place across the country in the past ten years. Support groups have been formed in almost every state to help us distinguish between the actuality of Alzheimer's disease and the myths about senile dementia. There are programs at the Andrus Gerontology Center in California, at Duke University, in Seattle, Denver, and New York. The most important contribution, I think, is that the organization is now national with a central telephone request line, and it deals with the actual disease rather than the folklore that has made us think of it as a natural consequence of aging. It's called *Alzheimer's Disease and Related Disorders Association* and you can find it in your local telephone book if you live in a major city, or you can call them for information about the nearest support group in your area: 1-800-621-0379 (In Illinois, call 1-800-572-6037). Information is also readily available about diagnosing the disease properly, services that you may need if your parent has the disease, memory, and aging, and most important of all, the support groups you will certainly need if the diagnosis is a positive one.

- AARP offers a booklet, *Coping and Caring: Living with Alzheimer's Disease* (D-12441), which includes a resource guide. (1909 K Street, N.W., Washington, DC 20049)

- The National Institute on Aging published several free brochures on the subject. Write: NIA, 2209 Distribution Circle, Silver Spring, MD 20910.

- You might read the book *The 36 Hour Day* by Nancy L. Mace and Peter Rabins (Johns Hopkins University Press), which describes the aspects of the disease, and gives advice on caring for persons with Alzheimer's. Also available from ADRDA.

- A recent book on the subject (1989) is called *When Your Loved One Has Alzheimer's: A Caregiver's Guide.* Written by David L. Carroll (Harper & Row), it covers an understanding of Alzheimer's, practical home care, coping and getting help.

- Also new and especially helpful is *Alzheimer's Disease: A Practical Guide for Those Who Help Others* by Judah L. Ronch (New York: Continuum), which is filled with sensitive insights into dealing with one's feelings as well as with illustrative examples and practical advice for choosing the most appropriate care.

There are also programs designed to help the children of parents who have had to move in with them by giving them a day off or a weekend away from the emotional and physical burdens. Programs that provide transportation for the elderly to the clinic or the doctor. Programs for mutual support. Programs for recreational activities. A national program administered by ACTION provides about seven hundred local offices throughout the country with about 300,000 volunteers who serve in community agencies and organizations. It's called *RSVP*, Retired Senior Volunteer Program and it has a dual purpose; it helps to enrich the lives of older people by giving them the satisfaction of helping others and it also helps local agencies to meet the needs of their communities. (ACTION, 806 Connecticut Avenue, N.W., Washington, DC 20525)

There are more, so many more, which can and do help, and if your problem is an extreme one and there is no other way but to find a nursing facility for your aging parent, many of the organizations I've listed above can give you the proper information so that you can ask the right questions when the time comes. At this point in my life, I suppose I might say, "I wish I had known" about all of this. But that would be twenty-twenty hindsight. One day, while sitting and discussing all of this in retrospect with Sheryl, I spoke of the research that I had done, of the groups and organizations that I had found, the people to whom I had spoken, the feeling that there was, indeed, help available to my brothers and sisters before that awful decision to place someone in a nursing facility has to be met, if it has to be met at all. And she asked, "If you had known all this during those years, would you still have insisted upon the solution of a nursing home?"

I might easily have answered, "Of course not!" But I must honestly say that I do not know. Though I *think* that I am now enlightened, it is difficult for me to go back to those days of depression and anguish and the tensions in our marriage created by the degenerating, incontinent patient, even though my wife was the one who bore the responsibilities. One of the books I mentioned earlier hit it right on the head with the title *The 36 Hour Day!* And, most of the people I have known who finally decided to place their parents in a nursing facility have lived for the rest of their lives with guilt and a feeling of having let their parents down when they needed them most. Possibly that would have been my emotional heritage too. I cannot answer it now.

Thus, if you and your family should make the very personal, very emotional decision to look for a nursing home, numerous publications are available to you. The National Retired Teachers Association, the Gray Panthers, and the organizations for the aged have all written pamphlets about evaluating and selecting a nursing home. The American Healthcare Association (1201 L Street, N.W. Washington, DC 20005) offers a free booklet, *Thinking about a Nursing Home?* and it includes good information about what to look for.

A fairly new concept is also available to middle-aged children of aging parents: *respite care*. It provides temporary nursing home care for children who must, for some reason, find a place for their parents while they are away on business or vacation, or through their own illness. It is not an easy place to find, for only a few facilities offer residential respite care. Short-term stays range from just a few days to several weeks, and you'll have to book the facility well in advance. A list of nursing homes that provide respite care is available (for eight dollars at the time of this writing) from American Association of Homes for the Aging, 1129 20th Street, N.W. Washington, DC 20036.

The problem I've discussed in this chapter is not, by any means, a hopeless one. We tend to forget that so very many of our parents are still quite active in their seventies and eighties and beyond. I see them all in my own little community as well as on the streets of New York. The neighbor's eighty-year-old grandfather, just out of the hospital after a gall-bladder operation and on his bicycle the very next day! The seventy-year-old parachute jumper. The surf fishermen who stand beside me in the ocean in the autumn, some of them in their mideighties, all of them outfishing me, a mere stripling of a lad. As we resent being made "old" before our time, so do they. And as the physical strengths begin to disappear gradually, our support is so very much needed *before* we scream "senility," and "put them in a nursing home!" I speak as much for myself as I do for (and to) you. I have not proven, after all, to be a paragon of clearheadedness and logic.

Summing up is difficult, to say the least, because each family's personality, each situation, is so different from mine or those of my (or your) friends and neighbors. The Colonial Penn Group asked Dr. Cohen to condense his thinking and his advice. In a booklet called *Bridging the Other Generation Gap* (available free from Colonial Penn Group, Inc., 5 Penn Center Plaza, Philadelphia, PA 19181), he concludes with some points to remember and I reprint them here with permission:

If You Are an Older Parent:

- Remain as independent as you can.

- Keep active and involved with others. Remember, use it or lose it.

- Your children are adults—don't try to take over their lives.

- Worrying brings you little—talk over your concerns with your children or a close friend.

- Your children are not the only ones able to help you manage.

- Getting help from a social worker or counselor is a sign of strength, not weakness.

If You Are a Middle-Aged Child:

- Encourage your parents to remain as independent as possible.

- "Doing it" for your parents can make them dependent—help them to do it for themselves.

- Your parents are adults—don't expect to change them to suit you.

- More open discussion of problems with your parents can usually relieve the tension that comes from not knowing what the trouble is.

- Other relatives and friends may be more than pleased to help out with your parents.

- More and more professionals are available to help you and your parents. Use them.

There is another thing to keep in mind, if you will. The "view from there" may be quite different from the "view from here." What is it like for *our parents* to look back at us from their point of view? What is their reaction if we rush in too quickly to help when no help is asked for or, on the other hand, when we are not there quickly enough when they feel they need us? Their answers can sometimes surprise us, even make us laugh if we listen.

Before you sadly consider the advice from Proverbs 23:22—"Despise not thy mother when she is old"—you might listen first to a part of a letter that appeared in an ad for the Colonial Penn Group. A California woman might well have been answering for many of our own parents. "The real shocker in aging," she wrote, "is seeing one's darling babies tottering around as white-thatched old codgers. I'm eighty-eight and I feel exactly the same as I felt at eighteen. *It's my darned children that depress me!*"

16 ✹ "Help! I'm a Prisoner in Paradise!"

Two weeks is about the ideal length of time to retire.

—Dr. Alex Comfort

My father had worked since he was eleven years old—and for seventy-two years more he knew nothing *but* hard work. As a young man of seventeen, part of an immigrant family living on New York's Lower East Side, he supported his mother, stepfather, and their assorted progeny by becoming a professional boxer at five dollars a fight (fifteen dollars for the main event). He slept on three wooden kitchen chairs pulled together for the night on the fifth floor of a walk-up tenement on Rivington Street.

It was expected—a natural period in the process of growing up—and he never spoke of it in later years. In fact, I only knew of his early career when I happened to read a sports column written by Jimmy Cannon, in which he longed for the early days of the superb clubhouse fighters. There, among the list of names, was that of my father. He had been known as "Kid" London!

Through seven decades he knew very little but his work and the support of a family. During the Depression, I remember that we saw little of him as he struggled with a tiny garment-manufacturing business for eighteen to twenty hours a day, still managing to send us to the mountains during the summer to get us away from the city heat, while he stayed behind to keep the struggling business afloat.

Even when the economic situation eased somewhat, and he was a respected and well-paid production manager in the garment trade, he knew very little but work. For a while he owned a dude ranch and, when he went there on weekends, he rode and played as hard as he had worked during the week. At the age of seventy-five, he was still entering 4-H club horseback-riding contests, while complaining of the indignity of having to be helped into the saddle!

When he was eighty-three, he finally retired, forced to slow down by the natural onset of physical aging. It must have been a terribly difficult, though necessary, decision. He had remained fairly active almost until the time he decided to retire. He had walked the twenty blocks to work, had communed with the retired executives, the hangers-on, and the drifters who sat in Washington Square Park, had frequented the restaurants that dot the city, and then suddenly decided that the cold weather, the gradual loss of hearing, and the muscles that no longer obeyed as quickly as they once did had forced him to make the ultimate decision. He and my stepmother moved down to where the palm trees wave in a tropical sun, where oranges and avocados, mangoes and lemons were outside the door for the picking, and where the seductive blue water of the swimming pool flickered just a few steps from the living-room door.

It would be an understatement to say that my father was miserable. The air in south Florida is often dripping with humidity; the house they purchased, with the fruit trees outside, was isolated, and neither my father nor my stepmother could drive a car. The swimming pool was covered with falling leaves and was constantly in need of care. And the man who worked only at work all of his life had no other real interests. The motor was idling. But his sense of humor and his quick mind were still with him. When I once telephoned to ask how he was doing, I could hear a plaintive wail come back over the long-distance lines, *"Help! I'm a prisoner in Paradise!"* At the age of eighty-six, he died as a result of the automobile accident of which I spoke earlier.

For a great many years, and even to this day, I keep saying that I will never retire. But that's what my father said, and at this stage in my life, I have also heard it from many friends, all of whom have said exactly the same thing: I will *never* retire. And now, they are retired. We are bombarded by the word. We hear it and see it every day. The radio plays the commercial for a large brokerage concern: "Thank you, Paine Webber, I've never been thrifty. Thank you, Paine Webber, I'm retired at fifty." I mutter, "poor guy," and go back to my writing. Their latest commercials hit retirement from yet another angle: they will help me plan for retirement whether I am twenty years away or just ready to call it quits tomorrow. Just call for a free consultation with a "financial advisor" (the current euphemism for a broker) and everything will be hunky-dory. (*Our* word for OK.)

The newspaper communicates its own urging and promises to all of us in full-page ads that offer me retirement villages as well as special discounts on the airlines and with the car rental agencies, reminding me that "It makes you glad you're fifty-five" (or sixty-five). Perhaps it is just that, as we enter the middle years and beyond, we begin to see the word *retire* more often because it means more to us at this particular time. Perhaps it was there all the time, but it was just passing us by. The Golden Years. The Leisure Years. Sitting back on our asses and reaping all the rewards to which we are entitled. Isolated in age-segregated societies "with dawn-to-dusk roving patrols, that assure you peace of mind," making certain that nothing gets in, or possibly that we don't get out. That, for a long time, has been my own hostile view.

But, there is another side, and my thinking has changed somewhat over these past two years particularly. Many people want to retire, actually want to relocate, possibly to end their work lives once and for all, or perhaps to begin a second career during midlife. A large proportion of our population is now choosing to retire at ages as early as fifty or fifty-five. For some it is normal, a looked-for, expected event, and surveys have shown that up to 70 percent are perfectly content with their retirement lives *if proper planning takes place* in the preretirement years! The figure was confirmed just recently in a study conducted by George Washington University, covering more than six thousand union members. About one out of four felt that they had retired too early. However, even in that group there were those who were still quite happy with the fact that they had retired, with only 12 percent who were unhappy if they were financially better off after retirement. (Rising, without surprise to 40 percent of those who were worse off financially.) But, here, as in every study on the subject, the warning to those who are even thinking of the major move, was "be ready and be sure!"

One of the funniest commentaries on the subject came from the *New York Observer* columnist George Lefferts, who suddenly decided to retire, moved south to warmer weather, went through ten days of discovering that it was not for him and then gave it up, returning to New York where, "I'm worried, anxious, overworked and feeling lousy. But I'm back in my own world, and enjoying a strange, perverse sense of peace." This, too, can happen.

Along with the enlightened social programs (now under attack from so many legislative directions), there came a societal expectation of planned obsolescence, very much as with electric appliances. Ready or not, we are expected to retire. It is taken for granted that we are suddenly unable to assume the same responsibilities, function as efficiently in the workplace or within the family unit, or keep our places in the "real" world of active, vital human beings as we did for so many years. Even the synonyms for this vaunted, supposedly idyllic "afterlife" give the lie to the broken promises of society. My favorite desk book, *The Synonym Finder* (Emmaus, PA: J. I. Rodale, Rodale Press) is a treasure trove of depressing words to describe the state of retirement: *withdrawal, removal, retreat, departure, shelved, rejected, castaway, discarded.* Then my eye is drawn to the words used for machinery, *throw out, scrap, junk, abandon use of, withdraw from service, disuse!*

Maggie Kuhn puts it well, as always: "We've been brain-damaged by a society that believes old age is a disease. When we turn sixty-five, we're trashed. . . . When I travel to my home from the airport in Philadelphia, I pass a junkyard where old cars are left to rust on a heap and then they're finally smashed by a society that wants everything shiny and new. America does the same thing to people."

For centuries American corporations have been the handmaidens of the idea of retirement, holding out the inviting picture of a life of leisure amidst sun-drenched horizons—demanding in return, for thirty years or more, the corporate attributes of conformity, productivity, performance (known as the bottom line), and subordination of personal life to the corporation's needs. Today, the problem is even worse, for if you remember my friend's description of the corporation as an economic machine, this time of great leveraged buyouts by corporate raiders has added to the problem of employee insecurity and potential forced retirement or job termination.

Immediately following the process of acquisition, and saddled with a huge, almost insurmountable debt, the first act of the new management is "to reduce the workforce"—in other words, to *fire* those who are excess and standing in the way of "progress." Other companies, after having moved their workforce to places like Houston, find later on that the market in oil, for example, has disappeared, and it strands the relocated families in a place where they cannot sell their homes, where their dreams have been shattered, and where their lives are destroyed both emotionally and financially. So much, then, for blind faith in corporate benevolence. If a company hurts, employees will suffer.

And still there is another factor. In spite of the fact that older workers have consistently been found to be among the most productive, the most talented, reliable, and adaptable, not to mention among the most loyal, millions of us have been forced into another type of unemployment, this one dictated by the calendar. For, make no mistake about it, as Alex Comfort so rightly declares, retirement is nothing more than unemployment and those of us who are unprepared for it will suffer the consequences just as surely as do minority teenagers who *want* to work but who find all doors closed to them.

Of course, I have seen situations in which I would be most anxious to retire—and to do it as quickly and as early as possible. Had I been unfortunate enough to be working for 30 years in the most impossible conditions of some of America's factories, I would be the first one out the door on my fifty-fifth birthday (or earlier if they would let me escape even sooner). The aluminum and steel industries, for example, boast assembly lines where the heat rises to over 150° F and the outside temperature of a summer day in Chicago seems cool at 95! Workers change shifts at the machines every twenty minutes and, in one aluminum plant where they recycle scrap, the lens cap on our camera melted as we were photographing the molten metal being poured into ingots!

The closed, noisy, dust-ridden cotton mills of the South, the dangerous working conditions of so many assembly lines, such as in the meat-packing industry, the lethal dangers of the chemical and asbestos industries would make me *run* toward retirement to escape from a world that paid me well but made me hate my job. Any alternative would be better than the job situations I've described, even sitting in front of a television set, beer in hand, letting my mind and my aching body slowly disintegrate.

This unhappiness, this unease, this dissatisfaction with the routine of our jobs even spills over into the white-collar and the executive areas of the corporate and government world. And, more and more of us are changing our lives in the direction of careers that are quite different from a computerized, impersonal world in finance, management, and material—meaningless consumerism. I shall have much more to say about that later on. Indeed, I have devoted an entire chapter to this phenomenon.

For a great many of us, however, the notion of leisure holds little meaning, especially if it is translated into doing nothing. There are millions of us who do not want to retire, either forcibly or voluntarily. There are many of us who will retire *only* to begin the new, second careers of which I've spoken. In the Harris study on aging it was found that the notion of leisure actually has less relevance among older people than it does among the young in our country; that retirement has more appeal for the young than for the middle-aged and old! It is no surprise to find out that most of us *want* to remain active, in spite of the societal myth that retirement means almost-total withdrawal from life.

Thus, in a time when one trend seems to indicate that more and more of us are deciding on early retirement, an opposite trend is taking us toward even later retirement than before, and both options exist side by side even though they seem to conflict philosophically.

In the first place, some of us who had planned to retire at an early age have found that the increased rate of inflation will not allow us the choice. Some corporate pension plans have just not kept pace with the cost of living, though Social Security and the governmental pension plans have built-in escalators based upon the inflation rate. But even some of us who feel that the nest egg is sufficient to allow us to stop working or to change direction are very much aware of the hazards inherent in the soaring costs of medical and hospital care; the future threatens to make these costs an impossible financial burden for those of us who live on a fixed income. It is even affecting the thinking of the younger generations, and there is a projection that many of the workers in the thirty-five-to-forty age group today may have to think of retirement no earlier than age seventy or seventy-five if they hope to live comfortably!

The trend toward later retirement has a minimally positive side. In 1986, the new age-discrimination law went into effect. It dictates that a worker cannot be retired forcibly until the age of seventy. However, it exempts tenured college professors, police officers and firefighters, and executives in policy-making positions who have held their positions for two years and who can retire on a pension of not less than $44,000. I use the word *minimally* quite deliberately, for the act does nothing, really, to prevent the corporations from *hiring* people over fifty or fifty-five who have lost their jobs through attrition or through leveraged buyouts. Though the company cannot *legally* use the excuse of age, there are thousands of other ways of making excuses for doing just that.

Some of America's companies are, however, slowly finding out what we have known for too long: that older workers are a great, untapped repository of know-how and experience. Our health is much better than it has ever been and we actually have better attendance and work records than our younger counterparts. But still another factor has made the companies more aware of just how valuable we are and has made them more receptive to delaying the retirement of older workers. The declining birth rate has made fewer and fewer younger workers available and ready to move up to positions of supervision and management. The corporate world is, first of all, a pragmatic one, and however youth-oriented it is, empty places on the corporate ladder mean less productivity. So, it is just possible that we are slowly being rediscovered. Overall, though, the record has not been a good one.

Certainly, there *are* times that Federal law provides some recourse for the worker. Standard Oil of California, for example, decided to reduce its work force and laid off 160 employees, all selected on the basis of age. Through a Federal suit, the company was forced to rehire 120 workers and pay almost $2 million in back pay, with reinstatement of pension and stock-purchase-plan benefits as well as insurance coverage.

Some years ago Greyhound Bus Lines made the statement that the human body begins to degenerate after the age of thirty-five (right in line with the *Esquire* article I mentioned earlier!). They began to retire their drivers in their fifties. However, because of the laws against discrimination in aging, they lost their case when the Labor Department proved that they had superb drivers who were over the age of sixty.

However, in another case, it was the government that contended that sixty was the magic age of physical dissolution, when the Federal Aviation Administration instituted mandatory retirement for commercial pilots at that age. As one pilot observed in a protest held in Washington, "One day you're fifty-nine and you're up there flying, and the next day you're out." The ruling is particularly ironic, since it was reaffirmed in 1989, and an interesting incident took place that one would think would make the FAA sit up and take notice.

If you remember, an airliner flying over Hawaii had a large section of its top fuselage blown away while in the air. Through incredible skill, the pilot brought the plane to a safe landing, and comments later on attested to the fact that it was only through his years of experience as a captain that the pilot could possibly have managed to prevent the plane from crashing. The captain was fifty-nine, one week away from forced retirement!

The entire problem has been studied by a variety of panels, and one made up of physicians concluded that there is "no special significance" to the age of sixty as a mandatory retirement standard. In fact, they strongly recommended that greater emphasis be placed on determining the ability of individual pilots to meet medical criteria for flying commercial jets, rather than on an arbitrary age. Another newspaper article, published right after the survey, made me smile again. It spoke of a man named Russell Green who had always had an interest in flying but just never could get around to it until later in life. He took his oral and flight tests with the FAA and passed. He now has behind him over two hundred solo flights in gliders. He's eighty-three years of age!

This whole subject of retirement is but another example of how preposterous it is to attempt to put an entire generation into a neat package of predictability. Some of us want to retire and some of us already have, and many of us will be dragged screaming into this vague mixture of stereotypes, myths, distortions, dreams, fantasies, fears, anticipations, and sudden discoveries of new realities when we finally do surrender.

My first experiences with retirees came when I roamed the shopping centers and the parking malls of Florida and Arizona and California about fifteen or twenty years ago. I spoke with the men and women who had settled there—some of them with dreams, some with resignation, some with the anticipation of finally doing what they had wanted to do and had worked hard to achieve. Depending upon the expectations and the acceptance of reality, these places are either anterooms to the grave or doorways to euphoria and castles in the air.

I remember meeting a man while standing in line in a department store in Miami. His first words were, "Are you retired?" I answered that I was not, and we went out to a shopping mall coffee shop to talk. He had owned his own company, and had sold it, had just retired a few months before. The realities were beginning to settle in.

"When I gave up my office, I gave up my throne," he told me. He was not unusual. The feeling of having somewhere to go, something structured to do, was gone and the adjustments were still taking place slowly but unmistakably. The office "perks" were still clearly recalled and "when I had to pay for the first tankful of gas, it nearly killed me!"

In the supermarkets the *couples* shop together, rather than the women alone who did the marketing while the husband played king in the office. Retirement, for both men and women, is suddenly finding a new face around all the time. The headline of a recent *New York Times* article summed it up succinctly: "In Sickness and in Health: But in Retirement?" The person who showed up for dinner only occasionally is now always there at dinnertime—and at breakfast and lunch too! People who barely saw each other are now living together twenty-four hours a day. And, what if the *wife* continues to work while the husband retires? Too much spare time hangs heavily and too many retirees feel like displaced persons, seeing the world much differently from the way they had expected to see it; certain that every minor ache is the first sign of disability or chronic disease. There is a disenchantment, the pinch of inflation, the children who visit too seldom or who make their duty-bound annual visit around Christmas. Gary Lee, a gerontologist and sociology professor at the University of Florida has commented that retirement may not add anything to a marriage and certainly won't improve a bad one, and that "for an event that is supposed to be a real change, retirement has surprisingly few and surprisingly weak effects. Basically, people are the same folks they were before they retired. They're just not working."

In my talks with Gerry Hotchkiss, publisher of *New Choices* magazine, he put it well:

> This is my personal observation—the CEO is the *least* equipped to retire. He has all the power and the glory. He is the one who is going to lose. Money isn't the real issue here. But power is the real issue. When he retires, he loses that power. Your secretary has done all the work. You become like a little child. In a sense you've had all these things done for you. Getting your stamps. Xeroxing a piece of paper. All of the little things that you take for granted. And now you have to do them yourself.

On the other hand Dr. Maxwell Jones in his book deals to a great extent with retirement. His title *Growing Old* is optimistically subtitled: *The Ultimate Freedom* (Human Sciences Press). And so, the overview and the reactions, as with everything else in our lives, are personal and very subjective. Some people are ecstatic about retirement and they remain that way through the subsequent years.

"Are there happy retirees?" Maggie Kuhn answers, "Yes I think there are. First of all, they have an income that is sufficient to offset the ravages of inflation. Also, they've had enough in their own past experience to enable them to define their goals and start again. Some people see old age as an extension of what they have been doing before, rather than a freedom, a new beginning for new roles, and a liberated kind of spirit of adventure and risk taking. It's an opportunity to rebuild and to try something entirely new." Maggie's last statement took on new meaning for me a few years later, when I began to investigate planned communities and the people who live and who work in them, and I have thus added an entirely new section to this chapter a bit later on, in order to pass on just what I found and my feelings about "new beginnings."

When we interview retirees about their past, they generally say that the most important thing the job brought them, next to the income, was the work itself, the feeling of being useful, and the activity that took place around them for at least eight hours a day. For some executives bordering on the workaholic, the *only* thing that satisfied them was their involvement with work—up to sixteen hours each and every day, weekends included.

When people do retire, the Harris study found, most do not want to be excluded from the world around them, nor limited to communities made up exclusively of people their own age. Reading those studies, sensitive developers have begun to build mixed-age communities rather than the traditional "retirement" pastures. Of as much interest are the figures dealing with what retired people feel are the most important steps to take in preparing for our later years:

- 88 percent consider it very important to have medical care available.

- 81 percent, to prepare a will.

- 80 percent, to build up savings.

- 80 percent, to learn about and investigate pensions and Social Security benefits.

- 70 percent, to buy one's own home.

- 64 percent, to develop leisure-time activities.

- 50 percent, to decide whether to move or continue to live in the same area.

- 31 percent, to plan a new part-time or full-time job.

One of the best series of preretirement and retirement pamphlets is published by the American Association of Retired Persons (1909 "K" Street, N.W. Washington, DC 20049) and is available for a small annual membership fee. They cover finance, income taxes, tips on retirement, health and insurance programs, housing, age discrimination, community service, widowhood and nutrition, and much, much more, with the list growing every year. They may start you thinking about all the areas that may become more important to you in the coming years. They may, indeed, help avoid what sociologists sometimes call "retirement shock."

We have to assume that if there is a spouse or a very special companion, that the both of you are very compatible. Don't discount the potential conflicts and readjustments when the retiree suddenly appears permanently in someone else's "space."

Dr. Erdman Palmore, professor of medical sociology at the Center for the Study of Aging and Development at Duke University, even recommends that you take a month off for a "trial retirement" in order to learn to develop new routines and work out the new territorial claims with your spouse or companion.

If you're working at a large corporation, you may find that counseling is available for preretirement employees, not only in financial matters, but also in planning medical coverage and handling the social and emotional problems that may arise. Some community colleges and schools of continuing education are also offering retirement counseling programs.

Possibly one of the greatest pitfalls in retirement is that of holding a totally unrealistic and unprepared view of just what is to take place, knowing full well that in any life-style situation there are going to be surprises. For example, too many people have found that the very same problems that dogged them in "real life" are now being met in their retirement communities—mainly due to improper or incomplete investigation of the move. The "Paradise" of my father may well carry with it exactly the same difficulties and problems that might confront him in Detroit or Omaha or Boston.

And yet, as Maggie asks rhetorically, "Are there happy retirees?" And, as I have tried to answer with some few examples of friends of mine, "Of course there are!" And generally, they are the people who have planned, who have other untapped interests, who know as best they can just what the future will hold for them.

It might be well for *you* to make a list of all the things that have interested you these forty or fifty or sixty years, aside from the work world and to begin thinking about just what it is you really want to do with your life when retirement hits or you decide to take the step. It could well prevent the story that my friend and accountant, Dave Ribet, tells of a telephone call he received from a friend who had retired to Florida. Exasperated, frustrated, and irritated, the man exploded on the telephone with, "Good God, Dave! How many sprinklers can I fix? How many rounds of golf can I play? How many times can I have coffee with the boys? I must come back to New York to have some *aggravation!*"

Retirement and Relocation: Another View

I suppose that, being a curmudgeon, and a confirmed New Yorker at that (a redundancy if I ever saw one), I had some very rigid views about retirement, and especially about the trauma of possible relocation to another state, another community. Influenced by the advertising in newspapers and magazines, lured by the headlines that promised Utopia in leisure worlds and golden-age villages, I had a fairly limited view of just what they really were like, and certainly of the vast variety that is available to someone who might well *want* either to retire and change location, or to retire, change location *and* career when well into middle-age. What I did not realize at the time, however, was that some forward-looking developers had begun to take into consideration the people who had feelings such as mine; for example, the desire and the need to remain with people of all age groups and to continue to lead a rich and productive life if I so chose. Indeed, there were some who were actually encouraging me to move my entire *business* to another state and to continue living my active life for as many years as I wanted to—and that my health allowed me to.

About three years ago, well after I had decided to make a very important change in my own career at midlife, and about which I shall expand upon in chapter 18, I was contacted by the people of ITT Community Development Corporation, which is developing a very large planned community in northern Florida. Having learned of my writing about midlife, they thought that I might well be interested in becoming a consultant to the Palm Coast Development on just the subjects about which I had written: retirement and relocation. We talked, but I had no idea of just what kind of community was being developed down there, between Daytona Beach and St. Augustine. And what I expected to find, I did not find—much to my pleasant surprise. On my first trip down to see if I really could and would become a consultant, and dependant upon my reaction to Palm Coast, I was startled to see people who were thirty and thirty-five years of age playing golf on the country club course. Somehow, I had never seen people so young living in a Florida community, nor had I ever expected to find them in a planned development! I found out later on that they actually worked there, in any number of the new industries that were springing up in the area.

I suppose that the second surprise was that I had always expected to find any planned community, especially in Florida, being made from a cookie cutter. Everything the same. A feeling of quiet nonactivity. And, certainly, everyone over sixty-five. Again, to my surprise, I found that this ITT unit was not only planning and developing a community the size of Washington, DC (or, to New Yorkers like us, the geographic size of several Manhattans), but was also developing several adjacent communities, each unique. Sea Colony, Matanzas Shores, and Hammock Dunes[sm] Private Community (Hammock Dunes[sm] is a service mark of ITT Community Development Corporation) all serve different needs, different budgets. But all, including the major undertaking, Palm Coast, are characterized by a basic environmental awareness—a concern about trees, water quality, birdlife—the qualities that make the best of Florida so attractive. The other quality I noticed was the diversity in age of the residents, in the variety of housing choices, in the options for work, shopping, medical care, golf, tennis, boating, fishing, surfing, cultural, and civic events. Not at all what I had imagined. And, I was impressed.

Did I become a consultant?

I became a consultant.

And it was then that my education was really to begin. In order to work with the ITT Community Development Corporation group and a wonderful man, Jerry Full, who was more of an environmentalist than I, no mean feat— and in order to write and produce a pamphlet that would eventually help people who were looking to relocate to any area outside their permanent homes, either for retirement or for recareering, I set out to learn more about planned communities, wide-eyed and bushy-tailed, as my grandmother used to say. And though I had already visited many of them in the Southwest and the West, including the famous planned community at Davis, California, my eyes were opened very wide by what I saw.

Sheryl and I took a ten-day auto trip in Florida, preceded by a visit to two of the most famous American planned communities—Columbia in Maryland, and Reston in Virginia. We played the role to the hilt; comfortable shoes or sandals, sports clothes that allowed comfort and freedom, camera around the neck, even a sailor hat to keep the hot sun off when we went from car to sales office. We were, of course, "relocating," we were "thinking of moving from New York" for various reasons: crime, crowding, filth, just change. We were authors who were looking for a place where "we might just settle down and write." We were potential buyers. We were tourists, and we visited every place we could think of from top to bottom, from east to west in Florida.

We spoke to salesmen and saleswomen. We looked at pure retirement communities like Sun City with its activities and trips geared only to us "older folk" whose kids had left home and might occasionally visit us once in a while when the weather got too cold up north. And, we visited planned communities that were still mostly undeveloped, but that "promised" a lush, exquisite, carefree life-style. Some had been in existence for twenty years or more. Others, believe it or not, merely had a golf course, clubhouse, tennis courts, ten or twenty homes and *signs* that boasted that these spots would eventually have a hotel or a supermarket or an industrial park.

We met hostesses, we met aggressive salespeople, we met some who claimed only "two pieces of property were left" even though all we could see were acres and acres of undeveloped scrub. We met salespeople who, knowing we were from New York, stressed the security aspects of their community, sometimes to a degree that frightened us and made us think that *their* crime problem must be much worse than that of our New York, drug-infested neighborhood!

We visited what seemed like every model home in the state of Florida and we learned very early on to "walk through" either the house or the plans given us and to re-create our daily life, in order to see if the house was adequate and would be perfect for our own individual life-style. We found model homes in which, in Sheryl's words, "every expense was spared" in the construction and the amenities. We learned to ask which items that were displayed were "options" and which were included in the price that was quoted. We also found many that were decorated in overdone baroque, but had mouldings that did not meet at the corners. In one model home we "walked through" and got to the kitchen. We opened the refrigerator door only to find that it would not open wide. A floor cabinet had been built in the way. In others we found the most exquisite contemporary appliances. And we met a large range of people, visitors like us, who were also "looking" for their ideal retirement or relocation home.

In short, we had a marvelous time. And, more importantly, we learned an awful lot about planned communities—and about which ones I might want to choose were I finally to relocate and where "we might just settle down and write."

Out of the trip came a booklet that I wrote with the Palm Coast people, *The Right Move*, which was then offered free on subsequent radio and television appearances (Palm Coast, ITT Community Development Corp., Palm Coast, FL 32051). I was amazed at the interest that listeners and viewers showed. Certainly, in places like Washington, DC, it was no surprise to me, for about one-third of the population of the city moves every single year (and especially in election years). But, the interest seemed to be as prevalent in Cleveland, New York, Boston, and Detroit as it was in Washington.

And so, I began to realize that the information about relocation, the tips about recareering, are not as available as I had once thought, and that my narrow view of places to retire or to relocate was, indeed, just that—parochial and really quite constricted. (Which, for any author to admit, must be a giant step forward!) There are not only different price levels, different age levels, different formats, but also different philosophies. There are, of course, a thousand different floor plans, all aiming at a different market segment.

And so, with the vast number of planned and unplanned communities available, what are some of the things that you might be looking for and what are the questions that you might be asking if you are one of the middle-aged or older readers who is planning a move? And, suppose you are thinking of also moving your business to another area, again for health or retirement or personal satisfaction reasons, how might you do it with some degree of intelligence and proper planning?

Of course, if you never plan to move, you might then skip right to chapter 17, where I talk about finances, and *everyone* is interested in that subject. Or, you might just stash the information away for some future time when you may well change your mind.

Choosing a Community

There are distinct advantages to the planned community concept, such as Palm Coast, since many of the infrastructure problems and the future blueprint of the community have usually been projected. Some, like Columbia in Maryland have grown substantially and have flourished. Others such as Reston have also grown, but have encountered many of the problems of that growth, such as a new major highway right through the middle of town on the way to Dulles Airport, an improvement in terms of the influx of taxable corporate property and, at the same time, a tremendous increase in the traffic through the area.

In *your* assessment of a community, one thing to keep in mind is the very real difference between a planned community such as Palm Coast, Columbia, or Reston. The latter prosper, generally, as alternative housing and business sites within *a metropolitan region,* such as Washington or Baltimore. Palm Coast, on the other hand, is largely self-sufficient, offering most of the jobs, the services, the recreation, and the housing—all the choices of a metropolitan area *right within its own borders.*

As you are deciding upon a place to which you might relocate, here are some other areas that might be of help in making your selection:

- A trip to the location is worthwhile. Stay at a hotel for a few days and walk around and ride around. Visit the local chamber of commerce and ask your questions.

- Read the local newspapers. They give you a very good idea of the quality of life in the area. If there is crime, you can be sure that the local paper will be printing the latest story. Look at the papers for the last year. You may be visiting during the only good month of weather. What is it like during the other months?

- Speak to people. The ones who live there are the people who can tell you what it's really like. But, try to speak with them at length in supermarkets, in parks, as they sit and enjoy the lake or the ocean. I found one woman in a community who told me how much she loved it, and about ten minutes later was expounding upon the teenage drug problem and how she never, never went down to that park after dusk!

- Read the bulletin boards in the community and get a copy of the local community newspaper or newsletter if there is one. You'll get a good idea of the activities that are available and just who runs them.

And, in the few days you spend there, here are some other questions that should be answered—and make sure they're answered to your satisfaction:

- Who is the developer? Is there a *master plan?*—take a look at it. What is the commitment of the developer to the infrastructure and the life-style of the community? Is there more than one developer? What is their history and background? Remember, the first person you'll probably be meeting is a *salesperson.* His or her job is to *sell.*

- Every developer will leave a community eventually and when that day occurs, how will the community be maintained? Who will pay for the upkeep and the new amenities as they are needed? How will the home-owners' association take care of the water supply, roads, sewage? Is that golf course, that tennis facility, that school in place now or promised for the future when the developer will be long gone?

- You will always be able to find out about taxes. Everyone is prepared for the question and gives the answer quite readily. But—what about *other* fees? I have found country club feels that range from free membership with purchase of land all the way up to an initiation fee of $17,000 plus yearly dues! On the other hand, there is generally a relationship between what you pay and what you get. On a golf course or a country club, cheaper fees often mean more members, harder-to-get tee times, more crowding. So, consider the trade-offs when you hear the costs.

- Does the community have light industry as a part of its planning—boat building, computer chips, etc.? The reason for asking is not only that *jobs* may be available as a result, but that the presence of industry helps to keep the tax base low. The classic case is that of Levittown on Long Island in New York State, where the planning included only residential areas. As a result, the tax base has climbed to a point equalled by exclusive resort communities. I found that at Palm Coast, for example, industrial parks are included in the Master Plan. As a result, property taxes there are among the lowest in the state.

• If you think as I do, you will want to find out if the various age groups are well represented, since the future may well depend upon the younger generations who are now moving into these communities. Are there schools—a sure sign that growth and vitality are factors?

• Is there housing diversity, so that a range of incomes are involved with the community and its growth and well being? You may want a $200,000 home, but if there are also $60,000 homes in the community then you're apt to find it much easier to attract teachers, police officers, and tradespeople. And, if you are looking for a $60,000 home, look to see if there are more expensive properties in the community, since they will insure the provision for public services when they demand them.

• What about shopping? Are there competing stores, rather than just one supermarket, where prices can then be controlled?

• The environment is a concern of mine—and, I assume, of yours. What is the commitment of the developer to that environment, in keeping sections green forever, in providing recreation, and other amenities for public use?

• Check on houses of worship, police and fire protection, recreation, and how close you are to other facilities—cultural and economic—and where major medical services are available, should you need them.

• One of the things that I learned to look for was the prevalence of *banks*. This may seem, at first, to be a strange observation, since I surely don't have enough money to worry about it. However, I have found that if *several* banks are in the community, it bodes well for the future. Banks just do not settle down in a town unless they have investigated the place and found it a potential growth area for business and for retirees.

On Moving Your Business

For many of us of middle age or older, there is a dream that just possibly we might be able to combine our own relocation with that of our business. There are times that I, too, daydream of doing all my writing on the Algarve in

Portugal, and just sending the manuscript to my editor by FAX. Perhaps some day. Perhaps not. In some cases, it is just not possible, of course, whereas for others the potential is very real and the move has been accomplished quite successfully.

While I was in Palm Coast, I looked carefully at the small and active industrial parks and I spoke with both residents and with John Gazzoli, an executive with ITT Community Development Corporation. I found—and he agreed—that most of the people who owned their own business down there were in their fifties, and many of them were also using the opportunity to involve their children along with them. John told me, "There are services that are lacking in some new areas, especially when they just begin to grow. The entrepreneur, wanting to start a new business, can often enlist his youngsters."

Indeed, some couples have brought their children down with them, getting them involved in the business as they move toward retirement, eventually planning to back out of it. John added, "In communities like ours, there are opportunities for a lot of businesses because not all of the niches have been filled. As a result, we see an influx of medical specialties, as well as a range of shops and services that have been started by retirees from up north, often employing not only their own children but also the semiretired residents here in Palm Coast."

I found someone who had opened the first veterinary service in the area; it was booming with the local pet population. Another opened the first card shop. And still another, looking at the industrial park, used his background as an ex-chef to begin a catering service directed to the small industries in the area and he took his children into the business with him. To me, the most amazing thing was the first view that I reported on earlier: the age range down there, much to my surprise.

John Gazzoli answered for me, "I don't think people realize it, but there's a tremendous attraction to bringing children and grandchildren with them when they move. The kids start visiting. They like it. The parents say, 'Well, what are you doing in New Jersey?' 'Well, I'm working as an accountant.' 'Why don't you come down here?' And the parents already have a base and if the kids can find a job, it expands just like a mushroom!"

Certainly, you have to investigate quite thoroughly before making a major move such as relocating not only yourself but your business. On your visit to the community, touch base with the people there who know of the need for services as population levels increase. For example, Palm Coast did not have any cleaners there a few years ago until a man came in to start one. There were no movie houses. No video stores. Each of them was started by someone who moved into the community and who realized that the population had reached a point at which each could be supported.

What about the negatives? What about warnings to the unwary? What about competition? I noted with interest that several new shopping centers were already springing up in the community and that all of them seemed to be busy. I asked John Gazzoli if he had any advice.

"The warning I give is that they have to make sure that the growth *is* going to happen so that the community is able to support whatever it is they're going to do. We try to put prospective business operators in touch with the new companies that have already been established in Palm Coast." His final advice was to check the master plan thoroughly to find out if the community is heading in the direction that will support the new business venture. "In other words, there's no point in opening an infant-ware shop if the development is aiming only at a very senior population."

So, just as if you are planning to retire, a move to relocate a business or start a new one also demands some tough questions, many of which you may have thought of. You'll want to know about land and building costs, labor costs, taxes, employee turnover and employee training, transportation costs, as well as possible state training programs that guarantee a supply of labor into the future. (Incidentally, that's a big business in Palm Coast. Whether you are thinking of relocating your business to Florida or to any other state, I might also recommend another booklet offered by Palm Coast, and I think you'll find it invaluable in your thinking and in providing questions that you might ask. It's called *The Bottom Line* and it's also offered free at the address that I gave a few pages back.

There are, of course, those of us who do not have a small business and who have decided to make that move at some future date, to change careers—many of them different from the ones in which we made our living right up to middle age—or for retirement with a desire to continue working. As I mentioned, I shall try to cover that large group in the chapter entitled, "What Do You Want to Be When You Grow Up?" There are different paths that you might want to follow.

And the Author: Does He Want to Retire?

Uh, no. Well, maybe no. Not yet. There are times when I go uptown in New York City and I am engulfed by the jungle of real-estate development run rampant, when people pour out of the buildings at the noon hour, or I am caught in a gridlock traffic jam while in a taxi and the meter runs faster than the latest, state-of-the-art IBM computer, and I think to myself that the answer must be "yes" or "maybe" and perhaps I should find that quiet place to write the world's next great novel.

And then I go to some new, incredibly good (and incredibly expensive) restaurant and I have a glass of wine, surrounded by the atmosphere of uncontrolled vitality, or I travel to some exciting location for my film work, and I realize at that point the answer is "no, not yet."

I try to look at where I am now, having passed my sixty-fifth birthday, and I cannot honestly answer the question of whether or not I will retire. Will I do all the things for which I've made lists all these years? I have never visited the Statue of Liberty, I am ashamed to admit, though it lies at the door of my city. There has been no time to go up to the Bronx Zoo to see the 150-pound baby elephant who was born there a short time ago (and is now, probably around 2,000 pounds!), no time to read some of the new books that pass me by in a frenzy of publishing mania, nor to reread some of my old favorites like *The Catcher in the Rye*. Indeed, no time to even read half the magazines that come in an avalanche each month, and yet I subscribe to more and more with each mailing that offers a bargain and a "new adventure in reading."

Somehow, though I can fully empathize with those of my brothers and sisters who *do* want to retire, I feel at this point in my life that I will continue to make lists that I cannot ever get to, jobs that I will never accomplish. I cannot see the end of my filmmaking, for I hope that I shall become even better as I age. And, with the new technologies of multimedia seven and ten screen presentations, there is so much new to learn and in which to become involved. I have books scheduled in my head for fifty years to come, including one that was born in four years of World War II and that I think is "different." I would like to do a novel, but I am still slightly wary of the challenge. Possibly I am too young to attempt it yet!

For my father, whose seed was responsible in part for creating my own neurotic, hypertensive personality, the years before his death were beginning to threaten. His Paradise was lost and, actually, was it ever there to begin with? But, until the very week of his death, he threatened to return, knowing full well that he would never do so.

For others it has been true Paradise. And for me, trying to project the future, I do not really know how I will feel in ten or twenty years—or tomorrow. Wherever I am for the moment is obviously the best place to be.

But will I retire eventually? Well, no. Uh, maybe. Maybe.

17 ✹ The Case of the Incredible Shrinking Dollar

Youth is the time of getting, middle age of improving, and old age of spending.

—Anne Bradstreet
"Thirty-Three Meditations"

A short time ago, on a film trip through California, our crew stopped for a quick, indescribably bad airport lunch while waiting for a connecting plane. Our assistant cameraman, about thirty years old, ordered his two hamburgers, French-fried potatoes, chocolate malt, and a dessert of fresh, out-of-season strawberries priced at around $3.50 for six plump, artificially grown fruit. Since he was obviously a fast-food aficionado, he devoured the first part of his lunch with gusto and then pulled the small bowl of strawberries toward him.

Tenderly, he lifted one red berry to his lips, took a single small bite, put it back in the bowl, and pushed the remainder away, untouched, in a single gesture of indifference. Curious, I asked him if they were spoiled or possibly tasteless. "Oh no," he answered, "that's all I really wanted." Our cameraman, Joe Longo, sensing my dismay at the waste, looked at me with a twinkle in his eye and silently mouthed the word, "Spoiled!" Being close to my age, Joe obviously understood exactly what was going through my head.

I am a child of the Great Depression, and I have never been able to shake completely the feelings that come with the memories of that distant time in our history. It is true that our family kept most of the anguish and despair from my brother and me. It is also true that later years more than made up for that struggle through the uniquely American experience that allowed an immigrant family to move into the middle class. As a child, I was only too aware that the times were formidable. My father had to work too many hours.

The urban reflections of the dust bowl and its gaunt, hungry farmers were seen in the faces of our city's apple sellers. I can still see my father's fearful expression when he ran from the house one morning to join the growing line at the shuttered neighborhood bank where a lifetime of savings had suddenly been sealed behind closed doors. I remember entire families being thrust out into the street, their furniture, their clothing, and their pathetically few other possessions piled on the sidewalk, even including the still-chirping pet canary, while the distraught mothers tried to comfort their bewildered children.

I cannot tolerate waste. Even the lettuce or parsley used as a garnish in most of America's restaurants, and left on the plate by almost all diners, to be thrown out, is a sin to me. I envision the farmer who grew the crop having nightmares as he contemplates the results of his efforts ending up as grist for a giant sanitation truck. Even today, I notice more and more young families who order huge amounts of food in restaurants, and leave much of what they ordered still filling the plates as they are removed by the waiter or waitress, the discarding of plenty in a too-affluent society, while the homeless and the hungry grow at an ever-increasing rate. The image of the young assistant cameraman and his strawberries keeps coming back to me.

So, in spite of the fact that I have joined the ranks of one of the most affluent of groups in American history, the insecurities of those early times remain with me, and I am convinced that everything in life is temporary. I wait, appearing to be secure, for the sword of Damocles to fall and take all away. My background asserts itself only too strongly in my reaction to watching the waste of food, the establishment of a pet boutique in a large department store chain that will be selling *tuxedos and wedding dresses for dogs*, and even the invention of throwaway items such as cameras and razors. It is something our children and our children's children will never understand.

It stands to reason, then, that someone like me—and I assume there are others who feel exactly the same way—would be concerned and terribly uneasy over the headlines that greet us each morning in the newspapers and magazines. If, as I stated in the previous chapter, my future as an older American is very much related to the financial structure that I am building as a person who has passed through middle age and is now entering the "magic" numbers decreed by Congress and Chancellor Bismarck, a promise is being threatened, and the threat seems to grow ever more serious year by year. We are being told that Social Security is in dire trouble. We are being told that it is not "fair" that some of us will be getting Social Security even if we have a private pension fund. We are being told that we—and you—who are next in line to depend upon this enlightened system of financial insurance, will probably find that the cupboard is bare! We are further warned by the Baby Boomers that *they* may not even have a cupboard at all.

For me, as for millions of others who are middle-aged and older, Social Security is an integral part of an overall plan that included private pension plans or an IRA (Individual Retirement Account) plus some small investments and insurance. If you take away any part of it, however small, our entire financial structure suffers. More important, perhaps, is that we are being fed a pack of myths and untruths about Social Security, and still more important, a trust and a pact that was made with us as much as forty or fifty years back is now in danger of having the rules changed. It has become difficult to plan the next twenty years or more without being constantly reminded of impending catastrophe. And, oh, how prevalent those reminders are!

It began as far back as the late seventies and early eighties. *Newsweek* magazine printed a cover story, "Can You Afford to Retire?" Other headlines compete for my attention, many of them on the first page of the newspapers, others on the op-ed pages or in the Letters to the Editor column, all of them bitching and complaining about the free ride that we are about to get:

"Turmoil in Pension Plans"
"The Crisis [*sic!*] in Social Security"
"Retiring at Age 65 a Receding Goal"
"Elderly Get Grim News for the Future"
"Social Security Should Benefit Only the Elderly Poor"

To top it all off, we have just completed a two-term administration that seemed to be totally insensitive to the needs, the fears, and the aspirations of so many millions of us, and we have been left a legacy of a Supreme Court that seems to be just as callous in the area of age discrimination. President Reagan set the tone when he made a TV address to the nation and stated, "I will not stand by and see those of you who are dependent upon Social Security deprived of your benefits. I make that pledge to you as your president. You have no reason to be frightened." And he continued to smile. Of course, only two days later, a White House spokesman stated that the president's pledge did *not* apply to those who were receiving the minimum benefit. I began to think that the president wasn't *smiling*, he was *laughing* at us.

His treasury secretary was asked at a meeting of New York financial writers just how he thought Social Security will be funded fifty years from now, and he replied, "I don't know. I'll be dead by then." As my grandmother used to say, "With friends like that you don't need enemies!"

The first signs in the George Bush administration seem to bode no better. Even though committed to "no new taxes," the president is firmly against doing very much about the Medicare "surcharge" levied against only one segment of the population—us.* Note, too, that if you call something a "surcharge" or a "supplement," it is no longer a "tax." And yet another trick of the last two administrations—this time in order to make them look good— was to include the Social Security fund in the general federal budget, thus making it look as if our astronomical deficit is smaller than it actually is. Here, too, we have been hoodwinked and lied to: the Social Security fund is a self-contained trust, and over the next seventy-five years, the projections indicate that we will maintain a surplus in the *trillions*, with enough time for the Baby Boomers to make arrangements for themselves.

What, then, are the reasons we are being given the warnings, told the scare stories, the words about "nothing to fear" while at the same time other words threaten the structure of an entire social system, even giving rise to organizations of the spoiled, mean-spirited young (such as Americans for Generational Equity), committed to taking away what is rightfully ours?

The Social Security Act, signed by President Frankin Delano Roosevelt in 1935, is one of the most outstanding pieces of social legislation in this century, providing dignity and a measure of security for more than 36 million working people. The statistics upon which it was based were viable and very practical.

For every thirty-five workers there was only one retiree, and the surplus grew large enough to expand the system to include additional trust funds for disability insurance, dependents and survivors, Medicare, and supplementary medical insurance. It was successful beyond the wildest dreams of Roosevelt and the Congress of 1935. It dramatically reduced the number of elderly poor to just about 15 percent as we enter this decade. It has provided a secure base for future financial planning for people in middle age, since it now also includes cost-of-living increases (COLA) at prescribed intervals. But now, we are being told, it has collided head-on with some sobering demographics.

They tell us that when it all began, thirty-five working people supported a single pensioner, and for the first twelve years or so, each worker was taxed

*An avalanche of mail has made Congress take a second look and either the surcharge will be reduced or the program discontinued or made voluntary.

only 1 percent on a maximum ceiling of $3,000 or $30 per year—small even by postdepression standards. As people began to live longer and retire earlier, the ratio plummeted and the burden was forced upon fewer and fewer workers. Today only three workers support the payments for each retiree, and the tax will probably jump to nearly 9 percent within the next few years, based upon salaries of up to $50,000 or more, with an additional burden falling on small businesses and farmers (who seem to have borne too much of a burden these past years without the help of Congress). Currently, the tax is at 7.51 percent.

The voices in Washington continue to tell us that other factors do not help matters. From time to time the unemployment rate jumps and Social Security comes under new attack. High unemployment reduces the number of people who pay taxes into the trust fund. And, with COLA, any rise in the inflation rate immediately results in larger benefits being paid to the retirees. Social Security again takes the brunt. And what about the latest cry, "My God! They're getting more out of it than they put into it!" Considering the fact that people are living longer as a rule, that may be true, but the complaint doesn't take into account those who die before sixty-five, and the fact that the same shriek is not heard when someone does the same in the stock market through capital gains!

It is no accident that I have used the words, "What are we being told?" for the more I watch the scenario unfold, the more I suspect we are being made the victims for a host of *other* governmental and personal problems in the economic area. So much has been written about the "crisis" and the voices of doom have been so loud and persistent, that most people over thirty do not believe that they will ever see even one cent of their Social Security taxes returned to them when they reach the retirement age—whether it be an early fifty or a later seventy. They are reading the same articles that we are, and in fact, many of the people in their thirties are *writing* the articles. I understand their being frightened. But it is without substance. There are other articles they should be reading, but probably are not, for they put to rest this generational conflict, and the figures are not at all ominous.

In the first place, looking at the projection of only 3.2 people working for each retired person, and only 2 workers for each retiree by the year 2000 is not a fact, but an assumption. Dr. Robert M. Ball served as commissioner of Social Security under three administrations in Washington, dating back to 1962, and then became a consultant in 1973. He stated in an interview, "More older people are likely to be working in 2020, and also more women. There will be fewer young people for the working population to support.

Fertility rates may change and so may immigration policy and productivity, all of which affect the picture. I refuse to accept that it's necessary to cut benefits now because this future problem is more or less inevitable."

In looking at the escalating annual tax on salaries that helps to pay for the trust fund, even 7 or 8 percent is not as high as the amounts paid by workers in some of the other industrial countries, and it is probably not an overwhelming burden. German workers, for example, already pay 8 percent for old-age, survivors', and disability insurance protection and, in addition, the general revenues of the German government pay for 19 percent of the cost of the system. More important, perhaps, is that—in spite of the attacks against the system by many of our younger people, a Harris study found that an overwhelming majority of the general public, young *and* old, feel that the government should help support older people with taxes collected from everyone. As a matter of fact, those under sixty-five were even stronger in their feelings than those over sixty-five! Ninety-seven percent agreed that "as the cost of living increases, Social Security payments to retired people should also increase."

This might be a good time, however, once again to point the finger the other way—at *us*. Most middle-class Americans have planned their financial retirement funds to include Social Security as a small adjunct to the income that they will derive from other investments, IRAs, Keogh plans, or income funds. We think of our retirement income too often in today's dollars, without taking into account the inflation spiral that continues to eat away at our "real" returns. And so, in planning, most of us think in terms only of the *interest income* without thinking that we must also be planning to *save* a part of that income to allow for inflation. Otherwise, too many of us find that the principal must eventually erode in order to keep up with the inflation rate. Just as Social Security includes COLA, so must our private pension funds. Unfortunately, that means we have to think of *savings* right through our lives!

It is complicated, but no one ever said that it would be easy. The realities of retirement-income planning, plus the constant flow of the current attacks against the Social Security system, somehow give me a feeling of unease, since my own future planning—just as yours—includes a variety of income-producing devices, with Social Security providing at least a small, sturdy anchor. Nevertheless, each time I read a new distortion, a little chill goes down the length of my spine.

Organizations like the Gray Panthers and the American Association of Retired Persons, and people like the late Senator Claude Pepper, have been in the forefront of putting many of the distortions and the myths to rest.

Unfortunately, most of what they print never hits the popular media, television and daily newspapers included. Reserves are projected to be about *$12 trillion* dollars by the year 2020, and this will help to ease the burden at least through 2030, when the first big wave of Baby Boomers have entered the system. Until that time, Congress will no doubt make some arrangement to avert yet another "crisis."

We should also remind those who are attacking the system that it is *more*, much more than just a retirement fund (for rich as well as poor). Social Security is also insurance against disabling illness or injury that can strike workers of any age group. It is a life insurance plan for widows and children. It is insurance against the appalling hospital costs that put us at the bottom of the list of industrial countries in the health care category. And, with COLA built in, it is a perfect hedge against inflation. There is no such insurance anywhere in the private sector. As a final note, and something that we tend to forget, Social Security provides *77 percent* of the total income for those who make less than $5,000 a year, and 75 percent for those in the $5,000 to $9,999 range. If we project that the median income for elderly households was *half that* of households headed by people in the fifteen- to sixty-four-year age range, then we begin to see that the fund is more important to many more Americans than "they" would have us believe.

Certainly, there will be dire consequences if we don't do anything before the twenty-first century hits us—or at least, in the forty years remaining until the Baby Boomers want and deserve their share. If the economy grows, so that Social Security takes a smaller percentage of our gross national product, there should be no surplus crisis. It is possible that the retirement age will be raised to sixty-eight by gradually moving it up month by month until the year 2000. Anyone retiring before that age would be severely penalized by reducing income.

Unfortunately, there are some very good arguments *against* this seemingly simple plan: some people are forced to retire because of ill health or "burnout" on the job—and it would be wonderful if we could first eliminate age discrimination on all levels of the corporate world before we decide to keep our employees there three years longer. In this area, as I've mentioned, our new, Reagan-oriented Supreme Court promises to be of little help. Judge Anthony Kennedy recently wrote the majority opinion in a case (*Ohio v. Betts*, No. 88–389) in which he stated that corporate benefit plans that treat older workers less generously than younger workers were valid, unless the employee could prove that the plans were adopted with the intent of discriminating. In other words, you can discriminate, but it's not discrimination unless you can prove discrimination. Somehow, I think that Justice Kennedy is no King Solomon!

There are some other options that have been put forward. They include eliminating the ceiling on additional earnings for retirees on Social Security; calculating the amount of retirement pay on actual earnings; enacting a national sales tax; phasing out student benefits (many of which are now gone); interfund borrowing from areas such as hospital insurance or from the general fund at market interest rates; changing the calculation of the inflation rate and cost-of-living increases; and broadening Social Security through universal coverage of *all* employees, both in the private sector and in the government. The latter suggestion would, no doubt, raise a storm that would make the corporate complaints seem like a whisper by comparison! Federal employees, for example, can take early retirement at age fifty-five with full benefits, and their cost-of-living increases are figured twice a year. Or—simply—tax Social Security benefits at the next "crisis."

The issues are phony, to put it quite simply. And, in actuality, I think that Social Security will be around for a long, long time and that no one will dare tamper with its fundamental concept. In the political arena, we middle-aged and elderly people represent the most awesome single-issue block of voters in the country today. Each of us is aware that we are affected by every suggestion, every option, and every word spoken by any administration or member of Congress. Even today, as this is being written—and I have no idea just what will be done—the Medicare "supplement" is being reviewed by Congress because of the avalanche of complaints from people just like us.

But the issues are also quite volatile and emotional, and they cross all age lines, and I think that the battle will continue, and the skirmishes will echo through the country long after this book and its readers are forgotten. I suggest that we all step back and take a good hard look before we accept the scare stories and the headlines that portend a quicksand of disaster. We, the middle-aged and elderly, should not refuse to carry more than our share of the drastic cutbacks and broken promises, while budgets are increased astronomically for cruise missiles, Stealth Bombers, and neutron weapons; while the sugar and tobacco lobbies manage to keep their own support systems afloat in Congress; and while the oil companies are targeted for special tax relief.

I have said that I am, by nature, suspicious and somewhat of a cynic, especially when it comes to what we are told "is good for you." I have worked, as you have done, hard and long to make my way in this world. As a former Depression kid, I carry with me the memories of the human problems that led to our great social programs—especially a Social Security system that has been called "America's most civilized project" and that is an independent and successful enterprise, quite separate and apart from the governmental blunderings on budget and the economy. I also retain my faith in the thinking and the legislative skills of a group of brilliant, enightened, and farseeing people who understand what it meant for millions to face a future of broken dreams, people certainly like the late Claude Pepper, like Robert Ball, and like Maggie Kuhn.

Maggie said to me in our last conversation, "Older people have paid into the system. It's not a charity and a handout, because we're benefiting from the payments that *we* made into it. *And, it's a contract that cannot be separated—a commitment to people*—(italics mine) that benefits people of all ages—the disabled of all ages."

Claude Pepper wrote, "Social Security is your rightful return on a lifelong investment in hard work," and Bob Ball added, "It is much more than an antipoverty program. Social Security is the base on which just about everyone in the United States builds protection against the loss of earned income because of retirement in old age, total disability, and death. Every private pension plan in the United States is based on the assumption that the pensioner will also receive a Social Security benefit, and individuals who are saving on their own, count on Social Security as a base for their efforts."

It is no accident, then, that the architects of Social Security created a payroll tax as the means of funding the system. Once we have contributed, then it is our *right* to claim the benefits when we retire, and we must be terribly vigilant to see that the government's part of the bargain is kept from now on, that the people who are attacking the system and its very concept be fought with every means available to us, for don't doubt for one instant that they would like to take it from us. Just read their articles and their diatribes, most of them written by well-tenured professors and wealthy economists or congressmen.

There has been no charity involved, no paternalistic funding by our companies or our government. We have paid the taxes for all these years. We are entitled to the benefits, and with all the cries of "crisis" continuing in the hallowed halls of the executive branch and our conservative "think" foundations, I have no doubt that our politically sensitive legislators will find a solution, should the need arise again.

Ironically, President Reagan (and now President Bush) had a penchant for quoting Franklin Delano Roosevelt. It might be enlightening for anyone who takes that road, or for the members of the White House economic staff and the elected members of Congress to look carefully at the statement that FDR made after Social Security had been signed into law. With regard to the tax structure of the system, he said, "Those taxes were never a problem of economics. They are *political* all the way through. We put those payroll contributions there so as to give the contributors a legal, moral, and political right to collect their pensions. With those taxes in there, *no damn politician can ever scrap my Social Security program!*"

As my grandmother used to say in order to make a point, "And that goes for your damned *cat* too!" Those of us who share these years are watching carefully to see if FDR will be heard throughout the land.

PART IV

New Beginnings,
New Horizons

On a barrier island there are familiar and very special harbingers of autumn. Early this morning, as I watched the ocean curl toward the beach, the small yellow school bus made its way slowly over the sand for the first time. The driver and I waved to each other. I looked toward the whitecaps to see if I might detect the first run of autumn bluefish in the surf.

The summer renters have departed, hauling their packed city belongings atop the little wagons down to the ferry dock, reminding me of Tevye in *Fiddler on the Roof* as he and his family left Anatekva, their household goods piled high on a rickety cart. Soon the ducks will form their fluttering lines as they head south. The monarch butterflies will make their annual migration, to fill the walks with orange-black wings. The purple beach plums hang heavy on the scraggly bushes near the sand dunes, and the August noises have given way to the insistent sounds of the September crickets and click beetles. It has become so very quiet and peaceful again.

I have passed my sixty-fifth birthday in the writing of this book, and I have had close to eight years to think about the change in life-style that I chose for myself during just such a September of reflection, self-evaluation, and contemplation. I have stated before that the very idea of change is usually quite difficult for me: Mental turmoil accompanies even the slightest digression from the status quo. If I cannot bear to see the furniture moved within a room, imagine my reaction when I first decided to rearrange my whole life-style!

They have been years of great change as well as a coming to a time when I am also at ease with that change and what it has brought for me. It has not been without its readjustments. But perhaps more important than my personal traumas or exhilaration has been the discovery that I am not alone in changing the direction of my life. There are literally millions of people of our generations who are taking stock: reevaluating their personal and business lives: finding new freedoms, new interests, new doors to open, new challenges. If we were not so damned invisible, the world would soon be aware that we are very much like the ocean that roars and churns not far from where I write—constantly changing; first roiling, then placid; searching its way onto the beach, withdrawing, then moving in again, constantly probing and resculpting the earth beneath it. I, who protest so much that I cannot tolerate change, find that very change exciting both in my piece of ocean and in my life.

18 What Do You Want to Be When You Grow Up?

For each age is a dream that is dying,
Or one that is coming to birth.

—Arthur O'Shaughnessy
"Ode"

The luncheon had already been in progress for over an hour and, for my part, I could have stayed in the restaurant the remainder of the afternoon. My companion, who had just turned fifty, was fascinating, easy to talk with, and filled with an enthusiasm and a life force that characterize so many of our contemporaries. We moved from subject to subject, leaning forward in our involvement, paying little attention to the captain and the waiters, finding much to agree on, laughing, probing. "Who are we?" he asked rhetorically. We agreed that we were very special generations and he continued, ticking off his points on his fingers.

"We lived through the thirties and we were seared by the Depression. We lived through the forties and we were scarred by the war. We lived through the fifties and we learned to keep our mouths shut and get along in the world. In the sixties—which we also lived through—we found that the flower children were successful at doing their own thing. In the seventies we saw that the kids of the sixties might have been saying something to *us*, and it began to have relevancy in our own changes. Now we're in the eighties and asking, 'How about me?'" And now, all of us—along with Jim Gallagher—are into the nineties, and the changes are even more complex, the opportunities more difficult to perceive in some areas, but more open in others.

I met Dr. James Gallagher after reading an article about him in the business section of the *New York Times*. He is chairman of a group called J. J.

Gallagher Associates, a career counseling company, and he and his staff
devote their time to "outplacement," the counseling of middle-aged executives who have been *separated*—a contemporary word to soften the real
meaning: *fired.* They are people who have devoted most of their lives to the
corporation, and being fired in their late forties or fifties is possibly one of the
most shattering experiences that can occur in their adult lives. Dr. Gallagher
equates it with the death of a family member, a serious injury, or being sent to
jail for a felony. And when I mentioned above that the changes today are
more complex than ever, I was specifically thinking of the new greed on the
corporate horizon, the leveraged buyout and the conglomeration of giant
corporations. The end result for the new company: huge debt. And the way
to pay it off: cut back. Cut back in every way possible, especially in the
"separation" (firing) of a large group of loyal, hardworking employees, particularly in middle management.

   In spite of this, what struck me most about Dr. Gallagher was his attitude,
his optimism, and, most of all, his conclusion that most fired executives,
properly counseled, can end up with even better-paying jobs, usually in a field
other than the one to which they have devoted so much of their working
lives.

   I was curious. Through my years in dealing with major corporations and
producing their films, I had seen many executives either fired after the age of
fifty or moved "sideways" into a job with no future. Some of these people were
clients with whom I had developed a long and close relationship and I
suffered right along with them. Some were forced to take early retirement;
others were the victims of cost cutting after disappointing annual profit
projections or the corporate indigestion created by the buyouts or takeovers or
mergers mentioned earlier. Several of my closest friends were passed over for a
vice presidency because they were too close to retirement and, after thirty or
forty years with the company, they watched silently as a replacement was
brought in from the outside to become their superior. For me, all of it was tied
together—the deliberate insulation of the corporation from humanity has
been evident all through my career, and the age discrimination in the
decisions only too obvious. The irony, of course, is that many of those
decisions to fire a long time employee were and are being made by people of
our own age, unaware that they may well be next (and in these years between
editions of this book, I have seen three separate cases where this has happened!).

   So I spoke at length to Dr. Gallagher, for I felt that if I could understand
what happens during a middle-age termination, and if Dr. Gallagher could be

so positive about such severe dislocations, what would his attitude be toward those of us who *voluntarily* decide to change our life-styles and those of us who choose to remain active in the corporate world past the age of "normal" retirement—either with the companies with which we've spent thirty years or more, or in a major shift to another field of endeavor? Because of the turmoil in the corporate world, there is an increasing number of executives who are choosing to leave and start out again on their own—either because of the merger potential or the fact that career goals have been stymied. And these days, this includes not only men but an ever-increasing number of women.

One of the things that fascinated me most during my lunch with Jim Gallagher and the subsequent telephone calls to clarify some points was the fact that the word *crisis* never once reared its ugly snout! And probably just as reassuring is the fact that all through these past eight years, I have seen several newspaper interviews with him and what he said then, at the first meeting, is still valid today.

"We live under a set of assumptions that make life livable—that the power will go on when we switch on the light, that the buses will run." He went on enthusiastically, "And we were given other assumptions, were we not? Start at the bottom. Keep your nose clean. Work hard. You will be successful. But those assumptions—as all others—do not take into account *change*." (There was that word again.) He leaned forward. "Look, if we've lived on this planet for fifty years or more, we've had to accommodate change—the aerospace revolution, the cold war, inflation, even the advent of television. We've absorbed them all into our family life, in society, education, and in government. Why not in our careers?"

He laughed. "I remember all my young life I lived under the assumption that FDR would always be president. I was led to assume that the presidency was a stable reference in my life. I was born a Roman Catholic. I was led to assume that, if I went to Communion for the first Friday of nine consecutive months, I would go to Heaven. Well, they've changed the rules! The mass is no longer in Latin. I can eat meat on Friday. I don't have to fast before Communion; I can have water or coffee first. *The constant is change!*"

And thus our assumption is that if we work hard and we stay with the corporation, always trustworthy, loyal, thrifty, clean, and brave, we will be rewarded. But one day, to our regret, that assumption is blasted. I have seen the looks on the faces of terminated middle-management executives who come to Dr. Gallagher's office. It is not a pleasant experience. And through all of this, remember, I am discussing only the people on the management levels. I have not even come to the problems met by those who are also fired (to use the proper word) and who come from the white-collar administrative staff or the blue-collar assembly line, still somewhere in their fifties, still active, vital, and ready to work. Overall, the very qualities that are lauded as major pluses in a presidential campaign—maturity and experience—are of little value in today's job market when it comes to the older employee.

According to Jim Gallagher, any fired employee goes through two major stages. The first one begins with disbelief: "This isn't really happening to me." This is followed by anger—threatening to "knock somebody's block off" or burying it deeply within, possibly to surface at the wrong time in a subsequent job interview, only to hurt the candidate's chances. Then comes a period of bargaining—trying to find a way to save the job, threatening to see the president, asking for time to look around for a transfer within the corporation. But bargaining is futile.

Dr. Gallagher illustrates the final point in the first stage, bargaining, with an anecdote from Dr. Elisabeth Kübler-Ross's work with hospital patients who were terminally ill. One woman bargained with her doctor to keep her well enough to attend the wedding of her oldest son, even though she could not survive her advanced cancer. Through the doctor's skill, her persistence, and a great deal of luck, she went to the wedding. When she returned to the hospital after the ceremony and reception, she met the doctor, smiled, and greeted him with, "Don't forget, Doctor, I have another son!"

During the second stage of the termination period, depression replaces the initial shock, followed by a gradual acceptance of the situation and the building of hope through sheer determination. It is during this period that the individual is forced to review his or her total past experience and to prepare for a job search, develop strategy, collect names, and produce an effective résumé. The move then is into the positive activity of a job search. The success rate, sometimes after another small dip into depression—usually about the sixth week—is amazingly good. Through intensive counseling, people are induced to search deeply, and many a new job reflects a talent in an area never even thought of before! This is a subject, incidentally, upon which I shall try to expand in my discussion of relocation and career changing.

The statistics are interesting, considering the fact that the trauma of being fired during middle age seems so hopeless and irreparable. Over the years, for those who have been professionally counseled by Dr. Gallagher's organization and others like it:

- With outplacement counseling, it takes about one week of job search for each $2,000 of annual salary before the individual is placed.

- About 60 percent of the executives and managers who receive outplacement guidance come through with new jobs in about twenty weeks, generally because this group is in a higher salary bracket than those in the first statistic.

- The most important factor in outplacement counseling, however, is that *about 85 percent find jobs at a higher salary than they had received before they were fired.*

I was impressed and curious about that last figure and I checked with an old friend in outplacement work in the Midwest, Joe Maloney, formerly vice president of personnel ("human resources," these days) at Brooks Brothers. He bears it out and says that it is not unusual. It is a remarkable statistic.

And in the final analysis:

- In spite of the fact that about 90 percent of all new small businesses fail within the first five years, 10 percent of their employees think it's about time to strike out on their own. (Up from 2 percent about eight years ago.)

Although some corporations provide outplacement services for their middle- and upper-level executives—possibly to assuage their guilt as much as for any other reason—others do not. There are some in-house seminars offered, many merely say, "Thanks a lot. We wish you luck. Please clear out your office by twelve noon." In these recent years, with more and more corporate cutbacks, mergers, forced early retirement (and optional retirement) plus the readjustment of thinking in the financial areas of companies due to ever-escalating costs of benefits, other support systems have come into being—all directed toward the job seeker who is over fifty. The task is still difficult in this society, but the support systems and the literature directed toward getting a new job may make the search a little bit easier. Many fifty-year-old job seekers are really as naive and inexperienced at job hunting as the new college graduates, since they are probably searching for the first time in twenty or thirty years.

- Operation ABLE (Ability Based on Long Experience) offers a network of community-based senior employment centers in eight cities and in the state of Arkansas. Many of its services are free. (Operation ABLE, 36 South Wabash Avenue, Chicago, IL 60603)

• The American Association of Retired Persons offers a pilot employment program, AARP Works, in over thirty cities, and the number is expanding. To get the latest information on the job-search workshops, write: Work Force Education, AARP Worker Equity Dept., 1909 K Street, N.W., Washington, DC 20049.

There are local self-help job clubs, such as Forty Plus (Now in seventeen cities), who use out-of-work professionals over the age of forty to staff the organization while they use its workshops, counseling services, and job banks to do their own job hunting. It is not free, however, and fees can be quite steep, from a small weekly charge up to as much as eight hundred dollars for annual dues.

On a more modest level, many communities have career counseling services in firms that provide advice for as little as thirty-five dollars an hour and up to as much as one hundred dollars for a short session. The AARP suggests that you check these firms quite carefully for references or write to the American Association for Counseling in Washington, DC, to get the latest information.

There are still other areas in which you can find help. From time to time, *Modern Maturity Magazine* (AARP) will print an article about job hunting for the over-fifty-year-old, with excellent advice about networking, résumés, the job search and the interview. There is also a free booklet (for members) on job hunting over fifty. It's called *Working Options—How to Plan Your Job Search, Your Work Life* (D12303). (Write to AARP Fulfillment at the address I've given previously.)

And finally, you would do well to check your local community college, continuing-education programs, and local vocational schools to see if they also offer seminars, courses, or just plain advice.

Well, then, with everything that I've written so far, with my natural hostility toward corporate "loyalty," with the problems of getting and holding a job after the age of forty or fifty, why, then, would I now recommend that another option you have in middle age (and even later) is to make that change *voluntarily*? To leave the job, to separate from the corporation, or to change your business direction and your career and to do it by yourself— without being given the "pink slip"? And, if you agree with me that your life-style needs a change—that it is time to do something with the rest of your life, that you only "go around this way just one time" and it would be nice to work at a job that gives some satisfaction, possibly in a place other than the one in which you are now living, why do you hestitate? The answer to that one is simple, and it goes back to the very beginning of this book: Because we have been taught to think that we are *too old* to start again.

As we grow older, we are conditioned to deny our own worth and the intrinsic values and attributes that we bring to our society, if only through our greater experience. The virulence of age discrimination in our culture begins to affect even those of us who should know better, when we hear *ourselves* declaring, "We have to make way for young ideas and young blood." We accept too quickly the words of the chairman of the board who fires two top officers in their seventies because they are "stagnating" and "not attuned to the times." The same chief executive officer was quoted in the *Wall Street Journal* as saying that the company needed "younger, more aggressive leaders," while being totally insensitive to his own age of sixty-eight! He is, as much as any of us, a victim of the youth culture in America.

The assumptions that Dr. Gallagher spoke of rule our lives and our attitudes about ourselves. We assume that we must live up to the expectations of others; that we must bow to the conventional ideas and criteria of our society. As Gae Gaer Luce said in her book, *Your Second Life,* "Our culture teaches us many ways to be unhealthy. . . . We are taught in first grade to stop feeling who we are ('You can stand in the closet if you're going to cry') and to give up our lives for good grades, reputation, and later, money."

Is it any wonder that we begin to dislike ourselves and to agree with the myths about aging: to doubt our abilities, to assume that a traumatic change in middle life does irreparable damage to our dignity and our life-style? Is it any wonder that a *voluntary* change of career at age fifty or later is greeted with "You must have guts!" or the observation that you must be living through your midlife crisis? It is another important area in our lives where the myths become self-perpetuating, and our assumptions begin to rule our important decisions, our behavior, and what we think, what we say, what we write, and finally what we do.

Our assumptions make us believe, for example, that *all* middle-aged people are heterosexual; yet many are lesbians, gay men, or bisexuals. Our assumptions about aging are such that we—the people in midlife and older—believe that our talents decrease as the years go by. Thus, in a newspaper review of a concert by the indomitable and everlasting Frank Sinatra, I read the line "but for a man of 65, his technique is remarkable." Angrily, I read on, and it was the next part of the review that showed the adulation that the writer felt, and

I wondered why Sinatra's age had to be mentioned at all: "In fact, every time this writer has heard him in recent years, his voice has seemed more secure and wider in range both for dynamics and pitch." Why was he surprised? Sinatra, now in his seventies still performs and seems even "more secure in his pitch."

However, too often, we tend to focus only on the brilliant and the powerful personalities in show business (especially), as well as in the corporate world and in government, in order to find the people who we think are *exceptions* to the rule of retirement at a specific age. Scientists and engineers do their most celebrated work late in their sixties and seventies. Writers, artists, doctors, lawyers, professors (and filmmakers) remain active into their eighties and experience some of their best years after the onset of middle age.

When I first began to collect the vast profusion of materials that fill my office, closets, and file cabinets, I thought I might complete a listing that would clearly show how vital we all are. Unfortunately about the same time I discovered two other things:

• The "exceptions" to the rule—the woman sports editor at age ninety-two, the eighty-two-year-old preacher, the ninety-year-old psychiatrist, the seventy-two-year-old architect, even my friend Harriet Herbst, who wrote a well-reviewed first novel (*Chocolate Mouse*, Mercury House) after the age of seventy, all smacked of tokenism, exactly the kind of publicity that perpetuates the myth that all these people are *exceptions*. It is the attitude of the popular magazines like *People*, purring, "Oh, aren't they cute?"

• In fact, people such as I've mentioned above are more the *rule* rather than the exception. Had I begun such a list, it would have filled the space of ten bookshelves, set in type much smaller than this!

Not only was President Reagan a prime example of a successful career change in later years (and what scriptwriter would have dared suggest that an actor could become president?), but I look at the list of directors in a company in which I hold stock (and which keeps going down in an up market), and I note that the eight men on the board are all between fifty-four and eighty-six. The one woman director has modestly withheld her age from the annual report.

The list of "who's who" in the corporate world, those who are "making way for younger blood," includes executives of some of the largest and most successful multinational corporations in the country. In the fields of publishing, communications, real estate, investment and finance, retailing, engineering and aerospace, there are so many chief executives who are over seventy that it must be embarrassing when they realize the extent to which they are marketing to the youth culture! Nor are they paying much heed to a statement made some years back by Arjay Miller, former president of the Ford Motor Company, who was quoted as saying, "I don't think anyone over seventy should be chief executive of a large corporation. It helps the morale of a corporation to have turnover at the top; there are a lot of young bucks waiting to be chief." Of course, the last part is true (with a lot of young "does" also waiting), but power is not given up easily and the older CEOs wait patiently for their "golden parachutes" before giving way.

Well, what about the rest of us? What about those of us of middle age or in our later years who do not hold the office of chief executive, either in the White House or in the board room of General Dynamics or General Motors? What about those of us who have never even become middle-level executives but have worked in the average office all our lives? What about those of us in our own businesses, in the retail world, in retirement, or in any career that suddenly seems to be giving less and less joy and rewards?

A report by the National Committee on Careers for Older Americans (*Older Americans: An Untapped Resource*) succinctly gave the all-too-common response of so many of us who have entered middle age, who have made our way through it, and who are now moving on in years: "Tragically, the other side of the coin is also commonplace. For whatever personal reasons, many highly trained and talented older people succumb to the depressing expectation that they should withdraw from life. . . . Sometimes these people are subject to their own or others' mistaken notion that their continued presence impedes the progress of younger people when, in fact, it is the younger people who benefit most by their continued leadership and example."

Certainly, as Gerry Hotchkiss, publisher of *New Choices* magazine said to me, "The younger manager hires people that he or she sees are going to be available through a continuum. If you or I go there, we're not the continuum they want. They're not sure how long you or I are going to be there. It's not a question of how long we *can* be there, but how long do we want to do this? They want twenty-five years—not five years." Particularly in this generation, the perception is that everyone working for a corporation is only trying to accumulate enough to finally leave and be free of corporate straitjackets. Gerry puts it, "Robert Townsend, in *Up the Organization* called it 'the Go Screw Yourself* money!'"

Well, let me set at least a part of the record straight. During World War II a great many older workers, including women who had not worked steadily since their teens, were employed in the defense industries while many of us marched off to Europe and the South Pacific. Studies of that era found that older workers had greater stability on the job, fewer accidents, and less time lost from work than did younger employees. More important, perhaps, is the fact that studies by the Department of Labor and the National Council on Aging concluded that older workers are able to produce work that is qualitatively and quantitatively *equal or superior* to that of the younger workers.

Older workers report more job satisfaction and less job-related stress than do younger employees. We are less likely to be absent, especially on the days when auto assembly lines turn out most of their "lemons"—Mondays and Fridays. The record shows, too, that we require less supervision, and that we have steadier work habits and a greater sense of responsibility and loyalty toward our jobs and our employers. Moreover, the reports indicate that we are less distracted by outside interests and influences, that we have fewer domestic troubles, and that we have a higher level of concentration than our young workers.

A few years ago I was hired to produce a film on the subject of "quality," and the sponsor of the project was one of the largest automobile manufacturers in the world. Armed with my questions, my camera crew, and my indomitable sense of optimism, I traveled to the assembly plant and, over the noise, clatter, and pounding—all the while dodging the slowly moving chassis—I tried to interview the workers about their feelings on "quality." My optimism soon vanished as the workers—particularly the *young ones*—met my questions with laughter, disbelief, and a series of unprintable responses for a film that would be shown to the general public.

"What would you do," I asked a young foreman, "if the people down the line forgot to punch the holes in which you put your grillwork?"

"We'd let it go by. If they don't do their job, we can't stop the line to do ours, can we?"

Another young man laughed and shouted loudly above the din, "Quality? Crap. I just want to finish this job this summer and get back to school!"

I came out of the project chastened, disturbed, and feeling much less naive. The older workers, either through being resigned, caring more, or carrying with them a stronger work ethic, were the ones who finally gave me the story that I was looking for. I drive a car that is now *twenty-three years old* and I dread the day that I will have to replace it, for I will have to insist on an automobile made only by older workers—and only on Tuesday, Wednesday, or Thursday!

How ironic! A culture of youth still persists in a society that has changed much already and is changing still. Billions of dollars have been thrown into the fight to improve nutrition, to increase the level of our medical care so that we can live longer, to increase our life span to the point where we are the fastest-growing segment of the entire population. Added to that, our own attitudes are changing, making us *want* to continue to pursue active lives, unwilling to sit out our middle and later years and our retirement, possessing a greater range of skills, talent, and interests ever before seen in an older population. How incomprehensible, then, that at this moment in time we are prone to aggravate this incredible waste of resources by demanding early retirement from the work force; that we exert subtle pressures to make way for the young; that we try every means to make millions of our population invisible and totally valueless! Look again at the quotation that I used at the head of chapter 2. Ken Dychtwald put it so well: "We've spent the last ten thousand years trying to grow old people, and now that we've done a pretty good job, we're embarrassed about it."

Too often in our lives we are driven to change or to take risks only by pain. Jim Gallagher believes that the forces that normally drive us are mostly negative: financial insecurity if we lived through the Depression or our parents told us the horror stories about that time; high need for achievement and tangible reflections of that achievement—good cars, homes, kids in college—a conviction that our children no longer consider us wise. Most of us are not, normally, risk takers. I number myself within that group.

"You don't have to be what you were before," he says. "You don't have to work in the same industry, do the same job. There are options that seem to be unthinkable when you're caught in the same track year after year." For his clients, it is the pain of termination that creates the need to take a risk. "But voluntarily or involuntarily," he goes on, "it may be time for a good change and your perceptions of that change may well move you into more rewarding work, even at this time in your life."

Time for a change. I thought I was very much alone, one of a kind, when I left the film company in which I was a partner, well over nine years ago. The responses from my friends ranged from the comment about having "guts" to "I sure wish I could do it. I envy you." Few were even the least bit pessimistic; most were enthusiastically supportive and optimistic. The remarkable discovery over these past years, though, is the fact that I might consider myself more unusual if I had stayed in the job for ten more years rather than making me move at the age of fifty-seven! Far from being alone, I find that I am surrounded by a peer group that is constantly changing, most often for a second career that is not at all connected with the first one.

A man named Frank Morgan worked at an oil company for eighteen years, did not get the promotion he wanted, left, and put his hobby of sailing to work for him in a new business. He bought the marina in a small town about seventy miles from Baltimore, and he now employs eight people in the height of the tourist season. At last report, I read that he has also started a real-estate company and was negotiating to buy a marine-supply company.

Husbands and wives are also making changes together, as Sheryl and I did. Tom and Marge Watson, who both worked for a major corporation, left their jobs together and ended up in Jacksonville, Florida, where they purchased a printing company with a partner—something that was a far cry from his specialty in the ski business and hers as director of employee relations—and the last report projected gross sales of over $5 million a year.

I had promised not to give specific examples, for the reader would then point to the *exceptions* again. However, in *Passages*, Gail Sheehy reported the results of a study made by Professor Judith Barwick of the University of Michigan, in which every one of the twenty subjects—all outstandingly successful men—had made radical career switches or had become social activists in middle life! Why is it that we so often think we are the unusual, the exceptions, only to find, to our surprise, that we are actually one of many?

In a lovely article in *Prime Time* magazine, Samuel Schreiner, Jr., wrote of his class of '42 at Princeton. He did not attend the reunion, feeling that he had neither the time nor the money, but in any case he was different in that he had recently resigned from a twenty-year job as an editor to pursue a career in writing novels. His assumption was that his classmates would all be at the peak of corporate careers, well settled, well heeled, privileged, and content.

Much to his surprise, a book arrived in the mail and the details of the careers were outlined. He wrote, "I was in for a rude and wonderful shock. Far from being unique, I found that more than 10 percent of my class had opted for new professions, new risks, new lives—in the years when you're supposed to stay put and accumulate juicy pension rights. Not only that, but the entries of all these 'dropouts,' including my own, reflected the joy of rebirth." He also reported that in every case the switch in careers involved reduced income and/or high risk with a remarkable increase in emotional rewards.

And so it has been for me. For over thirty-five years I had worked in television and film, the final fifteen with three partners in a company that was quite successful in the documentary field, and right before that with David Wolper, one of the pioneers of the contemporary documentary and a most memorable character. I had garnered my share of awards; my place in the industry was secure. I guess I had enough of a reputation to continue working in exactly the same way, structuring my life year after year in the same patterns, producing twelve or fifteen films each year, accepting the "perks": first class travel; freedom as an executive; guest lectures at America's universities; and a Fifth Avenue office hung with plaques, testimonials, and my Academy Award nomination. But something still bothered me.

When I first began the business of making films, I worked with young, vital, and visionary filmmakers, people who would not accept the first solution to a problem. The work was exciting and I was able to spend the time on each project that guaranteed that it would have my very best efforts. Something had changed over all those years and I had become a businessman first and a filmmaker last. Solutions to film problems were too easy; too *much* experience dictated my answers, my thinking, and the eventual product. What had become of the probing, the slow solution to a film problem, working with the young creators who stand at the edges of the motion-picture industry, eager to enter?

I guess I could have stayed. No one would have known the difference. But my life had taken another turn and my writing of books had begun to be successful. Unlike my college days, when I had filled a scrapbook with rejection slips, my weekend work at writing had begun to show results. After four years there were four books in print and I was living a dual life.

I suppose that, given my normal resistance to any change, I should have thought about it for a few months, mulling over so important a decision in order to give it time to fall into place. But I did not. It took but twenty-four hours to make up my mind. I called my partners together one Monday morning and I resigned. In one moment I was no longer an executive of the company with which I had worked for so many years. I had cut off the income, the staff relationships, the perks, and a partnership that had worked fairly well, considering that the personalities were so very different.

In a single instant I became an independent filmmaker, someone who wanted to do only two or three films a year for clients whom I liked and respected—and I wanted to do those films as well as I had when I was a young, director-producer at the age of twenty-seven. I was also, in that single moment, a writer of books in a world that is not known for treating most authors very well financially. In twenty-four hours I had cleared my office of the memorabilia, the files, the stacked papers, and the funny plaques that hung on the walls ("God So Loved the World, That He Did Not Send a Committee"), fifteen years of accumulated junk, birthday gifts from the staff, unnecessary memos, vague corporate letters, and my ashtray that said, "Thank You for Not Smoking." It took nine cardboard cartons to pack what I wanted to keep and take back to my city apartment that could ill-afford to store it all until I had located a working space. It took eight more cartons to haul away the old magazines, out-of-date files, and an accumulation of trivia that I had not looked at in fifteen years. The day I left, a letter arrived from my dear friend and cameraman, Peter Henning, with whom I had worked for twenty years. It read, in part, "Welcome back to the trenches!"

It has been a remarkable nine years. I was convinced that we would starve and we have not. (The Depression syndrome again.) We dubbed our new corporation, Symbiosis Inc., a description both of our work habits and our marriage. (And it is constantly misspelled by correspondents, suppliers, and government agencies, as well as mispronounced by almost everyone.) My old clients have remained with our small company and we are booked for films through the middle of next year. We have produced documentaries at Lourdes, at Guadalupe in Mexico, for Sunkist Growers in Japan, Hong Kong, and California, visitor center films for Duke Power, career guides on fashion and art, and we have just published our fifteenth book! And do I worry? *You bet I do.* I worry each and every year. The administration of even a small company takes a great amount of time. The government gets its share of the forms and the correspondence—as does the accountant, the lawyer, my suppliers, the bank, and the efforts toward getting new projects.

But there is also some time to think, time to write, time to escape and fish without feeling the guilt that I have left three partners to fend for themselves. I have been, in fact, busier than ever and the financial rewards have been greater than I had ever expected (so far!). And, of course, there has been the readjustment. The uptown office does not exist any longer. Midtown has become a voyage into discovery and turmoil.

I work at home or in my little room on Fire Island and I have had to adjust to being around twenty-four hours a day rather than going out to an office at 7 A.M. For my wife it has been more difficult, or at least it was at first, for suddenly I was thrust into "her space" and "her time." The work schedule is of my own choosing and my disciplines are self-imposed, else I would not get anything done. The filmmaking has become a joy again, now that I have put the businessman's hat in the closet and returned to the job of producing films of which I can be proud and in which I have once again played a vital role. My wife has become active in our small company, both in the films and in the books that she has always written, and since we generally get along well together, my being constantly at home has not been so great a burden as expected, at least not for me. We have even learned to use that time together for some delightful escapes, and there are days when we walk down to Little

Italy, just a short mile away, and have a lunch that makes us feel that we are back in Rome for just an hour or two. It is a pleasure that was not available when I worked in midtown Manhattan.

After nine years, am I content with the change? The words of Sam Schreiner's Princeton class might well be my own: "Excited beyond my wildest dreams." I have never regretted the change and seriously wonder if I might have done it sooner. A few years back, soon after forming Symbiosis, I walked uptown to an appointment and I began to think. Dodging the New York traffic, I made a list on a scrap of paper, then stopped to sit in a large plaza, using still more paper to compile *three* lists: *The Things I Miss, The Things I Don't Miss, What Has Replaced the Things I Thought I'd Miss.*

I was surprised to see the shallowness of the things that I missed. Was I really unable to list more than I had, after thirty-five years? I miss the vitality of uptown Manhattan, though it is there for me to savor just twenty minutes away, whenever I want to leave home. I miss the uptown characters, like the man who beats his snare drum on the street, or the rock and rap musicians and the mimes who perform at noon in front of the public library. I miss the constant parade of New York women—attractive, well dressed, vital, and so very individual. I miss the perks, sometimes, though that feeling left me very quickly. I do not travel as much as I did, so the first-class seats are not quite so important.

I did miss some of the people for a while, but I have found that "corporate divorce" is very much like the marital type. It is better for both sides not to keep the contacts alive. And with corporate divorce there are no children, so visitation privileges are not a factor! Occasionally, I have run into one or two of my ex-partners on Fifth Avenue and we exchange pleasantries, but it has been a long time now, and we have very little in common except some very fond memories.

I do miss the availability of a staff, a full array of people who are there to do my bidding, but I am learning to cope by myself with the aid of my wife, and for a short time, a remarkable production manager, Tina Gonzalez, who later moved on to American Express as an executive and eventually a regional vice president based in Hong Kong. But I still use the systems that she set up when she was with us.

If I were called upon to detail the one thing that I miss most, I would name the shallowest of them all. I miss using the company Xerox machine that was right outside my office door! I now have to walk four blocks to take my manuscripts to a small, crowded copy shop. Now *there* is an epitaph for a career of thirty-five years: *He Misses the Xerox Machine.*

And the things I do not miss? I don't miss the office politics, for you can put any two people together in an office, give them a water cooler around which to congregate, and the lives and loves of all are open to scrutiny and discussion. I don't miss the constant business lunches with people I don't like and with whom I have nothing in common (including the crabgrass on their lawns), the aimlessness of conversations at our table or overheard—and no business being done at all, though the main purpose of the luncheon was to discuss "the deal."

I don't miss the endless and worthless corporate meetings that take place all over America and of which I was a participant for so many years. I also don't miss the routine of the office, though the disciplines now are more severe since they are my responsibility. I don't miss being responsible to three other partners and a staff of twenty-two. Though I am running my own business now, and am busier than ever, I don't miss the "businessman" I left uptown at the office.

The things that have replaced it all are diverse, complicated, though no longer new to me after all this time. Most of all, the freedom that I found by making that change cannot be equated with anything in my past business life. The decisions, the responsibilities, the rewards all belong to Sheryl and to me, and we share them together. My films show, I think, the effort and the thought that now go into them. I like to think that I will have more time to expand, to think, to stretch my imagination, but I have been too busy to accomplish any of it yet. My clients are of my own choosing now, and they are people with whom I love to share coffee or a glass of wine in front of the fire or on a terrace that overlooks the entire city. I have made time to visit Mother Mary Bernard and Mother Genevieve at the Little Sisters of the Poor residence, because the film we produced for them has also made them our friends.

All of them are people with whom I spend my time because I *want* to, rather than because of a sense of corporate duty. After over forty years it is a personal perk that I think I well deserve, just as I feel that those little Italian luncheons that break up the workday are one of the rewards of having made the decision to be on my own.

And as for the Xerox machine, even that has been replaced with an unexpected dividend. Though the shop is four blocks away, and it is crowded and inefficient, it has become a personal journey each time I take a chapter or a letter or a newspaper article over there for copying. I am now friends with the young rock musician, Santo, who runs the place with his wife Margaret, and he comments on each chapter of the manuscript as it goes through the machine. As a matter of fact, it is not even a *Xerox*—I note that he uses a *Kodak* copier! Somehow, my copies look even brighter than they did before, back at the office! And when the job is finished, my bonus walk takes me to the string of Korean greengrocers on the way home, to look, and to purchase the fruits that are colorfully in season.

I like to think now that my change was possibly a catalyst for other friends. Soon after the decision to change my life-style, the calls and the letters began to arrive from friends, from acquaintances, from clients, from people who had disappeared from my life as much as ten or fifteen years before. One call was from a senior executive of one of America's top ten corporations, a friend whose career I had followed with interest over twenty-five years as he rose from advertising agency vice president to a leader in his industry, one quoted in trade journals and lauded for campaigns that feature tunes you and I hum after watching his commercials. Over lunch he informed me that he, too, wanted to change and that my decision had spurred his own. He was retiring at the age of fifty-five to pursue a career as a *scuba diving instructor!* His plan was to take four executives each week to his second home in the Bahamas (flying his own plane to get them there), put them up in his house, and give scuba lessons in the clear blue waters. He would then fly back to pick up another group the following week!

My friend, Malcolm, switched from the lucrative career of writing music for commercials to the nether world of Broadway and wrote a hit musical his first time out! A chemical engineer studies law and becomes a public defender, while a middle-aged lawyer becomes a filmmaker. A bank executive leaves the world of finance to strike out as a free-lance writer and in three years has made an indelible mark in the travel field with his books and his articles. A recent letter from him tells me that he has now written *twenty-six* travel books. A public relations director of a large hospital in Memphis opens a small shop that deals in gold and jewelry and in one year moves to the center of the city to expand. My last contact with him tells me that the shop has once again grown and is now the busiest in his area. A biochemist, who left the field to become a mother and raise two children, returns to school after their teenage years and becomes the director of a counseling service in California. This was topped for me recently by the story of someone with whom I've worked on promotional films. The mother of *eight* children, she spent her entire life raising them and being the support person for the family, including her husband, who was a successful surgeon. In her *fifties*, she went back to work and is now the director of a successful, progressive, dynamic science museum in the South.

Possibly the most unusual career change I've heard of recently is that of a successful executive who quit his job at age fifty and went to India to produce pornographic films! You can be certain that his family has used the term "midlife crisis" more than once in describing his move.

And so I am not alone. Indeed, I am not alone. Many of us are paying heed to the thinking that we are stalled at middle age, irrevocably mired in the quicksand of routine, security, and the inability to take chances. As longevity increases, more and more of us are looking for a second career, and finding it. Age is no longer a barrier.

However, there is a "however." There are some of us who do not want to continue to work—either at our primary, long-term careers or in a second career. There are some of us who feel that way and who can *afford* not to work. But, I would like to add one more thought to this area of just what it is we want to be when we "grow up." The American Medical Association issued a report that most of us will agree with and they concluded that, "There is a direct relationship between enforced idleness and poor health," and that the retired are returning to the work force, either in businesses of their own or in volunteer work in the community.

Many of our elder citizens have mixed feelings, however, about being asked to volunteer their services, and I blame them not at all. President Bush, in his "thousand points of light" concept has declared that volunteerism can cure the ills of society, the problems of homelessness, the health care crisis [sic!] and just about everything else that is wrong with America. Frankly, I cannot agree for a great many reasons, not the least of which is the fact that volunteerism is really a cop-out for all the things that the government has withdrawn in the social area these past eight or more years. I think, too, that we all want the dignity of being paid for our work, just as we did when we were younger and beginning the career climb. Nevertheless, if local communities could learn to take advantage of the retired people who want to help, they could increase their total volunteer programs by as much as 50 percent. In one area I do agree with President Bush, since I have been an activist since my teens. He feels that the true measure of success in the future might well be the judgment of what a person has given back to his or her community during their lifetime. Amen to that.

For those who are interested in volunteer work, there is an organization that can help you find a range of opportunities. Currently boasting almost half a million volunteers, ACTION includes VISTA, the Foster Grandparents Program, Retired Senior Volunteer Program, the Senior Companion Program, and it currently has ten regional offices across the country. (AC-

TION, 806 Connecticut Avenue, N.W., Washington, DC, 20525) One of the reasons that I admire them is that many of their programs include young volunteers as well as seniors.

A few years back a symposium was held on the subject of "The Future of Older Workers in America," funded by the Work in America Institute, Inc., and the Andrus Gerontology Center of Los Angeles. At a general workshop Jerome M. Rosow, president of the Work in America Institute, made the prediction that "society in the next century will be begging for older workers—there won't be anyone but older workers. They may have to pay them a premium to keep them from retiring." Because of the decline of the birth rate, he feels that by the turn of the century (not too far off) we will have a work force of which 60 percent will be older workers.

We are the elders of the tribe now; we are more experienced, somewhat wiser, and the logical group to be dealing with the problems of our society as well as its productivity. We have been trained in law, corporate structures, medicine, and a thousand other crafts, skills, and professions, not to mention the upbringing of our children and our vast experience in managing family life. We are men and women who should logically be utilized in jobs that deal with discrimination, functional illiteracy, deliquency, alcohol and drugs, as well as continuing or changing our careers in the business world if we so choose.

Is it easy? Of course not. My grandmother, as well as yours never promised that life would be easy, and it probably has not been to this point. I remember the discussion I had with my friend, Malcolm, after he made that move from commercials to the ogre of Broadway. "It was not just guts; it was a necessity," he said. "I couldn't look at myself in the mirror. Every time I booked a vacation, maybe once a year, I'd try to gauge when I could safely get away. It's getting to be August. Maybe they'll all be away. Maybe I'll book seven days someplace. So I'd book, take a limo to the airport, but every time, twenty minutes before the flight, after I'd gotten my seat assignment, I'd find a phone and say, 'Did anybody call? Maybe Pepsi, maybe Burger King?' And in the back of my mind I'd have a battle plan. If someone called, I knew where my luggage was, how could I get back into the city. No more. *No more!* I don't have that any more!"

And, after the move—after the first startling look at the fact that you have broken the ties with the past? Malcolm reported, "The amazing thing is—it's such freedom! When you've spent years doing everybody else's laundry and all of a sudden you've got your own basket and your own clothes, it's a whole different ball game!"

New Locations—New Careers: Transferring Your Skills

There are a great many in our generations who want to do a complete transformation of life-style, not only in changing their careers, but in moving to another location, either for semiretirement or for weather considerations, family, or health. Too often, however, that move results in a great many disappointments insofar as getting a job in another state is concerned. If the market is glutted and in the midst of a downturn such as the Southwest after the oil boom burst, or if the influx of people is larger than the job market can comfortably accommodate, such as the Sun Belt, then the projections are generally quite pessimistic. However, there are ways to overcome the problems and thousands have successfully moved to places such as Florida and have either continued their working lives or have quite effectively started to earn a living.

I would not have been quite so reassuring about all of this, had I not begun my work with the people at Palm Coast. Until then, I had had the usual feeling about Sun Belt communities, and especially about the problems of staying active. In an earlier chapter, I mentioned my talks with John Gazzoli, and his advice about *research* and the probing of the *needs* of a community can lead to the start of small, new, very successful businesses in the developing communities around the country. Not only has the veterinarian successfully made a move to the community, but the start-up of many new businesses has been the result of previous *avocations*, rather than vocations—a complete switch in job orientation based upon hobbies, interests, and pastimes. This is exactly the same thing that has happened in outplacement, as I've written. Thus, Palm Coast, for example, now has small businesses that produce stained glass, plastics, electronics, lighting fixtures, medical equipment (pacemakers), and even a subscription fulfillment center—many of them transfers of businesses to one of the industrial parks, but others the result of a change in direction for the owners.

However, suppose you don't want to go through the problems of starting a business, or suppose your financial situation is such that you just can't start one. Suppose you are someone who has to work—or who wants to work, remembering that there is a "direct relationship between enforced idleness and ill health." There are, in fact, ways to get a job, and it requires the same patience, the same research, the same probing, and the same deep thinking that starting a business entails.

While in Palm Coast during several of my trips there, I tried to find out just what the "formula" is—just how people who have moved there and to other planned communities have established new work patterns, new job opportunities, new beginnings. One of the people with whom I've been working is Tom Bailey, vice president and director of Employee Relations with ITT Community Development Corporation, and an expert in just this area. "The formula," he commented, "includes not only flexibility in salary needs, but also in the fact that even though you did one job for thirty years, you can transfer some of the same skills to *different* kinds of work. Adaptation to a new work environment can be very rewarding."

He gave me some concrete examples of people who have had an avocation at home and who changed careers as a result: a gourmet cook—transferable to an upscale, exclusive restaurant. Almost anything related to the tourist industry has also been a good basic grounding for working in the Sun Belt. People who do electronics and home repairs have found a way to transfer their skills to jobs in other states.

"The key point," Tom said, "is to achieve as much flexibility as you can in looking for job opportunities. It's amazing how many skills people have picked up over the years that are transferable to other positions. Some of those skills may be from former employment, but many come from a person's hobbies, his or her avocations, or adult education classes."

People our age have experiential education in addition to our formal years at college. Vocational schools and local educational facilities from kindergarten to college are anxious to get hold of people who have worked in companies and can bring to them the skills that you just don't pick up at college. People who have worked in large corporations are usually quite service-oriented, and probably realize more than anyone else just how important customer relations are. It's also a good transferable skill. People who can teach, people who have financial background, people who know computers or communications, people who can write, may have better opportunities of finding an employer who can use their talents.

Knowing that the trend is toward more and more retirees and middle-aged (as well as young family) relocaters to want and need work, the most innovative thing that Palm Coast has done is to develop a "Job Bank." It is being copied by communities all across the country and it would be well to check it out before making your decision about where you would like to live—and to work.

The companies in the various industrial parks and retail centers at Palm Coast compile a computerized list of potential job applicants and their backgrounds—listing the skills that they might have used in any number of different areas. The job of the personnel people, of course, is to fit the people available into the existing needs. Tom explains:

> The companies here draw upon that bank and it gives them a steady supply of applicants. We have about forty thousand people who have bought property here, and about five or six thousand who have expressed interest in relocating here as jobs become available. It not only helps the employer, but it helps the applicant because it puts their names in front of the potential managers.

On one of my visits, I started to compile a list of the types of jobs that had been successfully recruited at Palm Coast and the surrounding area of Flagler County. It includes accounting clerks, cabinet makers, clerical, computer operators, data-entry operators, draftspeople, educators, electrical engineers, electricians, real-estate salespeople, landscape maintenance, mechanical engineers, production workers, nurses aides and RNs, protective and security services, retail sales, and restaurant employees. And all of this, in addition to the people who own and run the small shops and businesses in the area.

The best suggestion I can give to anyone who is planning such a move is to visit the place that's been chosen. Check out all the things I've cautioned about previously—the true year-round weather, the local newspapers, the job market, the housing market and its diversity, the age groups and their diversity, infrastructure and recreations. Do it on a vacation if you have finally narrowed down your choices to one or two states or planned communities. There is always a hotel or a motel near the place you've selected. And finally, ask the people who *live and work there* just what their feelings are about your potential new home.

And, above all, sit down and make a list of all the hobbies, interests, avocations, sidelines, and recreational pastimes that you've been involved with all of your life—and the life of your companion. You may be very surprised to find that you really do have a transferable skill. It's not too farfetched to think that your public-speaking attributes and anecdotal talents might well make you mayor of the town to which you've chosen to move!

19 The Graying of the Campus Green

I grow old learning many things.

—Solon
Fragment 22

It is difficult to believe that the volatile generation of the sixties is just about two decades past. I have always loved to teach, to lecture to young students, to conduct seminars on filmmaking, and to exchange ideas and opinions with the future leaders of my profession. To this day, I try to squeeze in the time to teach at least one course a year at New York University as an adjunct assistant professor in the Department of Arts, Sciences, and Humanities. But it is of the sixties that I remember my lectures and seminars during that time with a very special sense of joy and excitement. For, with all the talk of hippies and flower children and revolution, the students of that period had a dynamism and a probing sense of disbelief that made an establishment professor fair game for their questions, their curiosity, even their rudeness. It was wise to be well prepared for any lecture. Some of my readers, now well into their forties, might remember the days of which I speak.

I remember one session at NYU with an undergraduate class in film production. When I entered the room, everyone was reading a newspaper, magazine, or paperback, challenging me to make them put the reading materials away, to give them something important enough to make them listen to *me*. At first I was angry at the lack of respect, for when we went to college, the entrance of the instructor was the signal for immediate attention. Then I laughed and *turned out the lights!* Unable to read any longer, they put the newspapers and magazines aside while a film was shown, and the class was under way.

Question periods were equally as exciting and challenging. In a two-hour session, forty minutes would hardly be enough time to field the queries that ranged from what kind of film stock was used in the documentary to "How can you sell your soul to make films for America's money-grubbing corporations?"

As all things change, this too has changed. The first thing that occurs to me now is that many of those in my class are actually money-grubbing with some of America's money-grubbing corporations, and many of them now have a family consisting of a conservative, average wife or husband plus an average two-and-a-third children! The other thing that has changed quite radically is that I find that the students of this era now just sit there and listen. Once again the professor has become God and whatever is given as gospel is written down as such. Well-washed, establishment faces look up in blank and accepting trust, and I sometimes feel that if I were to state that "sex is the cause of acne," they would dutifully write it down in case it came up in the final examination. It is now a waste of time to schedule a long question-and-answer period, for it is generally filled with long, awkward silences, while the questions that are bothering them are quickly asked during the short, five-minute break in the hallway outside the classroom. I once thought that it was *I* who had changed for the worse, until I compared notes with others who teach. The establishment has settled on the heads of our new student generation and it is the *teachers* who are the revolutionaries.

As long as I'm in my "curmudgeon mode," I might as well cover one more point that has begun to disturb me in the past two or three years particularly. With the advent of videotape and the proliferation of VCRs, a great new pseudoindustry has evolved—the pirating of copyrighted shows. For those of us in the industry, this means a loss of income, for the royalties that are rightfully those of the old collaborators are, in essence, lost forever. The society as a whole has now begun to tolerate dishonesty, I suppose, but it is amazing to me that I have had students who also pirate videotapes on their home machines. The fact that they are about to enter an industry where this will eventually affect *their* income does not seem to bother them, and in discussing this in classes, I have been met with a feeling that I am a "dinosaur." After all, "Everybody does it!"

There is, however, an area of brightness in all of this. During these past ten years or more, I have been invited to speak to classes and seminars in the field of continuing education, to adults who are holding other jobs while attending school or who have decided to go back to college for a variety of reasons. Some return to improve their chances for advancement in their own professions; some to change careers; some because there has been a smoldering interest in their lives since they were teenagers, an interest never fulfilled for diverse and personal reasons. I have the utmost admiration for them, since they work a full day, come to class in the evening, and yet never miss their deadlines on homework, and they are always anxious to engage in discussion. The professor, in turn, can do no less than to give his or her utmost commitment.

The good news also is that in these continuing-education classes all over the country, the age group has changed, and I now see before me the faces of men and women who are more mature, more interested, more committed and more concerned with learning as much as they possibly can. It is because they have *chosen* to go to school; for them schooling is not just another unavoidable step in the process of growing up and leaving home. The ages range from about thirty up to the late seventies and even into the eighties. At a recent seminar for adults, the most exciting questions were asked of me by a man of seventy-two who had always wanted to know more about film directing. This was *his* chance to go back to college! Suddenly, I began to see the vitality of the 1960s without the hostility, in addition to an intensity of motivation and an intellectual stimulation for teacher and student alike.

How rapidly the world of education is changing! And we, as always, are a part of the sudden change. There was a time when we went to school at the age of five or six, graduated from high school or college and then pursued a career until retirement—single-minded, rigidly programmed through our lives—to rust away until death. We were again the victims of a self-perpetuating myth that said that our intelligence and our capacity to learn were declining after the age of thirty or forty. "You can't teach an old dog new tricks," my grandmother used to say, "There's no fool like an old fool," and other adages of ageist folklore, too many of them still in circulation today.

How surprised she might be to discover, as the researchers have, that, much to their surprise, there is actual proof of an *improvement* in intelligence and the functions of learning as we age! The *speed* of our performance may decline, but the *capacity* to learn does not diminish when we have passed the invisible barrier of age forty.

Marty Knowlton, one of the founders of Elderhostel, becomes angry when the subject of waning intelligence is mentioned. In one of our telephone conversations he mentioned the findings of colleges at which Elderhostel classes are conducted. "All of us carry with us that ugly myth that you lose your capacity to learn, that you begin to learn less and less, when in fact the opposite is true. As you get older, you learn better. Experience doesn't diminish the mind; it *increases* your mind. Experience *creates* the mind. Shouldn't your mind be better at sixty than it was at 30?"

Somehow there has been a new liberation in the spirit of learning, of achieving our potential, no matter how late in life, and the return to school by people of our generations has been nothing short of astounding. *More than half* the full-time and part-time college students in the country are adults, and though the term *adult* also includes students from 25 through 45, vast numbers of middle-aged men and women are also returning to the classroom. The colleges and universities have been quick to spot the trend, for they have been in a period of decreasing enrollment as the Baby Boomers graduate and go on their way to Wall Street. Promotional materials now include the older student as a target, and continuing-education programs are flourishing and expanding.

Dr. James C. Hall, dean of University College at Pace University in New York, added, "Continuing education is just a dynamic view of life. People continue to change. Development doesn't stop at adolescence, and *learning* is a part of development. Continuing education is a function of people developing . . . and not necessarily just in the schools."

Millions of us have gone back to class at community colleges; in our churches and synagogues; in our professional organizations; in our libraries and museums; via television and videotape instruction; through correspondence courses; through private lessons in the languages, the arts, or even tennis; as well as in schools in the armed forces and in prisons!

Colleges, in addition to seeing their young financial base gradually disappear, also began to suffer an increase in dropout rates. With the alternative of total extinction staring them in the face, they began to realize that changes would have to be made if they were to appeal to the adult student, and to the people who were living right on the perimeters of their own campuses. Our life-styles are quite different from those of college-age students, needless to say. Curricula that took into account the fact that most of us worked during the day, and could not attend classes at normal hours, had to be developed. Administrators had to realize that the usual battery of entrance exams and testing procedures were quite valueless for people who had interrupted their schooling as much as twenty or thirty years before, when college kids like us wore bobby sox. Suddenly, there are "weekend" colleges springing up all over the country; morning and evening classes held especially for adult students who commute to work, and new methods of independent study, such as closed-circuit, interactive television, field work, correspondence study, videotape cassettes, and private tutorial teaching.

One of the most important innovations I find is that most schools and colleges are beginning to acknowledge that our *life experience* is worth analyzing as a prerequisite to reentry into the academic world. Thus we find that many universities are admitting students not only without regard to age, but with a good hard look at such criteria as motivation, creativity, and job history, rather than on the standard college admission guidelines of tests and high-school grades. Evaluators are now giving credits for business experience in blueprint reading, writing, management, labor relations, marketing and cost control, as well as for self-taught skills like painting and sculpture.

For colleges and universities, many of the changes have been a breath of fresh spring air. In these educational institutions, originally designed for the children and the youth of our society, it is *we* who are preserving the jobs of thousands of professors who had been trapped in a diminishing job market— many of them in our own age group—by this sudden influx of a vital and totally new breed of student. And for those of us middle age and older who are the new scholars, the innovations in the educational system have opened up new and exciting horizons. After all these years, we are going back to school!

At Pace University in New York, an older student named Henry Seymour told me, "I'm learning as quickly as I did when I got my master's degree in 1937, but it just takes a little bit longer to write it down when I take an examination." I asked him if he learns more slowly, and he answered with, "No, I just think I'm more *thorough* than I was back in 1937."

He was but one of many. Retired for a year at that time, he had spent forty-one years as an international executive with a major pharmaceutical corporation, working and living in Colombia, Ecuador, Venezuela, Mexico, Brazil, and Greece. "There are various reasons that I went back to school. First of all, I don't want to sit and do nothing. Second, I think that the acquisition of knowledge is an end in itself. And third, I want to look around and get a job." His majors included International Business Management and Taxation and he also mentioned that it was the younger students who turn to *him* for help because the subject is so complicated.

For younger adults, the desire to make more money or to improve their professional positions is what sends most back to school after so many years away from the classroom. Dr. Hall said, "No matter what they tell you, if you probe deeply enough, you find that it's the major reason. However, there are people who have reached a stage in life where they are finally able to pursue something that has always been a second interest in life: physics, astronomy, finance."

Actually, in our age groups, only a small percentage are going back to school for academic credits or to get a degree eventually, but when we do return for completion of a bachelor's or a master's degree we often show ourselves to be superior in both performance and the ability to learn, regardless of age.

The return to school of people of our generations also serves to break down the barriers of age segregation, since the mix of all ages is of benefit to everyone, young or old. The young can learn from the experience of the mature, seasoned adult, while the returning student remains in touch with a society that is always in a state of flux, however incomprehensible it may sometimes be to those of us who grew up in simpler and more naive times.

I read of a high school in Harbor Springs, Michigan, that opened its doors to the elders of the town, allowing them to sign up for any high-school class, either for credit or just for fun. Some of the adults are invited to give guest lectures; they share the library, lunchrooms, school band, the classes in microcomputers and ceramics, and most of all, the wisdom of the years. "Suppose a student is writing a term paper on the lumbering industry in Michigan," a counselor said in an interview. "Imagine how much more alive the material will become to a student when he or she can sit down and talk to a man who has run a sawmill for forty years!"

On the college level, several schools have also begun to offer intergenerational programs, and the reports are sometimes quite amusing when researchers investigate the adjustments that are necessary on both sides of the age fence. Many of the older students have thrown themselves not only into courses like mathematics and philosophy, but also into the more exotic forms of learning—like belly dancing and mountain climbing. One older student at the campus of Western Washington State University summed it up: "We had stereotyped ideas about young people, about 'hippies,' and some of our first classes were a shock. I walked into my math class late. The students were lying all over the floor on their stomachs, on their backs, every which way. I learned soon afterward that the fellow who was sitting in a chair leading the class wasn't the teacher. The teacher was down on the floor with the students! This was a whole new world to me."

For the younger students, it was also a revelation to find that the older classmates were far from over the hill. It has the additional result of making them unafraid to grow older, and even makes them envious of the attitudes of the elderly students. One of them said, "How very free they are!" Another commented, "You can't believe how much more interesting a class in history is when there's an older person in it who has lived through the Depression or who has heard a father or grandfather talk about the time right after the Civil War or World War I."

These experiments in education are continuing all over the country, both in the area of reentry for middle-aged students taking the normal curriculum and in programs specifically designed to bring the older American back into the mainstream of learning—for a degree, for expansion of one's intellectual potential, because of a long-deferred desire to learn, or just for fun. Community colleges in Miami, Los Angeles, and New York, as well as Duke University, Fordham, the University of Maryland, Aquinas College in Michigan, New York University, and Baruch College are just a few of the institutions that have joined the list of innovators. As Dr. Douglas Rich, the former director of the Bridge Project (unfortunately discontinued just a few years ago) put it, "The fact remains that when we isolate any group of people from the established norm, we usually are contributing to their ill health; however different any group may be, our society is most healthy when such groups remain among us."

For those interested in part-time degree programs, there is a publication that gives the information for every area. It's called *Who Offers Part-time Degree Programs?* and it's available from Peterson's Guides, Department 8355, PO Box 2123, Princeton, NJ 08543-2123 or telephone 1-800-EDU-DATA for the current price and instructions on how to order.

The nondegree student who wants to return to school for whatever reason has a choice so vast that no single writer can begin to sort it all out. My office floor is piled high with university and college bulletins that offer courses from the Culture of Morocco, Wraparound Second Mortgages, Investment Banking, Techniques of Book Editing, and Advertising Workshops to such esoteric and diverse subjects as Psi Phenomena, the Holographic Aspects of Consciousness, I Ching, Tarot Reading, Neighborhood Restaurant Tours, and Beginning Backpacking. All this in addition to "readin', 'ritin', and 'rithmetic!"

Even in my own personal life, I had reason to take advantage of the courses offered over a most diverse range of subjects. The New York real-estate market, as you might have read, has gone berserk with everything in sight being converted to either a cooperative or a condominium, and the total experience a classic example of greed, rampant gentrification, and lack of planning by developers and city officials. As soon as we had word that our building was slated for conversion, both Sheryl and I went to school. My own course in cooperative conversion was given at Baruch College and it prepared me well for the next three years of negotiation and aggravation.

One of the most innovative and exciting developments in expanding the boundaries of the learning experience has been with the group known as Elderhostel, founded in the early seventies by Marty Knowlton and some of his associates. It is based upon the best European tradition of education and innkeeping, but is designed for the elder citizen over sixty who remains active, on the move, and hungry for new knowledge and new friends.

The program has now expanded to all fifty states as well as Canada and forty foreign countries. The number of Elderhostels has also mushroomed to slightly under 200,000 and the first programs to be held in Russia are to begin about the time that this is being written. During the late spring, summer, and early autumn, when colleges are emptiest and lying dormant, regular members of the college faculty teach a wide variety of courses in the liberal arts and sciences—for example: Mark Twain Studies, Astronomy and Mythology, Philosophy of Religion, Vitality and Fitness, Saving Planet Earth—and so many, many more that reading the catalog is a delight in itself. The foreign courses cover everything from contemporary society in the country in which you study, but also ancient civilizations (right on site), local history and color, and a wonderful course called *Rhinos, Butterflies, and Mangoes*, offered in Nepal.

On each of nearly four hundred campuses, the Elderhostelers live right in the dormitories, eat in the college cafeterias, and share their schoolwork with other summer students. It has grown so rapidly that Michael Zoob, the vice president of the nonprofit organization calls it "The Elderhostel Phenomenon" and he says, "It's gone above and beyond the program. It's almost a movement. The hostelers come into the classes with the mental energy and drive professors never see in their undergraduate classes. There are no grades. They don't need the course for a major. They come for no other reason than the love of learning. That's what liberal arts is all about!"

One of the most delightful letters ever received by the group read as follows:

> I stumbled on the material about your program in the *New York Times*.
> It met a definite need in me.
> I am retired.
> I am bored.
> I don't know how to play.
> I can't settle for gymnastics, crafts, and pep talks by twenty-year-olds on how great it is to be a senior citizen.
> I would still like to be a being in the flow of life. Your literature seems to hold out that hope. Do please send it to me.

And the reader of this book might well do the same. It is an impressive, delightful, dynamic organization with groups of people to match. Write to: Elderhostel, 80 Boylston Street, Suite 400, Boston, MA 02116, or telephone 1-617-426-8056. You might also find the catalog in your local library.

There is a growing hunger to keep learning. And the opportunities have burgeoned for us through educational programs given right in our communities, in outreach programs, and in innovative concepts such as Elderhostel. I find that most of my older friends are involved in some kind of educational experience—whether in taking just one course a week or in spending several weeks of the summer months on campus with others who share that hunger and that vitality. It was brought home to me once again on a bus.

For some reason, as you have noted, my mini-adventures always seem to take place on a New York City bus, just as I described at the very beginning of this book. This time I was on the Fifth Avenue bus, and a lovely woman in her early sixties sat down next to me and took out what seemed to be a school program. Ever curious, I looked over her shoulder to read, "Institute for Retired Professionals," and I engaged her in conversation to find out where she was heading. The program was begun at the New School in New York in 1962 and membership is open to people who have recently retired from professional or executive careers. It has since spread its innovative thinking to such universities as Harvard, Johns Hopkins, Hofstra, and the University of California at San Francisco and San Diego. For all these retirees, the prime thrust seems to be an indelible restatement of the words of Willard Wirtz: "There must be more to life than twenty years of learning, forty of earning, and the rest, just waiting!"

I looked with her at her program for that week. Her subjects included German Literature, Hebrew Conversation, Watercolors and Acrylics, and T'ai Chi! At Twelfth Street she spryly leaped off the bus, waved once, and headed down the street to school. Thinking of her program, I mused: Why was I having so much trouble with beginning Spanish? Somehow I could no longer use the lame excuse, "Well, I suppose it must be because I'm getting older!"

20 Madison Avenue Discovers Middle Age—At Last!

> If there were dreams to sell,
> What would you buy?
>
> —Thomas Beddoes
> "Dream-Pedlary"

If you've spent the greatest part of your working life in the field of selling or marketing or advertising, then I think you will agree with me that we (the author included) have a tendency to develop an egocentric conceit about the customer. We "know" the buyer from the looker, the person who will drive the car out of the showroom from the "tire kicker." We can "tell" the poor from the rich, the bargainer from the impulsive buyer. We are, after all, experienced, with that uncanny perception that comes from years of dealing with people, and we are—as often as not—*wrong*. Prejudging has been the downfall of too many salespeople.

A friend of mine lives in Grand Prairie, Texas, and each year she makes a trip to New York to catch up on the theater, to dine in her favorite restaurants, and to visit some of Manhattan's better stores. She tells of a visit to an exclusive Fifth Avenue department store and the purchase of a new wardrobe for herself and her husband. The young salesman in the shirt department, who also "knew" his customers, had obviously pegged her as an out-of-towner and his hauteur was exceeded only by his indifference and lack of warmth. Her selection completed, she handed him her credit card. He looked up, his suspicions confirmed, and he asked, with a small supercilious grin on his lips, "Grand Prairie? Wherever on earth is Grand Prairie?"

Calmly, she answered, "Oh it's between Arthur and Irving."

An eyebrow rose slightly and he continued undaunted, "And whatever do you do in Grand Prairie?"

"Oh, we just sit on the porch and watch the oil wells go up and down, up and down!"

Of course, this being at the height of the boom in the Southwest, yet another stereotype took over at once and the word *oil* made the salesman reflect that everyone from Texas is rich! His manner changed, he whipped out his card and gave it to my friend. "If you ever need help in our store, just look me up!"

It is not at all unusual. Even today, just try wearing a pair of faded blue jeans when you visit an exclusive clothing store or go to buy a custom automobile. Your image will not fit the mold, and in a recent series of training tapes that our company made for Brooks Brothers' forty-five stores, we warned salespeople, particularly in suburban locations, that today's family who shop together on a Saturday may very well not look like the old "Brooks Brothers Image." So it is with age.

One of my old dear friends and a longtime client during the 1960s was the late Rosanne Beringer, president of Welcome Wagon International, over eighty years of age, and one of the most successful executives in the country long before the advent of the token female managers in American industry and the current small crop of female CEOs. She kept a very low profile and every time I'd suggest that *Fortune* magazine or *Forbes* might well want to do a story about her, she refused firmly.

She telephoned me one day to tell me of an incident that had occurred in the Memphis Lincoln-Mercury showroom, and since Ford Motor Company was also a client of mine, she thought I'd be interested. I was.

"Young man," she indignantly sputtered. (She always called me "young man" when she was angry.) "Young man, you should call those clients of yours at once and tell them this story!" She had gone into the dealership with her daughter, wanting to purchase a brand-new Lincoln. She looked, she touched, she sat in the seat, she handled the wheel, and all the while not a single salesman came over to assist her, even though the showroom was quite empty. For over half an hour, ignored by the staff, she looked at the car. Finally, angry and distressed, she left, walked across the street, and purchased a Cadillac!

To the salespeople she "obviously" was not a buyer. *No woman of eighty* walks into a dealership, ready to whip out a checkbook, and pay cash for a brand-new luxury car! In the sagacity of their conceit, the salesmen had pegged her as a true "tire kicker"—a looker, but not a buyer. Had the prospect been a well-dressed *man* of about fifty, he would have been duly pegged as a wealthy chairman of the board of a major corporation, and the rush to serve him would have mauled fifteen salesmen in the stampede!

To those who claim to reflect the images of our society—the advertising community, the marketers, the purveyors of communications—two entire generations (ours) have been dismissed for a long time as "tire kickers." Until now, the advertisers have considered us so unimportant in their scheme of things, in their analyses of "cost per thousand" that we do not even exist in the mailing lists! Ken Dychtwald, the author of *Age Wave*, and the new "guru" of our generations, puts it well, when he says that "we have more people over the age of sixty-five in the United States today than the entire population of Canada . . . and yet, everything in the marketplace is designed for the *young*." Though we have forty million Americans with arthritis, *buttons* are designed for young, supple fingers. He also mentions the design and the technologies of public transportation, of the steps to public and private buildings, typeface in newspapers and magazine, tamper-proof medicines for our kids, traffic lights and pedestrian cross signals geared to the pace of the young.

Not too long ago, a group that is active in the furtherance of the rights of women looked desperately to purchase a list covering the ages of forty-five to sixty-five, and nowhere could one be found! Certainly they could have acquired lists for the aged, adolescents, college students, middle-income liberals or conservatives, gun owners, gun haters, and cat fanciers, but the demographics did not exist for "Women, Age forty-five–sixty-five." That was a mere eight years ago.

But the face of aging is changing, so possibly is the awareness of the advertising community. Every so often the sleeping giant of Madison Avenue, comatose in Rip Van Winkle isolation these past twenty-five years, is shaken awake by discovery and revelation. But it has taken place very slowly (and in some areas not at all, even today). The *Harvard Business Review* published an article by Rena Bartos, a senior vice president at J. Walter Thompson, titled "Over Forty-nine: The Invisible Consumer Market." Stephen J. Frankfurt, an old and talented friend from my early television and film days, and now a top executive in creative planning at Kenyon & Eckhardt, has effectively spoken and written to his industry on "The Maturity Market"—us—the people from age forty-five and up to sixty-four. Ken Dychtwald has been lecturing to groups all over the country in trying to wake them up to the fact that the over-fifty market is now worth more than $800 *billion* a year! They have also discovered:

- That seventy-seven percent of all financial assets in America are held by people over fifty-five.
- That sixty-eight percent of all money market accounts are held by people over fifty-five.

- That eighty percent of all the money in savings and loans institutions are owned by people over fifty-five. (And thank God they're all insured, given the history of the S&Ls.)

Certainly, there is a pocket of profound poverty among the aged as well as among the children of our country. Certainly, too, we have seen our government pull back from helping the people who are struggling to meet even the simplest of daily needs. It is an area in which I personally become very angry, for this is also a society that could help, if it so desired. But, in spite of it all, an interesting phenomenon has taken place, and it has resulted in the most affluent group of consumers, who have come slowly from a state of sheer invisibility, so long neglected, too often insulted, perpetually ignored, to a place in the market as the "active affluents" or the "active retireds." Why? Why have we gone so abruptly from the back door of the marketplace to become the fair-haired, albeit rapidly graying, favorite children of the business community? The reasons, of course, are simple and what surprises me is that it took so long to discover them:

- There are lots and lots of us and we are growing rapidly as a group.

- *We have lots and lots of money.*

Another attitude of Madison Avenue has also resulted in the late discovery of us as a market. The pundits who control our advertising and who claim to know us well have always held that our buying habits were established during our own years in the "Pepsi generation" and they cannot change now. As Hubert Pryor, former editor of *Modern Maturity* magazine, put it, "Clearly, if that were the case, everybody in the maturity market today would be using Kolynos toothpaste, driving an Essex, reading *Liberty*, and drinking sarsaparilla."

What the marketers have failed to uncover is that, in Gerry Hotchkiss's words, "I don't know any people our age who are concerned with *longevity* as such. They're more concerned with the *quality of their lives*, making it as rich as possible for as long as possible."

These feelings, these attitudes of the people of our generations make us, as a result, consumers the likes of which the advertising world has never quite seen before. We have postponed much of our lives until now—the children had to be diapered, raised, schooled, and prepared for the world. For the most part they have gone on to lead their own lives. For the first time we do not have to make sacrifices for them. Steve Frankfurt, in a speech before the

Western States Advertising Agencies Association in Monterey, California, commented on the continuing erosion of "the Puritan, work-oriented ethic" and stated that we are becoming more self-indulgent, putting more emphasis on "having it now." He went on to say, "For the first time since taking on the responsibilities of marriage, the couple is free to think about themselves, what *they* want or need, how *they* want to spend their money, what kind of car *they* can now have." He calls it, rightly, "mom-and-pop time"!

In spite of the myths about us, we are in excellent health for the most part, and are reported to watch our waistlines and diets more than any other age group. Less than 1 percent of us are listed by the census takers as being seriously ill. We are, in fact, the single greatest market for luxury items and for travel, even if we don't appear too often in the ads. If you take the cruise ships to Alaska, as I have for various film assignments, you will find that fully 85 percent of the passengers on the ship are our age or older! We also demand more luxury in our travel. We've put away our backpacks forever. *Fully 80 percent of all luxury travel is by people over fifty!*

A short time ago, *New Choices* magazine did a survey that was directed at the advertising and travel industries, that are still showing twenty-year-olds romping on the beaches and lifting one another out of the clear, blue water of the Caribbean resorts. The figures are fascinating. In *every single category*, the age fifty-plus group (in the income range of $30,000 or more) had a higher percentage of involvement and spent more money as a result, than the general population. Here are some examples:

	Total Population	Age 50+
Domestic Travel in Last Year	50.2%	63.4%
Foreign Travel in Last 3 Years	15.3%	25.6%
Traveler's Checks Bought in Last Year	14.3%	24.7%
Foreign Travel/Schedule Plane	9.9%	17.1%
Domestic Trip/Scheduled Plane	16.4%	23.1%
1–14 Nights Motel/Hotel	29.3%	35.8%
Rental Car	7.8%	12.0%

In all categories, including the use of credit cards, amount of money spent on the trips, activities while traveling, the fifty-plus group showed higher percentages than the general population (except in sailing, where each was equal at 3.5 percent).

We also actively buy a thousand or more categories of products that range from swimming pools to investments, from boating equipment to restaurant dinners, from second homes to magazines, newspapers, luggage, and automobiles. In fact, the group over fifty is more apt to own two, and even three, cars than any other segment of the population. We love to entertain; we're active in gardening, fishing, bicycling, tennis, camping, and photography. And I noted with interest a statistic in the *Harvard Business Review* that we "not only invest in stocks and bonds, [but] are the only segment of the population that is above the norm for buying diamond rings." *Sarsaparilla and Liberty magazine indeed!*

There are, of course, a few checks and balances to all this, and I write of them so as not to be vulnerable to the reviewer or the reader who shouts, "Yeah, but. . . ." Our generation, for the most part, has been able to own our own homes for some time now, in spite of the fact that the post–World War II period was no picnic either, and I have been trying to tell some of our young people that. Housing was a mess. It just didn't exist. But, now we find that even second homes are quite common in our list of assets, and young people are complaining (sometimes rightly) that they might never be able to afford a *first* one, no less a second.

However, these homes that are used to determine our total worth are really paid-for, mortgage-free assets. As a result, many in our generation are what Ken Dychtwald calls "brick rich," and are paying the current high tax rates on property and assets that are not at all liquid—*unless we sell.* Thus, even though our *total worth* may be around a figure that would have astounded us as younger people, we somehow don't *feel* rich. And we are not about to sell!

There is another danger in this discovery of our generation as an affluent, vital, active part of the consuming public. It might well be hurting the truly homeless and the elderly poor. For a while there was the myth of *every* person over sixty-five subsisting on a diet of dog food; this is giving way to still another pernicious distortion, for I have begun to read about it in popular magazines like *Newsweek* and newspapers like the *Wall Street Journal.* The new myth portrays *everyone* over the age of fifty as affluent and totally independent. America would like to get rid of the image of the poor forever!

An article in *Forbes* magazine tried to debunk the idea that a large number of our elderly are in need of help from the government, a growing attitude in these days of "too much governmental control over our lives." By using selective and exceptional cases (which every author uses, of course), *Forbes* gave the distinct impression that we are *all* well-heeled, living in the lap of luxury, buying condominiums and sailboats, and becoming filthy rich in the stock market.

I sense in this shifting perception of an entire group, a potentially harmful result, equally as damaging as the myth that we are all in penury. It is the reason that the attack on Social Security becomes more pronounced and vociferous. It is the reason that we have seen the rise of such mean-spirited ageist organizations like Americans for Generational Equity.

This feeling was echoed by Cyril F. Brickfield, executive director of the American Association of Retired Persons, who wrote, "Normally, we would welcome the efforts of those who seek to correct misconceptions about older citizens. But the new myth makers go too far. Rather than just explode the old stereotypes, they are creating new ones. They are implying that just because the elderly have made substantial gains, they can now afford to make major sacrifices, such as giving up some of the cost-of-living protection provided by Social Security."

Like you, I try to balance my feelings of being a part of this affluent generation of ours with my conscience and continual awareness of the social problems with which I grew up. I do enjoy my role in an age group that is, overall, less dependent upon others than are the very young and the very old. At the same time, I look with admiration, faith, and some dependence upon the people who will be described in the following chapter, to make certain that the myths of middle age and the elderly are destroyed forever, but without being replaced by other societal straitjackets that reflect the self-interests and the narrowness of those whom we elect to govern us, those who communicate to us, or those who merely try to sell to us their products.

If we are a newly discovered market, I will revel in it and smile as the Baby Boomers and the television "Pepsi Generation" seem to be turning gray, or as I note a *Wall Street Journal* headline that advises its readers, "Advertisers Start Recognizing Cost of Insulting Elderly."

And, in these past years, I have also noted with interest and amusement even the slightest changes in approach and in attitude toward us by Madison Avenue. I note that Polaroid began selling a camera for the grandmother who was graduating college. Advertisers have begun to discover that the *toy market* is a great one for people our age, for how many grandparents have bought expensive playthings (no batteries included) for their darling grandchildren? *Modern Maturity* magazine now has the largest circulation of any magazine in America (*Reader's Digest* was first until recently), and it looks now as if *Lear's*—geared to "the woman who wasn't born yesterday—may be on its way to being a huge success. *New Choices: For the Best Years* now speaks to over 1,600,000 readers each month, and the responses to both advertising and editorial copy is, to put it mildly, phenomenal. Recently, they published a request from a missionary asking for used Christmas cards for his Bombay community, and they were deluged with over 250,000 cards!

So, it is not all bad and I shall accept all of this for now, waiting suspiciously for a change of the fickle heart by Madison Avenue should they discover another group to love. For the moment, it will do. My mother loved me as her son, good or bad, my wife in "sickness and in health," my German shepherd dogs for my loyalty and devotion. Now I am overjoyed with my new experience. I am finally being loved for my *spending power!*

21 ✸ Man (Person?) the Barricades!

You're wrinkled babies! Sniveling! You're the elders of the tribe. What are you doing for the tribe's survival?

—Maggie Kuhn

I remember it as a rainy day in April. I had come into New York from my island especially to attend the meeting, and the warmth of the YWCA lobby in midtown Manhattan felt comfortable in the early spring chill. Convinced in my usual grumbling pessimism that I would be the only person to show up on a day like that, I was pleasantly surprised to see the milling, vital women who had already arrived, shaking off umbrellas, picking up pamphlets, signing the register. A charming registrar came up to me and asked if, perhaps, I might be in the wrong place. No, I told her, checking my folder, I assume that this was the meeting of the Older Women's League? She nodded, smiled again, and went back to her desk.

The huge hall was packed, rain notwithstanding, with probably over four hundred women, attractive, alive with humming anticipation, all of them between the ages of forty-five and sixty-five. Four hundred women—and me. For I realized, looking around, that I was the only man present, an obvious fact brought home still further when the meeting began and Jo Turner of the OWL National Board greeted the group with, "Good afternoon, sisters," then, turning to look directly at me, "and *brother!*"

It has been a long time since that rainy afternoon and I have watched with interest as groups like OWL have sprung up, expanded, increased their political power, and made themselves heard in a world that continually strives to make our generations invisible. Suddenly, too, I have watched with awe as

258

middle-aged men and women have begun to protest, very loudly, very effectively, not only through their organizations but also as individuals, as busload by busload they have become the massed verbalization of the things that threaten us most.

From the protests in the early eighties, such as Solidarity Day in Washington, DC, when a quarter million people marched, drove and bused to the demonstration, to the most recent one that came as this book was being revised, the huge gathering to support *Roe v. Wade*, the faces were not the same as those we saw in the sixties. Not at all. The ages were vastly diverse, and the middle-aged and elders took their places alongside their younger sisters and brothers. One man, about fifty years old, wearing a hard hat, sat on the Mall and commented, "I thought the protest marches were for kids who had too much time on their hands. They'd come down here, have riots, smoke marijuana, and tear down the system." But there have been many middle-aged faces during the years that have seen protests on a great number of issues, many of them having little direct bearing on the issues of age and aging. In a recent article in *Mother Jones* magazine, a Baby Boomer wrote an article that seemed to be the typical contemporary, spoiled, cranky complaint that Mom and Dad had it all, but they—their children—would never have a house, never be able to afford a new station wagon, would never pay as little for rent as dear old Mom and Dad did (though Mom and Dad probably made one-tenth their salary), and that they had also inherited a huge national debt, also the fault of Mom and Dad.

However, there was one interesting box within the article, and in it the author did make some sense. She wrote that Baby Boomers had forgotten how to *fight*. "Young people could have learned a thing or two from the elderly: also squeezed by inflation in the seventies, they organized, voted and lobbied Congress. As a result, Social Security benefits have been indexed to the cost of living." Of course, one of the excuses she gave was the fact that they were all "raising kids" while we older folk had plenty of time to protest!

I think what I have been most awed and impressed by is the fact that, for the most part, it is the *women* who are leading the battle on ageism, while we men lag far behind in our activism. Possibly, too often, the male has been involved with his career (just as the Baby Boomer is so busy raising children), quite confident that nothing will ever change, that life will continue as it has, that problems cannot affect us under the protective umbrella of a male-dominated, male-oriented legislative and corporate world. And then, one day, the roof falls in and we are shocked and surprised and cast adrift. Is it because women, on the other hand, have always been discriminated against in the society—economically, socially, and legislatively? Certainly, for the women in our group, it has always been a continuing struggle to achieve equality in the business world run by men. In fact, women earn less money today, as compared to their male counterparts, than they did twenty-five years ago! In 1955, the earned income of women was about 64 percent of that for men in equal jobs, while today it is about 59 percent. The unemployment rates of professionally trained women are two to five times higher than for men in the same field and with the same degree of training. And all this in spite of (or because of) the dramatic growth in the numbers of women returning to the job market since World War II. So, if women's voices are the loudest ones being raised, perhaps it might be well for *all of us* to listen.

"It's a call to political action," Maggie Kuhn says, "but not as vested interests, not as a self-serving group. It's a call to a new kind of political responsibility for the survival of society . . . because *age* is a universalizing force and a universal human experience. Not all of us are black, not all of us are women, not all of us are minorities. But we're all getting *older!*"

When she was sixty-five, Maggie Kuhn was forced to retire from the editorship of a church magazine. Wounded and angry, she fought back and gathered five friends to form an organization that would battle to change the laws, as well as the attitudes, that make up a pattern of age discrimination in our country. It was the press that teasingly referred to the tiny group of battlers as the "Gray Panthers" and the name stuck. A decade later, the group is more active than ever, and though the organization has always been in the forefront of the fight for generational equality, more than *half* the membership is under sixty-five. And, if you were to comment on Maggie's age, she would probably put you down with the fact that Susan B. Anthony was eighty-four when she culminated her lifetime battle by organizing the International Women's Suffrage Alliance in Berlin. Margaret Mead remained a dynamic, strong, vocal force well into her seventies. The list is endless.

The important question, of course, is: Does it do any good? The Gray Panthers have been active in *all* areas of society, and their current agenda includes the subjects of peace, of house care reform, and housing policy, all of them areas that are not confined to the field of aging. But they have also been active in the antiwar movement, antinuclear protests, in health care, racism, sexism, and all the other forces that demean people and dehumanize them, regardless of age. Protest is an effective weapon.

- Under pressure from the Gray Panthers, Congress raised the permissible mandatory retirement age from sixty-five to seventy. They have also promoted new workforce concepts—job sharing, phased retirement, sabbatical leaves, and midcareer changes to allow people to work at any age.

- A four-year study of nursing homes exposed the shocking conditions that prevail in so many of them; there are Panther networks monitoring their own local nursing homes and the agencies responsible for enforcing reforms. For years they have been in the forefront in seeking alternatives to placing our elderly parents in institutions, for they have believed, as I do, that 40 percent of nursing home patients could live successfully in their own communities if homemakers, hot meals, and minimal health services were provided.

The Gray Panthers have also been involved, along with many other organizations, in fighting any proposed cutbacks in the Social Security programs, as well as lobbying for national health insurance, consumer protection, and intergenerational housing. The latter theory is practiced by Maggie herself. "Our rigid age segregation—the 'ghettoization' of young and old people—is contrary to the larger public interest," she says. "Ultimately it will destroy the sense of community when you have more and more old people living in isolation."

The idea is not an easy one on which to expand. Though it has worked in some areas, including an experiment at Bucknell University (in which older students returning to college shared living quarters with younger ones), much of the zoning in the United States prohibits more than two or three unrelated people from sharing living quarters (though some courts have struck down local ordinances as restrictive). In Yugoslavia, the *komencias* provide older persons without relatives the support of a younger family of their choice. The agreement provides care to the older person until death, at which time the property and estate are inherited by the younger people. It is a subject that is gaining acceptance here in the United States, especially in times of very tight housing and a runaway inflation rate. We may all see the day in which surrogate families begin to play an ever-increasing role in the aging process.

I have commented earlier on what seems to be a growing trend in the planned community concepts, where formerly all of them were geared to retirement families over the age of fifty or fifty-five. Communities such as Palm Coast in Florida have broken the old "Sun City pattern" by mixing age groups, and it has been quite successful. It has worked, too, because these new communities are also taking into consideration the continuation of careers or the changing of direction in those careers as well as offering lifestyle and relocation to warmer climates.

Of course, I am now a Gray Panther and have been one for at least ten years. I am, to say the least, quite proud of it. The membership fee is minimal; their newspaper, *Network*, gives me joy and keeps me up to date, and I am still constantly amazed by the fact that Maggie's schedule has not let up one bit, even though, as she notes, she now travels with a companion. If you'd like information, write to the Gray Panthers at 311 South Juniper Street, Philadelphia, PA 19107.

There is much in the fight to gain our rights, to be heard in our crying out for equitable treatment, that stirs a faint undertone of ambivalence in me. I have always considered myself a battler when the need arose, though living in a world where evenhandedness and compromise are often needed to survive or to achieve even a small measure of success. I have written letters to the editors, to corporations, and to my Senators, most often without success, sometimes with notable recognition—and I continue to do so, perhaps with even more frequency these days. However, I have found that too often the lone voice of dissent is easily squelched, while the strength of an organization or a programmed campaign is triumphant through the powerful voice of sheer numbers.

My ambivalence occurs when I roundly condemn the people who think differently of using pressure tactics when they develop a strong following of activists to convince networks, for example, that certain types of "jiggle" programs and TV violence are unsuitable for the chaste American family, or that Tipper Gore's campaign against suggestive rock lyrics smacks of hypocrisy. On the other hand, I strongly support the groups and organizations that are pressuring these *same* networks to end their silent support of ageism, sexism, and racism. I accept my hostility and my anger with "the other side" because I feel that they preach censorship and boycott, though they deny it vehemently. Then I look at *myself* and ask why I am any different when I refuse to buy the products of a manufacturer because of the company's role in creating a horrendous oil spill, or in "pushing" supplemental feeding to infants in Third World countries, or in the delivery of dangerous birth-control devices to these same people when our country has banned them from use. Am *I* then not supporting a boycott? Of course I am!

But it is not natural (human nature) to think that *they* are unfair and that *we* are right, while they think that *we* are unfair and *they* are right? At times like those I merely set my stubborn jaw and mutter the line from Voltaire, "Your freedom ends where my nose begins," and I go back to do battle, firmly convinced that *they* are wrong and *we* are right!

At the meeting of the Manhattan chapter of the Older Women's League,

Natalie Priest, a superb actress and then chairperson of the AFTRA (American Federation of Television and Radio Artists) Women's Committee, asked a question of the audience:

"How many of you saw the Oscar broadcasts the other evening?"

Several hands went up. I was surprised at the small response, since I was convinced that *everyone* else watched Hollywood's inflated image of itself, even if I didn't. She went on.

"Did you notice the absence of anything in the commercials? Do you realize that there was not *one single older woman* in a commercial in a broadcast that was two-and-one-half or three hours long?"

Earlier in the book, I devoted an entire chapter to the problems of the media and just why I consider them an enemy of the aging. This is a prime area in which strong protests are being mounted by groups interested in halting the stereotypical, distorted images and the omission of older people, and older women in particular, from network and cable programs and commercials. Interestingly enough, I seem to notice even more sensitivity on the part of the networks these days to the letters of complaint that come to them not only from well-organized groups, but also from individual viewers and consumers.

The Gray Panthers, always in the forefront, have had a National Media Watch Committee since 1973, administered by a remarkable woman in her eighties, Lydia Bragger. Culling information and research from viewers all across the country, they have met with network officials and advertising agency executives, the National Association of Broadcasters, and the select committees of the Congress of the United States. They use blowups, film and videotape clips, and transcripts of programs and commercials and they document their complaints with the figures acquired from their watchers across the country. In addition, universities around the country (such as in Georgia and Maine) have developed courses on media-watch monitoring.

AFTRA and Equity, in conjunction with the Women's Action Alliance, a countrywide consortium of women's groups, are still active in a project to make women aware of how they are (or are not) being represented on television and radio. Their monitoring over the years has confirmed a fact that will probably come as a surprise to no one: the older woman is the least represented of all categories in the entire world of television commercials. As Natalie Priest says angrily, "We are confined to doing an occasional ad for hemorrhoids, false teeth, and Geritol!"

Progress has been slow, but some protest letters have actually brought results. AFTRA has suggested a program of "Orchids and Onions"—letters written to the television station, the manufacturer, or the advertising agency. Send an "orchid letter" when you want to praise them, or an "onion letter" if you've got a gripe. Most local stations are listed right in your telephone directory and all products have mailing addresses right on their labels or on the box.

The Women's Action Alliance itself, the umbrella group for the AFTRA/Equity watchdogs, was founded in 1971 as a national organization committed to "furthering the goal of full equality for all women. We work toward this end by providing educational programs and services that assist women and women's organizations in accomplishing their goals." You might want to look at both their publication lists that include listings of other women's organizations, women's centers, programs on alcoholism and drug education, and referral information. (Women's Action Alliance, 370 Lexington Avenue, Suite 603, New York, NY 10017)

For the male of my generation it is difficult (but I hope, not impossible) to shed the cloak of chauvinism. Brought up in an era when the roles of gender were carefully drawn, it was the *man* who supported the family, as did our fathers and our grandfathers, while the woman remained at home to nurture, to tend, and to mother. We men may give lip service to the idea of equality, but too often it is lacking in our actions, even today. It is very much like Jim Gallagher's story of the navy petty officer who stormed, "I don't care how many changes they make around here, as long as they don't do things differently than they've been doing them!"

As Dr. Elizabeth Most, a retired professor of social work, said in a speech to OWL members, "Being married generally meant isolation from the world outside and having practically complete responsibility for home and the rearing of children. . . . Magazines gave us an idealized picture of ourselves. . . . They presumed that we could accomplish miracles in the home no matter what budget and yet present ourselves of an evening relaxed and ready to seduce the husband." There was, of course, laughter at this point. Then she went on, "From childhood on, we perceived ourselves through the eyes of men . . . a perception of inferiority and self-abasement, for along with the rhetoric and the pedestal, the reality was scullery work for most older women!"

Consider that most women of our generation spent twenty years or more in the administration of the household, management of the family budget, supervision of the cuisine, directing the "client relations" involved with entertaining business guests who were suddenly there for dinner, serving as purchasing agent for everything from the weekly groceries to furniture, doubling as transportation captain for the kids and the friends of kids, being the doctor, nurse, and paramedic, as well as the executive vice president of the family. What happens when such a woman comes out into the marketplace *run by men* to look for a second career? She is considered *unskilled.* Unskilled, middle-aged, and relegated to the lowest-paying jobs, while the men are just reaching the height of their careers at the ages of forty or fifty!

I have a sometime fantasy in the form of a short playlet in which the normal love relationship leading to marriage is replaced by a job interview, much as it would be in a corporation.

The homemaker applicant sits before the male interviewer, hands demurely clasped on her lap, her legs together, hair combed neatly.

SHE: What does the job entail?

HE: I'm offering you a position as "homemaker." You'll have to clean, shop, plan, be nice to my mother and father, be the social hostess, give birth to the babies, stay at home and care for them while they're young, be nice to my boss, keep the checkbook balanced—

SHE: *(interrupts)* What does the job pay?

HE: *(baffled)* Pay?

SHE: I mean, what is the salary, what are the perks?

HE: *(annoyed with the effrontery)* Well, it doesn't pay any *money.* What I'm offering is a lifetime job with security, a chance to be a companion, a helpmate. We don't demean the job with *money!*

SHE: *(rises and begins to leave)* I think I'll look somewhere else!

It doesn't take a feminist to understand, then, why organizations like the Older Women's League have become active. Through a reevaluation in middle age, or through divorce or widowhood or just plain free choice, a woman discovers that she is on very shaky financial ground. An angry woman rises at a meeting and recounts her own experiences: "We've been out of the job market for years. We go to an employment agency and they say, 'Where is your résumé?' *We have no résumé,* except for having successfully, I hope, raised a family!"

The Older Women's League, over these past years since my discovery of the group that rainy April day, has expanded as a nonprofit advocacy group, with greater emphasis now upon lobbying in Washington. However, there are more than 120 local chapters around the country dealing with advocacy and with local problems; most of them are listed right in your telephone directory. They've been involved in the fight to make Social Security benefits equitable for a surviving wife after the death of her breadwinner husband, for increased pension rights for widows, and for some access for health insurance for the divorced or widowed woman. The common thread that runs through all of these is the cry to recognize the value of a woman's work, whether paid or unpaid; to focus on the economic plight of women in their later years, and to attack the inequities in public policy.

At OWL there are no age limitations, even though the organization was founded for women between forty-five and sixty-five. There is a member in New York who is eighty-seven, and both her fifty-seven-year-old daughter and twenty-nine-year-old granddaughter also belong. As Jean Phillips, former president of the Manhattan chapter, told me, "A lot of young women want to join us. They say, 'I can see myself in a few years!' They say that it's been bad for their mothers and *they* don't want to end up that way."

For women reentering the job market after divorce or widowhood, another source of help and guidance is the Displaced Homemakers Network, Inc., 1411 K Street, N.W., Suite 930, Washington, DC 20005. Their *Program Director 1* provides a listing of centers, programs, and projects around the country that offer services to the displaced homemaker. Their newsletter, *Transition Times,* is a further source of information to members, with subjects covering reading materials, new books, films, conferences, and current legislative issues of interest to older women.

We are, none of us, valiantly fighting the battle alone. Not by any means. There are also large and effective organizations with memberships in the hundreds of thousands—and, indeed, in the millions—that are also involved in the struggle against ageism. Possibly they don't have the "personality" of the groups I've mentioned, but they do have the clout of the establishment and the knowledge and experience in Congressional lobbying that most of us lack as individuals. Many have been fighting the conservatism and the rigidity of organizations like the American Medical Association—which was against Medicare when it was first brought to the floor of Congress and which has been against other programs of national health insurance that might aid the elderly and the indigent. Americans for Democratic Action has joined the battle for equal pay for women. Many of the groups listed in this chapter have raised their voices on the issue of the integrity of Social Security. And in these past few years, we have begun to hear again the massed voices of the unions, the National Association for the Advancement of Colored People, the National Organization of Women, Republicans, Democrats, and Independents. We are not, by any means, alone!

The National Retired Teacher's Association and the American Association for Retired Persons have a membership of over thirteen million, and the

National Council of Senior Citizens numbers well over three million. There are others, including the National Association of Retired Federal Employees, the American Association of Homes for the Aging, the National Council on Aging, and the National Caucus on the Black Aged. For the middle-aged reader who does not want to get personally involved in the activities of groups like the Gray Panthers or OWL, or who does not yet want to march on Washington, these larger organizations provide an outlet through membership, and no matter how small an effort that seems, it is important in this battle that affects us all. What the young author wrote in *Mother Jones* seems to be quite true: "Young people could have learned a thing or two from the elderly."

If we are aware of the societal treatment of the middle-aged and the elders—and how can we not be aware?—if we are not to be relegated to the status of second-class citizens in a culture that reveres and idolizes youth; if we are not to be pushed aside when we reach the age of forty-five, we *must* speak up, each of us.

We *must* make ourselves heard, else *we* remain the first and foremost enemy of our own age groups! There is so much to do. We vote in larger numbers than our younger citizens, who still do not fully understand the democratic process. We have isolated the problem of our invisibility by becoming more aware of the myths and angry at the stereotypes, many of which we have been carrying firmly within our own heads. We even have the support and the goodwill of many of the young people, in spite of the ever-growing attacks by groups such as Americans for Generational Equity and the Letters to the Editor that begrudge us everything we have worked for and fought for all our adult lives. Most of all, I feel that we are beginning to evolve a sense of self.

Certainly it is frustrating when we are surrounded by so many groups with their own self-interests and voices that clamor to be heard. The farm lobby, the real-estate lobby, the tobacco lobby, and the gun lobby, as well as the "pork barrels" and the continual filibusters on continuing aid to the poor defense industry, foreign governments, and the development of new, sophisticated, very expensive space technology, seem to dominate the daily headlines. There are times, then, that we feel that our thin voices are being drowned out by a cacophony of political boom boxes. Of course, it is no fun to fight and lose. It is sad to put energy and time and thought and emotional strength into the battle, only to find that we are not being heard even half the time. It is difficult to start all over again, right from the beginning. But it is the quality of our survival for which we fight. It would be truly sad if we refused to fight at all.

Chrysalis Awakening

Barbara Hertz, Publisher, *Prime Time* magazine,
August 1980:

"Unlike the kids who are trying to find out who they are and what the world is all about, we *know*—we've been there. Over the years, we've stockpiled knowledge, experience, and good sense, and we're set to put them to good use. In ways no other midlife generation has known before, we are active, involved, and venturesome, with the capacity for enjoyment that few youngsters can ever know. . . . At last it's time for me!"

Gerry Hotchkiss, Publisher, *New Choices* magazine,
January 1990:

"What she said is right. She's right. It *is* time for choices, the freedom to have those choices. Presupposing that you are reasonably well cared for financially, that you're healthy, it's wonderful to get to an age where you know who the hell you are. You no longer are trying self-identification. I have a friend who just reached his sixtieth birthday and suddenly realized his mortality. Possibly he had twenty-five more years. It didn't frighten him. He said to me, 'It freed me!' "

It is, perhaps, more difficult to end this personal accounting of a journey than it was to begin it, when hundreds of empty white pages lay in wait beside my restless typewriter. For, as the days and the weeks have passed, and the anniversary of more than a year of writing went by unnoticed, I realized that this discovery of middle age would continue to unfold unabated, even as the chapters were concluded and long after the book was published. What I did not know at the beginning was that I was then fifty-eight, but would have passed my *sixty-fifth* birthday in the revision of the book—that much of what I thought at first would have changed, but that so much would have remained the same.

During the first writing of the book, and then during the months of the "second *Second Spring*," I was able to become more aware, more observant, of the continual growth and vitality of our generations, more cognizant of *us* as a very special group of people. It is just possible that before this book, and in my own personal way, I had also been infected with the virus of invisibility and self-doubt in a country that venerates youth.

But, not once during the original research, the writing, and now, eight years later, did I discover what might be described as *typical of us;* not once could I determine at what exact age we turn from "young" to "middle-aged" to "elder" with all the myths and all the stereotypes that the labels connote. After all, by every standard of our esteemed and revered sociologists I have actually passed that marked point of entry into "elder" from the long journey through "late middle age" or whatever label they now give it. But I still feel the same as I did yesterday and I am still as active as ever, both in my documentary films and certainly in my writing.

We are so often concerned with dividing our lives into chronological segments that we violate the concept that living has an essential *wholeness*, a continuum in which the same social, psychological, and economic factors that affect us as young people are still with us all through our adult lives. As the great baseball pitcher, Satchel Paige, so wisely inquired, "How old would you be if you didn't know how old you was?"

In the writings of the Talmud, of Confucius, and of the Greek poet and lawmaker Solon, we read again and again that the years of middle age—from forty to sixty-five—allow the greatest potential for proficiency and achievement, the greatest contributions to society, the greatest fulfillment in terms of our capabilities and our interests. And though Confucius and Solon set longevity at age seventy, the Talmud wisely foresaw our longer life span and recounted our virtues until the age of one hundred, with a mere fifty as the time for giving counsel and sixty for wisdom. I am reminded of the blessing given by my grandmother and others in my family as they intoned, "You should only live and be well until 120!" Even the 100 years of the Talmud were not enough for her!

It was brought home to me quite delightfully once again at the seminar of the AT&T Pioneers in Montreal, when one of the participants spoke up:

> My mother worked until she was eighty-three, same as your dad. She had to stop working. At eighty-six, she was going on every bus trip she could find and she said, "I go because I want to help the old people on and off the bus!"

The ancient sages were not wrong. If we probe deeply, we find that chronological age has not altered our perceptions of ourselves as individuals. Except for the inevitable physical changes, we are not much different at forty-five or sixty-five from the way we were in our youth. It is the reason, I think, for the success of the current advertising campaign of *New Choices* magazine: "This is how they look. This is how they feel!" Often, too, we find that life has turned out much better than societal myths have led us to expect, and we think of ourselves as the *exceptions* rather than the *examples* of millions who feel and think and react and enjoy life in a freedom of spirit that only comes with reaching true maturity.

We look around, and suddenly it is a time when the children are grown and on their own. Oft-postponed pleasures are there within our grasp. Suddenly it is a time to enjoy the family while maintaining a sense of freedom, the likes of which we have never experienced before. It is, for most of us, finally, a time of stability and financial independence. But most of all, perhaps, it is a time when we begin to understand our own wisdom and our own maturity. Bernice Neugarten called it, "the conscious processing of new information in the light of what one has already learned and the turning of one's own proficiency to the achievement of desired ends." She concludes with the thought that it is a time when we begin to create our own rules and our own norms.

Eleanor Roosevelt, on her seventy-seventh birthday, was heard to say, "Life was meant to be lived. Curiosity must be kept alive. One must never, for whatever reason, turn his back on life." Interestingly, in this past eight years, I have found that very few of us *have* turned our backs. Quite the contrary—the vast majority of us have just begun to discover ourselves in ways that we never thought possible.

When I left Maggie Kuhn that rainy day in Philadelphia, the interview over, Maggie fluttered from desk to desk, taking calls, having her next speech copied, and then she stopped for one last hug of good-bye. The fire was in her eyes again and she spoke of *now.* "Now you can finally say what you want to say and no one will berate you. You can say it in the way you want to say it and no one will scold you. Now . . . it's a time for *now!*" It was not until weeks later that I found a similar uplifting line in *Passages,* in which Gail Sheehy wrote, "The motto at the stage past fifty might well be 'no more bullshit!'"

And thus, in the euphoric years of passing through middle age, the time has been one of discovery. I have learned to listen to the voices around me, to hear the chorus of the others of my age and of those whom we consider "older," and I have found that so many of us have suddenly begun to realize that we have spent far too much time trying to be what society thought we should be, trying to be younger if youth demanded it or the advertising suggested it, trying to be more agreeable if our children nagged about it, trying to fit the mold of *everyone else's* idea of who we are and how we should feel and what we should think. As Gae Gaer Luce wrote, "We victimized ourselves and blamed our age."

Look around you, as I have done and as I continue to do. Listen carefully, for we have much to say that is worth hearing. We are really terribly attractive; we are certainly more interesting than we were at the age of twenty! I walk into an elevator in a condominium in Florida and a handsome, gray-haired woman gets on with me. I notice that around her neck she wears a gold charm on a chain. It reads: "10½." I smile as I get off, wondering what friend or lover or husband had the good taste to compliment her with the gift and to recognize that she certainly is *more experienced* than Bo Derek!

In the pages of *Vogue* not too many years ago, I saw a photograph of one of my favorite people, a nun by the name of Sister Serena, with whom I had once produced a touching and effective documentary film about retarded children. Standing there in the photograph, probably sixty years old at the time, with her dignity, her sense of wisdom, her elegant and beautifully expressive hands clasped before her, she made the models who adorned the pages of the rest of the magazine look shallow, vapid and insignificant by comparison. How very beautiful she looked!

The poet Robert Penn Warren commented that, at this stage, you "make terms with life, you get released." And a woman student at a university, then fifty-four years old, said to me, "You have a chance to really explore where you have never been before. You have a freedom!"

Finally, we have earned the right to our emotions, to our opinions, to our freedoms. Suddenly, we can even be *imperfect!* Some of our frustrations go back as far as our childhood, and suddenly, suddenly we find we are free. A woman of sixty recounts to me, "I had a mother who was very strict. I didn't know what it was to play with the neighborhood children or to go out. . . . (I was) always in the house praying or going to church. So now it's time to go out and enjoy myself and to make the best of these years of my life."

For so many of us the "good old days" are, indeed, *now.* Over and over again I discover how true this is. I read the letters from my friends and the printed comments in newspapers that seem to repeat the same theme of liberation: "I have time." Now there is time to try so many of the things we've postponed, and for each of us it is a different need, a different goal; we march to a different drummer, each of us, without the tyranny of ambition that colored our youthful lives.

We are at an age when we are more in touch with ourselves and with our feelings and with our needs than at any other time in our growth. And we are at an age when the dreams of our years are finally within our reach.

There is a primitive society in Southern Africa—the !Kung San—that forbids young adults to eat the eggs of the ostrich, believing that it will make them insane. It is a special treat reserved only for the very young children and for the people of middle age, an unwritten link of kinship between the first generation and the last. Only when the adult has entered the middle years can he or she savor the taste of what has been withheld for generations. Then, and only then, are they allowed to eat the ostrich eggs. Well, during the writing of this book, I reached that stage in life and I finally felt that I was entitled to those ostrich eggs—to enjoy them finally, and to savor them, and I tried not to rush through it. Indeed, I have "eaten" of ostrich eggs throughout these past eight years and I continue to enjoy them as this new edition nears completion. How marvelous to feel that the "me" generation is finally really "me"—that it is all of us of our age!

Since so much seems to happen to me on the buses of New York, what occurred as I was completing this manuscript was no exception. An elderly messenger climbed aboard the Third Avenue bus. He was about seventy-five years of age, and as he made his way down the aisle of the bouncing vehicle, his thin, flat package clutched under his arm, he let the entire gathering of passengers know his very valid philosophy and I laughed along with the rest. "Live each day as it comes," he proclaimed loudly. "Stop looking for tomorrow. *This afternoon* ain't here yet, and you're lookin' for tomorrow!"

It is, indeed, today that matters. It is now, and for some the eating of the ostrich eggs will take the form of using the children's inheritance and setting off on a trip around the world. For others it will be a chance to change careers, to go back to school, to learn how to bake pizza, to garden—or just to sit. "For age is opportunity no less than youth itself," Henry Wadsworth Longfellow wrote. For each of us, no matter what our choosing at this stage of our lives, the opportunity will be personal and it will be rewarding.

Yes, I shall miss these friends I've made, the ones who fill the pages of this book. I have tried to communicate their deep wisdom, their vitality and zest for life, and I have learned much from them, not only about *them*, but about myself.

And for me? What will there be in these new discoveries, in this new awareness? Certainly, I hope there will be still more books, and certainly, the production of the documentary films I love so much—especially those that deal with the fascinating lives of the people in this world of ours.

But, what of now? What of this moment, now that I have a feeling of joy and of weary achievement? For now, I turn to a quotation that I used in a book that my wife and I wrote a few years back, little thinking then that what *began* the philosophy of one book would *end* another on exactly the right note. For now, only for this moment in time in my journey that has taken me through the middle years and has placed me on the doorstep of yet another transition through the age of sixty-five, I turn to a quotation from Thoreau and it is the last one I shall burden you with:

Everyone should believe in something.
I believe I'll go fishing.